'This book is a milestone for approach[...] logically for evangelicals and others. C[...] I know, it stands out in ambition and penetration, breadth and depth. Although not written with the specialists in mind, the book is aware of the prevailing debates and the issues at stake. The final five points represent extremely healthy and fruitful guard rails. I hope this excellent contribution from, and to, evangelical theology will be studied, appreciated and assimilated.'
Pietro Bolognesi, Professor of Systematic Theology, Istituto di Formazione Evangelica e Documentazione, Padua

'Thomas Aquinas is one of the greatest theologians of all time, whose impact on the Roman Catholic Church has been enormous and pervasive. Protestants have been more critical and eclectic in their attitudes to him, and this book tells us why. Leonardo De Chirico analyses the diversity of approaches to Aquinas, and argues that evangelicals must be alert to what he has to offer them but also careful to understand how much of what he says is incompatible with a theology rooted in Scripture alone. Students of both theology and philosophy will greatly benefit from this even-handed and clear assessment of a system of thought whose compromises with Aristotelianism challenge Protestant minds seeking to be subject only to the revealed Word of God.'
Gerald Bray, Research Professor, Beeson Divinity School

'Evangelicals have had an "unresolved" relationship with Thomas Aquinas, vacillating between outright rejection and (recently) a protestant Thomist renaissance. In this insightful, balanced book, Leonardo De Chirico offers an eclectic approach, providing an evaluation not only of Thomas but also of his reception in both Roman Catholic and Protestant thought. Within, he rightly calls Protestant theology to avoid a simplistic approach and engage Aquinas as a necessary theological interlocutor while being guarded against the "full outcome" of his system.'
Cory Brock, St Columba's Free Church, Edinburgh Theological Seminary

'Thomas Aquinas, Doctor of the Roman Catholic Church and her quintessential theologian, as well as Western Christianity's philosophical and theological giant, continues to fuel conversation, controversy and confusion today. Within the evangelical tradition, there has sometimes been a hesitancy to engage with Thomas. The sheer amount of intellectual effort required to wade through his significant literary and theological contribution, and a nervousness about appropriating the intellectual champion of the Roman Catholic Church, has meant that evangelicals are often ill-equipped to traverse Thomas's thought and theology.

'As an Aquinas "renaissance" occurs within evangelical thought, De Chirico acts as both expert tour guide and commentator, walking the reader through the forces that impacted Aquinas, his works, the various interpretive traditions once Thomas became "Thomism", and how evangelicals may thoughtfully engage with Aquinas in a careful and considered way. De Chirico brings together his years of experience as a theologian, pastor and academic to provide a book that the Evangelical Church needs today to re-engage with Aquinas with nuance, sensitivity and an informed perspective.

'Ultimately, this book calls for evangelical maturity that avoids injudicious infatuation or ill-considered disparagement, giving readers the tools they need to navigate the world of Thomas Aquinas.'
Rachel Ciano, Dean of Academic Development, Mary Andrews College; Lecturer on Christianity in History, Sydney Missionary and Bible College

'There is a growing number of evangelicals who advocate for a retrieval of the theological insights of Thomas Aquinas (1225–1274), the philosopher par excellence of the Roman Catholic Church. This has led to the emergence of even a Reformed Thomist movement.

'Leonardo De Chirico balances the evangelical romance with Aquinas, appreciating the aspects that are in line with the Christian faith but rejecting those which have generated serious departures from the biblical faith in areas of Catholic soteriology, ecclesiology, sacramentology and devotions.'
José de Segovia Barrón, former President of the Theological Commission on Spanish Evangelical Alliance

'Why is a thirteenth-century Roman Catholic theologian having a twenty-first century moment among evangelicals? Engaging with Thomas Aquinas answers this and much more. Leonardo De Chirico introduces the thought of Thomas himself and surveys how Roman Catholics and Protestants have assessed and appropriated his legacy through the centuries. Most importantly, readers will find here wise, charitable, yet cautionary advice for evangelicals tempted to become Thomists.'

Kevin J. Vanhoozer, Research Professor of Systematic Theology, Trinity Evangelical Divinity School

'This book guides us round the breathtaking architecture of Thomas Aquinas's cathedral of theology. There is much to admire: the solid pillars on which it is constructed, the soaring buttresses, the magnificent elevation, and the beauty of the stained glass through which light filters. Our guide indicates how magnificent this achievement is.

'However, there are also some features which leave him uneasy. Has the design of the Scripture blueprint been faithfully followed? Are there not sombre places where the divine architect says we should not venture? Does the construction not have some inherent flaws? Leonardo de Chirico makes us sensitive to the beauty, without forgetting the dangers.'

Paul Wells, Emeritus Professor, Faculté Jean Calvin, Aix-en-Provence

ENGAGING WITH THOMAS AQUINAS

Leonardo De Chirico (PhD, King's College London) is the pastor of Breccia di Roma, lecturer in historical theology at the Istituto di Formazione Evangelica e Documentazione (IFED) in Padua, Italy, and the director of the Reformanda Initiative. Additionally, he blogs at www.vaticanfiles.org. He is the director of *Studi di Teologia*, an evangelical theological journal that has been in publication in Italy for forty years, and the author of *Evangelical Theological Perspectives on Post-Vatican II Roman Catholicism* (2003), *A Christian's Pocket Guide to the Papacy: Its Origin and Role in the 21st Century* (2015), *A Christian's Pocket Guide to Mary: Mother of God?* (2017) and *Same Words, Different Worlds: Do Roman Catholics and Evangelicals Believe the Same Gospel?* (2021).

ENGAGING WITH THOMAS AQUINAS

An evangelical approach

Leonardo De Chirico

APOLLOS (an imprint of Inter-Varsity Press)
Studio 101, The Record Hall, 16–16A Baldwin's Gardens, London, EC1N 7RJ, UK
Email: *ivp@ivpbooks.com*
Website: *www.ivpbooks.com*
© Leonardo De Chirico, 2024

First published 2024

British Library Cataloguing-in-Publication Data
A catalogue record for this book is available from the British Library.

ISBN: 978–1–91067–474–1
eBook ISBN: 978–1–91067–475–8

Set in Minion Pro 11/14pt

Typeset in Great Britain by Fakenham Prepress Solutions, Fakenham, Norfolk

*Inter-Varsity Press publishes Christian books that are true to the Bible and that
communicate the gospel, develop discipleship and strengthen the church for its mission
in the world.*

*IVP originated within the Inter-Varsity Fellowship, now the Universities and Colleges
Christian Fellowship, a student movement connecting Christian Unions in universities
and colleges throughout Great Britain, and a member movement of the International
Fellowship of Evangelical Students. Website: www.uccf.org.uk. That historic association
is maintained, and all senior IVP staff and committee members subscribe to the UCCF
Basis of Faith.*

Contents

Introduction

To engage with Thomas Aquinas (1224–74) is to approach one of history's greatest theological giants. Thomas is second only to Augustine in his influence on Western Christianity. More specifically, Roman Catholicism has for centuries held Thomas as its vital intellectual champion, the most thoughtful, profound and comprehensive voice of Roman Catholic thought. Already canonised by Pope John XXII in 1323, only fifty years after his death, he was proclaimed a Doctor of the Church by Pius V in 1567 for being the Roman theologian whose thought was seen to have defeated the Protestant Reformation. During the Council of Trent (1545–63), the *Summa Theologiae* – his outstanding work – was placed symbolically alongside the Bible as evidence of its primary importance in formulating the Tridentine decrees and canons against the doctrine of justification by faith alone. In the seventeenth century, Thomas was considered the defender of the Roman Catholic theological system by Robert Bellarmine, the greatest anti-Protestant controversialist, who influenced entire generations of Roman Catholic apologists.[1] In 1879, Pope Leo XIII issued the encyclical *Aeterni Patris*, with which he proclaimed Thomas as the highest expression of philosophical and theological science in a climate marked by a harsh confrontation with modern thought. There is no other theological figure who has received such admiration and who has exercised such an impact.

Turning to the twentieth century, the Second Vatican Council (1962–65) established that Thomas should be the supreme guide in theological studies leading to the ordination of priests: 'The

---

1   See my 'Robert Bellarmine and His Controversies with the Reformers: A Window on Post-Tridentine Roman Catholic Apologetics', *European Journal of Theology* 31:1 (2022), pp. 21–42.

students should learn to penetrate them [i.e. the mysteries of salvation] more deeply with the help of speculation, under the guidance of St. Thomas, and to perceive their interconnections' (*Optatam Totius*, n. 17).[2] In addition to being the theologian most repeatedly cited in the documents of the Council (734 times compared to 522 citations of Augustine),[3] according to the Roman Catholic scholar Thomas Guarino, Thomas provided the Council with 'the bases and structure' of its dogmatic Constitutions.[4] While Thomistic *language* was arguably absent at Vatican II, Thomas's *ideas* were in plain sight. His doctrines of 'analogy' and 'participation',[5] appropriately reinterpreted by the Council, are the cornerstones of the Roman Catholic theology that emerged from the Council and was developed further in the following decades. On the one hand, everything is considered more similar to than different from the rest (this is analogy); on the other, everything participates in the other rather than being a stranger to it (this is participation). Thus Vatican II 'updated' the legacy of Thomas, finding in his thought and work powerful tools for the service of the relaunched vision of the Roman Catholic Church.

Pope Paul VI (*Lumen Ecclesiae*, 1974) and then John Paul II (*Fides et Ratio*, 1998) expressed a deferential appreciation by identifying Thomas 'as a master of thought and a model of the right way to do theology' (*Fides et Ratio*, n. 43).[6] This is all to say that in recent and less recent history the Church of Rome has appropriated Thomas in a persistent and convinced way, elevating him as the Catholic theologian *par excellence*. It is no coincidence that he is traditionally called *Doctor Angelicus* for the 'celestial' tenor

---

2 Decree on Priestly Training *Optatam Totius* (1965) https://www.vatican.va/archive/hist_councils/ii_vatican_council/documents/vat-ii_decree_19651028_optatam-totius_en.html (accessed 18 December 2023).

3 In the *Catechism of the Catholic Church* (1992), Augustine is instead the most quoted Father, while Thomas comes second.

4 T. G. Guarino, *The Disputed Teachings of Vatican II: Continuity and Reversal in Catholic Doctrine* (Grand Rapids, MI: Eerdmans, 2018), pp. 25, 74, 200.

5 See T. Tyn, *Metafisica della sostanza: partecipazione e analogia entis* (Bologna: Edizioni Studio Domenicano, 1991).

6 Encyclical letter *Fides et Ratio* (1998) https://www.vatican.va/content/john-paul-ii/en/encyclicals/documents/hf_jp-ii_enc_14091998_fides-et-ratio.html (accessed 19 December 2023).

of his thought and angelic chastity. Thomas is in himself a giant; Thomism is an ocean of almost immeasurable size.

In the light of all this it is no surprise that Pope Francis issued the explicit invitation 'Go to Thomas!' to participants of the International Thomistic Congress (21–24 September 2022) during an audience at the Vatican.[7] In his address, the pope extolled the thought of Thomas Aquinas as a sure guide for the Roman Catholic faith and a fruitful relationship with culture. In so doing, Francis stood in the wake of recent popes in emphasising superlative appreciation for the figure of Thomas while adding his own. Francis indicated the need not only to study Thomas but also to 'contemplate' the Master before approaching his thought. Thus to the cognitive and intellectual dimension he added something of a mystical one. In this way, Pope Francis caused Thomas, already a theologian imbued with wisdom and asceticism, to be seen as even more Roman Catholic. This mix best represents the interweaving of the intellectual and contemplative traditions proper to Roman Catholicism.

This persistent influence of Thomas is still only one side of the story. Grafted onto Thomas's work, several interpretative traditions of his thought have developed, giving rise to various versions of 'Thomism'.[8] The Thomistic traditions have accompanied the flow of the history of Roman Catholic theology over the centuries and have indicated different, sometimes even conflicting, appropriations of his thoughts. One thinks of the rigidity of nineteenth-century neo-Thomism, which tended to systematise Thomas within a square philosophical grid; alternatively, one could refer to the fluidity of the *nouvelle théologie* in the first half of the twentieth century, which read Thomas in a dynamic and sapiential

7 C. Hall, 'Address of His Holiness Pope Francis to the Participants in the International Thomistic Congress, Organized by the Pontifical Academy of Saint Thomas Aquinas', The Vatican: https://www.vatican.va/content/francesco/en/speeches/2022/september/documents/20220922-congresso-tomistico.html (accessed 10 May 2023).

8 On the history of Thomism, see G. Prouvost, *Thomas d'Aquin et les thomismes: essai sur l'histoire des thomismes* (Paris: Cerf, 1996); F. Kerr, *After Aquinas: Versions of Thomism* (Oxford: Blackwell, 2002); S. Vanni Rovighi, *Introduzione a Tommaso d'Aquino* (Rome-Bari: Editori Laterza, 1973, 1999), pp. 137–58.

way, almost wanting to recover the 'real' Thomas by rescuing him from the too schematic reduction of previous forms of Thomism. In any case, doing theology *ad mentem Thomae* (according to the mind of Thomas) has been one of the highest ambitions in Roman Catholicism, even if what it meant to interpret his legacy has given rise to lively internal debates. Some have suggested a list of seventeen different types of Thomism throughout history.[9] When reflecting on the twentieth century, McGinn lists many interpretative tendencies of Thomas, such as 'Strict-Observance Thomism' (in the wake of *Aeterni Patris*: R. Garrigou-Lagrange), 'Revived Thomism' (M.-D. Chenu, Y. Congar, H. de Lubac), 'Metaphysical Thomism' (J. Maritain, E. Gilson) and 'Transcendental Thomism' (P. Rousselot, J. Maréchal, K. Rahner).[10] Throughout the various streams of Thomism we see that Thomas is alive and well in contemporary Roman Catholic thought.

As already hinted, when Thomas is referred to, so many possible avenues of enquiry open up that it is almost impossible to govern this complexity in a coherent way. And yet, without taking Thomas's theology into account, it would be difficult to say anything meaningful, not only as far as medieval theology is concerned but also with regard to modern and contemporary Roman Catholic theology. This is yet a partial recognition of Thomas's importance. In fact, similar statements about the past and ongoing relevance of Thomas could be made with reference to both medieval and modern philosophy and ethics.[11] The above-mentioned International Thomistic Congress had as its theme the exploration of the resources of Thomist thought in today's context. Thomism is not just a medieval stream of thought but a simultaneously solid and elastic system. All seasons of Roman Catholicism have found Thomism inspiring for the diverse challenges facing the Church of

9   T. Rowland, *Catholic Theology* (London: Bloomsbury T&T Clark, 2017), pp. 43–90.

10 B. McGinn, *Thomas Aquinas's Summa Theologiae: A Biography* (Princeton, NJ: Princeton University Press, 2014), pp. 186–209. See also S.-T. Bonino (ed.), *Grandi opere del Tomismo nel Novecento* (Rome: Urbaniana University Press, 2020).

11 For an overview see J. Finnis, *Aquinas: Moral, Political, and Legal Theory* (Oxford: Oxford University Press, 1998).

Rome, including the Reformation first, the Enlightenment project second, and now post-modernity. We hear more about Thomas and Thomism later, not only in historical theology and philosophy but also in other fields of knowledge that were once far from the previous interpretative traditions of Thomas. The point is that no one can grasp basic academic discussions in theology and philosophy without having Thomas and Thomism as conversation partners. It is with this in mind that the present volume seeks to engage with Thomas Aquinas, offering an evangelical approach informed by an evangelical theologian who has been working on Roman Catholic theology for twenty-five years, and, more recently, working towards an evangelical appreciation of pre-Reformation theology, including Thomas.

Evangelicals have had an unresolved relationship with Thomas. The Protestant Reformers of the sixteenth century had a critical/ sympathetic approach to Aquinas (including Martin Luther, for whom Aquinas was the embodiment of what it meant to be compromised with Aristotelian philosophy but who was nonetheless conversing with the medieval tradition). A more eclectic and critical approach was followed by subsequent generations of Protestant theologians. The pendulum of twentieth-century evangelical scholarship has swung between strongly negative appraisals of Thomas (e.g. F. Schaeffer, C. Van Til) and, since the 1980s, rather more appreciative receptions (e.g. N. Geisler, A. Vos).

In current evangelical studies, there is something of a love story with Thomas emerging, especially regarding his theological metaphysics and epistemology. The evangelical interest in Thomas can be traced as beginning with apologists attracted to his epistemology in defending an evidentialist view of the relationship between faith and reason against the presuppositionalist school that was critical of any linear and only mildly disrupted view of that relationship. Then came the turn of evangelical theologians looking at Thomas's metaphysics in accounting for the 'classical' doctrine of God over against what they perceived to be the slippery slopes of popular evangelical authors presenting unresolved (and perhaps unintended) issues in their Christology and trinitarian theology.

Both evangelical groups, the evidentialist apologists and the self-declared 'classical' theologians, have found inspiration in Thomas and launched a kind of Thomas 'renaissance' within evangelical circles. Thomas could not be avoided by previous generations of Protestant scholars, given his stature and importance for theology. Yet Thomas was read with selective and theologically mature eyes. Today there is an increasing tendency to think that you cannot be properly orthodox (in the 'catholic' sense) if you don't embrace the fundamental tenets of Thomism as such.

In the face of the pressures from secularisation and the identity crisis felt in some evangelical quarters, Thomas can be perceived as a bulwark of 'traditional' theology that needs to be urgently recovered. What is often overlooked is that Roman Catholicism has considered Thomas as its champion in its anti-Reformation stance and its subsequent anti-biblical developments, such as the 1950 Marian dogma of the bodily ascension of Mary. Rome regards Thomas as the quintessential Roman Catholic theologian and thinker, and this is something that the evangelical Thomists seem to gloss over.

Today some look at Thomas with great admiration and want to be identified as evangelical 'Thomists', while others think that Thomas is a misleading theologian, being at the root of all the errors of Rome. What should we make of this entire discussion? Are Thomas and Thomism(s) the same? In what ways does evangelical thought need to be aware of the strengths and weaknesses, if not dangers, in Thomas Aquinas? How can the Roman Catholic Church's chief theologian be at the same time a significant reference point for evangelical theology, indeed for all Protestant Christians? On the other hand, is it possible to dismiss him as totally unreliable when most Protestant theologians across the centuries have dealt with him eclectically, i.e. sifting what is good and rejecting what is deviant?

'Go to Thomas!' is an invitation that even a growing number of practitioners of evangelical theology are taking up. The point is not to study nor avoid Thomas uncritically. Rather, it is necessary for us to provide the theological map with which one approaches him. Furthermore, it is necessary to develop an *evangelical* map of Thomas Aquinas. If Rome considers Thomas its chief architect, can evangelical theology approach him without understanding that Thomas stands behind almost everything Roman Catholicism believes and practises?

These, among others, are the questions behind the present research project. This book is intended to provide a (hopefully) informed and thoughtful engagement with Thomas Aquinas that will speak into the ongoing evangelical conversation on the significance of his work and legacy.

It will be an engagement, not a simple introduction or a bird's-eye survey. There are lots of books that already do that job in a reliable and readable way.[12] Nor will it be a monograph concentrating on a single aspect of Thomas. All engagements are encounters that assume some distance and proximity, degrees of familiarity and estrangement. This engagement will focus on the framework of Thomas's theology and its long repercussions on the history of Christian thought, trying to have an evangelical account of theology as its viewpoint. I am sure that readers with philosophical expectations may find the book lacking the thoroughness of a medievalist. I am more of a generalist church historian and only tentatively entered a field (medieval philosophy) in which I am not an expert. Readers looking for a careful analysis of the whole of Thomas's theology will be disappointed because they will find the book sketchy and selective. Although I will defend my choices and consider them intellectually plausible, I am aware of the complexity of grasping the scope and depth of Thomas's theology and presenting it fairly. If one adds to it the varieties of Thomisms present in academic theology, the possibilities of failing to meet expectations increase exponentially.

This evangelical engagement with Aquinas will take the following shape. The first chapter ('The life and work of Thomas

---

12 E.g. F. Kerr, *Thomas Aquinas: A Very Short Introduction* (Oxford: Oxford University Press, 2009); E. Feser, *Aquinas: A Beginner's Guide* (London: Oneworld Publications, 2009); T. M. Renick, *Aquinas for Armchair Theologians* (Louisville, KY: Westminster John Knox Press, 2002); J.-P. Torrell, 'Thomas d'Aquin (Saint)', *Dictionnaire de Spiritualité*, vol. 15 (Paris: Beauchesne, 1991), cols 718–73.

Aquinas') will briefly introduce the medieval historical, religious and scholastic context of Thomas's theological existence, coupled with some of the key events of Thomas's life that shaped his work. All the major contours of his prolific written output will be introduced to gain a fair picture of the immense richness of his thought and legacy.

The second chapter ('Sources and synthesis of Thomas Aquinas's thought') will explore the intellectual world that Thomas inhabited, with special references to the three main sources of his work, i.e. Holy Scripture, Aristotelian thought, and various patristic traditions, from Augustine to Pseudo-Dionysius and beyond. For each main source, a case study will suggest one major way Thomas develops what he has learned from others. Out of those streams, in an unsurpassed combination, Thomas made an amazing synthesis whereby biblical exegesis and commentaries, philosophical analyses and constant interaction with the Church Fathers were blended into something original. The *Summa Theologiae*, though unfinished, will be examined as reflecting the most comprehensive theological work that has come out of his intellectual genius.

Chapter 3 ('Roman Catholic appropriations: from veneration to magisterial affirmation') will investigate a selection of the ways in which Roman Catholic magisterium and thought across the centuries has read, interpreted and appropriated Thomas. From the early canonisation by John XXII in 1323 to the late encyclical by John Paul II, *Fides et Ratio* (1998), Thomas has been the North Star in Roman Catholic theology, albeit with multiple nuances in, if not true conflicts over, the exact and intended significance of his legacy.

Chapter 4 ('Protestant readings of Thomas: circling around evangelical eclecticism') will try to do a similar exercise regarding the reception of Thomas in Protestant thought. From the early reservations to the extensive engagement with Thomas found in the Protestant tradition, from the twentieth-century criticism to the apparent early twenty-first-century love affair, Thomas has always been a test case for Protestant identity in its interaction with pre-Reformation theology and how Roman Catholicism eventually appropriated it.

The fifth chapter ('Legacy and critical issues: the contours and the trajectories of Thomas's architectural thought') will wrap up and further elaborate on some of the most important questions that emerged from the research, dealing especially with the degree of identification between Thomas and Roman Catholicism and the need for an evangelical discernment in coming to terms with it. The nature–grace interdependence will be dealt with as representative of Thomas's system of thought and assessed critically from an evangelical viewpoint. Attention will be given to his doctrines of analogy and participation as they have been reclaimed and developed since Vatican II. Furthermore, Thomas's theological method will also be subject to critical review. Since Thomas's thought is a rounded and consistent 'system', any evangelical approach to it needs to develop a systemic awareness while being open to interacting with aspects of it.

Finally, chapter 6 ('Thomas Aquinas for evangelicals today') will ask the question of whether evangelicals can be identified as Thomists and provide five guidelines to encourage evangelical engagement with Thomas that is theologically generous and critical at the same time.

I wrote this book from the office of Rome's Istituto di Cultura Evangelica e Documentazione (ICED). It is located 300 metres from the impressive buildings of the Pontifical University of Saint Thomas Aquinas (the so-called Angelicum), one of the world academic centres for Thomistic studies and run by the Dominican Order. The Angelicum is where Karol Wojtyła, who later became Pope John Paul II, studied. It is where thousands of students from all over the world are trained in Thomas's thought. Just another 250 metres away in the other direction, ICED is neighbour to the Pontifical Gregorian University, the flagship university of the Jesuit Order, which was also heavily influenced by Thomas's theology. It is here that Pope Francis studied, though he never finished a degree. I used both libraries in my research for this book. ICED physically stands between two giants of Roman Catholic academic theology: one institutionally dedicated to Thomism in its more rigid version, the other shaped by Thomism in its more creative form, especially from the second half of the twentieth century. ICED was therefore the ideal place to research and write this book as an evangelical theologian. While writing, I was always reminded of Thomas's impact on the Roman Catholic Church, which considered Thomism (Roman Catholicism) and Protestantism antagonists, and for good theological reasons. Next to the Angelicum is the church dedicated to Saint Dominic, the founder of the order to which Thomas belonged. On the façade of the church is a statue of Thomas. Inside are statues of Mary, devotional chapels and a plethora of Roman Catholic pictures and symbols indicating the cult of the saints, Mary and prayers to the dead. As part of the university entitled for Thomas, where sophisticated courses in philosophy and theology are taught, there is a place of Roman Catholic worship stemming from the same source: Thomas. Thomas remains at the centre of both academic and devotional practices: a high view of God and high view of Mary and the sacramental Church; lofty theological discourses and devotions like rosaries and novenas. This served as a reminder that when dealing with Thomas, we should pay attention not only to his alleged Christian theism or to his being part of the 'great tradition' but also to his being a champion of everything Roman Catholic, even the things that are most alien to the evangelical faith. In other words, while it is foolish to promote church history 'cancel culture' or 'throwing the baby out with the bathwater', when engaging with Thomas, at the same time, a mature theological evaluation will seek to grasp what has emerged from the work of the Angelic Doctor (Thomas's nickname in Catholic circles) as a whole.

This book originated from the courses on medieval theology that I taught at the Istituto di Formazione Evangelica e Documentazione in Padua in the academic years 2021–22 and 2022–23. I wish to thank colleagues and students for the fruitful interactions over the material presented. Thomas is a demanding dialogue partner in academic studies, and IFED has been the ideal place to engage in such an endeavour.

My friend and colleague Clay Kannard has helped me immensely, not only by reading the manuscript and editing the oddities of my written English but also by supporting me in prayer and Christian fellowship, his desk being next to mine.

Finally, a heartfelt thank you to my wife, Valeria. This is not yet the book I want to dedicate to her (if God will ever allow me to write it), but the fact is that I could not have written it without her support, patience, affection and irony. I call it love, which has been ongoing for thirty-three years. *Grazie.*

1
The life and work of Thomas Aquinas

The twelfth, thirteenth and fourteenth centuries are conventionally considered the historical age that reflects the transition between the Middle Ages and the Modern Age. It is often regarded as a time of twilight (the *Autumn of the Middle Ages*, as the famous book by Dutch historian Johan Huizinga puts it),[1] when culture was marked by pessimism, cultural exhaustion and nostalgia rather than rebirth and optimism. This is only one side of the coin, though. There is also a very different picture in the popular imagery that sees the Middle Ages as the most accomplished synthesis between Christianity and culture, faith and spirituality, philosophy and theology, etc. It is considered a period of history to draw inspiration from in our own disrupted time characterised by fragmentation.[2] Twentieth-century authors such as J. R. R. Tolkien and C. S. Lewis have contributed to a certain idealisation of the Middle Ages as a time infused and imbued with Christian symbols, an imperfect yet real bridge between heaven and earth and a rich reservoir of wisdom.[3] Whether this perception of the Middle Ages is realistic or merely an aestheticised and enchanted reinterpretation of it is a matter of ongoing discussion.

---

1 J. Huizinga, *The Autumn of the Middle Ages* [1919], tr. R. J. Payton and U. Mammitzsch (Chicago, IL: University of Chicago Press, 1996).

2 One can think of the founder of the Catholic University (Università Cattolica del Sacro Cuore) in Milan, Father Agostino Gemelli (1879–1958), himself a fervent neo-Thomist, who coined the term 'medievalism' to indicate the need for modern culture to take the Middle Ages as a model to overcome its tensions. See A. Gemelli, 'Medievalismo', *Vita e Pensiero* 1 (1914), pp. 1–24.

3 C. R. Armstrong, *Medieval Wisdom for Modern Christians: Finding Authentic Faith in a Forgotten Age with C. S. Lewis* (Grand Rapids, MI: Brazos Press, 2016).

However one views the world of the Middle Ages, this is the world of Thomas Aquinas. He was a medieval man fully immersed in his time's historical and cultural dynamics. Before diving into his life and work, it is important to be familiar with some general traits of the religious medieval background he was part of, especially regarding the scholastic method and mendicant orders.[4]

The religious medieval background

The extent of the reach and claims of papal power largely dominated theological reflection in the thirteenth century. Under Pope Innocent III, the Fourth Lateran Council (1215) took place. Among the many issues addressed, various dissenting movements were condemned, including the 'evangelical' one of the Waldensians, and the line that the Roman Church took on the age-old debate on the meaning of the Holy Supper was decided: the bread and the wine were thought of as changing nature (transubstantiation) into becoming the body and blood of Jesus. Taking a definitive position for the sacramentally 'realist' readings of the Supper, the Fourth Lateran Council introduced the category of 'transubstantiation' to explain the supernatural change of nature of the human species, without the accident of the same undergoing any modification, and attributing to the clergy endowed with the sacrament of the order the power to bring about such a change – claiming that the bread and wine of the Lord's Supper truly become the physical body and blood of Jesus while maintaining the appearance of bread and wine. Since then, Roman Catholicism has stiffened its sacramentalist theology, combining the sacrament of Holy Orders with the sacrament of the Eucharist based on categories largely inferred from Aristotelian physics, i.e. the 'substance' (nature) and the 'accident' (appearance). The dogmatic definition of transubstantiation was accompanied by the devotion of the consecrated wafer, which resulted in the feast of *Corpus Domini* (the Body of the Lord) or

---

4   For an overview, see P. J. Leithart, 'Medieval Theology and the Roots of Modernity' in W. A. Hoffecker (ed.), *Revolutions in Worldview: Understanding the Flow of Western Thought* (Phillipsburg, NJ: P & R Publishing, 2007), pp. 140–77.

Corpus Christi (the Body of Christ). Thomas wrote a liturgical text to celebrate this feast.

The issue of the extension of papal power was intertwined with political claims in the ongoing conflict with the Holy Roman Empire. The medieval climax of this clash occurred at the First Council of Lyon (1245) when the emperor Frederick II was excommunicated and deposed based on the alleged power invoked by the pope to possess a 'general delegation' from Christ to loose and bind anything, without exemptions. The theological legitimacy of such a move was also followed by military actions aimed at regaining the pope's temporal power over the territories around Rome and present-day Latium. This was the first nucleus of what would become the future state of the Church.

The Crusades also belong to this period and need to be understood against the background of the discussions about the attributions of papal power. Historically, the Crusades were a series of military campaigns, typically promoted by the papacy, which took place from the eleventh to the thirteenth century. They began with the initiative of Pope Urban II in 1095 in response to an appeal by the Byzantine emperor, who had asked for help in countering the advance of the Turks on the eastern front. The Crusades can be seen significantly as a response to the Muslim conquest of 'Christian' lands (particularly Jerusalem, the site of the 'holy sepulchre') with the goal of stemming the Muslim advance.[5] For the Crusaders, the Church granted the remission of their sins and the protection of their property and families. Beyond these religious purposes, the Crusades were also a way of affirming the pope's military power and capabilities. They were also wars of conquest, inspired by the feudal nobility in search of possessions and income. This encounter with Islam is another feature that can be seen in Thomas's work, especially in his *Summa against the Gentiles*.

---

5   C. Tyerman, *God's War: A New History of the Crusades* (London: Penguin, 2007). A different interpretation of the Crusades is suggested by R. Stark, *God's Battalions: The Case for the Crusades* (San Francisco, CA: HarperOne, 2010).

The scholastic method

The dynamism of thirteenth-century theology must be placed in the broader context of the renewal of culture that followed the reintroduction and circulation of texts by Greek and Arab authors. Since the first centuries of Christianity, Plato's and Neoplatonic writings had been among the most influential philosophical traditions that Christian thought had dealt with. From the twelfth century, the rediscovery of Aristotle and Aristotelianism quickly became the main interlocutor and incubator of theology. Theology had to confront, often not without compromises, classical Greco-Roman thought, both in the universities established in various European cities and the theological schools associated with churches or abbeys.

The circulation of *Libri naturales* by Aristotle (384–322 BC) in the universities introduced a new challenge for the theology of the time. They were a collection of Aristotle's treatises (e.g. on physics, meteors, the soul) in Latin translation. The thought of Aristotle was both read directly and mediated by the Arabic commentaries of Ibn Sina (Avicenna, 980–1037) and Ibn Rushd (Averroes, 1126–98), and, as a result, philosophy knew a renewal, or rather a transformation, of its methods and categories. Theology was deeply impacted by this process and morphed itself accordingly. The traditional and centuries-long reliance on Platonism, mediated by Augustine, had to become acquainted with the thought structures of Aristotelianism, which was being taught in universities and had acquired a 'scientific' status.

If the threads resulting from the interweaving between the birth of universities and the diffusion of Aristotelianism are united, one begins to understand the institutional and intellectual context that gave rise to the scholastic method.[6] University lectures were made up of *lectiones*, orderly presentations of the subject taught, and public *disputationes*, which required an argumentative style and a

---

6   M. Grabmann, *Die Geschichte der scholastischen Methode* (1909–1911). I had access to the Italian edition: *Storia del metodo scolastico, vol. 2: Il metodo scolastico nel XII e all'inizio del XIII secolo*, tr. M. Candela and P. Buscaglione Candela (Florence: La Nuova Italia Editrice, 1999).

formal setting. Once the lessons became copied texts to be studied and distributed, they gave rise to their literary genre. Furthermore, the *disputationes* started as appendixes to the lectures and tended to acquire their own autonomy concerning the exposition of the subject as such. The texts of the classics (Plato, Aristotle, the Church Fathers) were commented on, and these comments formed a body of interpretations that flowed into university teaching and academic discussions.

Comments to ancient texts could be integral or occasional (*scholia*) and form *sententiae* that summarised the thesis supported by the author or commentator in his teaching. They were also used to stimulate further discussion. In commenting on texts, *dubia* (doubts) could arise; they highlighted the problematic passages of a given text and called for a *solution*, which was the result of the analysis of the various arguments in favour or against and on the basis of the weight of *auctoritas* (authority) of their proponents. The topics covered were *quaestiones*, which, if substantial and lengthy enough, could become subjects in their own right and not just extensions of the comments on previous texts.

Around and within the university, a community of teachers and students was formed who practised the scholastic method in their study and research. In these processes of transformation, theology adapted its didactic and argumentative strategies to the scholastic procedures that were becoming mainstream. Scholasticism also shaped the epistemology of medieval theology to the point where theology was recognised as a *scientia* (science) among other academic disciplines. Specific to theology, the scholastic method favoured the deepening of the relationship between faith and reason and the rational analysis of the contents of the Christian faith. The specific scholastic process of distinguishing, weighing and arriving at the solution of the problems posed became the pattern of theological analysis. In studying Scripture and Christian doctrines, ontological questions and logical issues took precedence over the historical-redemptive understanding of the biblical message. In essence, scholasticism was a systematic way of organising theological knowledge. It was also a method for resolving the real or apparent contradictions of tradition by seeking to harmonise faith and reason and by demonstrating the fact that the truths of faith do not contradict the logic and reason established in a Neoplatonic and/or Aristotelian way. Thomas became a master in doing theology the scholastic way.

The mendicant orders

The thirteenth century was also the time when new religious orders were formed and began to thrive. This is especially true as far as the mendicant orders – the groups whose members were committed to a lifestyle of poverty and travelling for purposes of preaching and others forms of ministry – were concerned. The recovery of evangelical poverty (*altissima paupertas*) and the preaching of the gospel to the people were two axes that dissent movements (e.g. Waldensians, Albigensians, Lollards) would use in their polemical stance against the institutional Church, causing a repressive response from the ecclesiastical authority.[7] However, poverty and preaching were also the guidelines for forming movements within the established Church. Instead of being fought against, they were integrated and approved. On the one hand, there was the Franciscan movement, born with the preaching and life of Francis of Assisi (1181–1226)[8] from which the 'minor friars' (or Franciscans) dedicated to poverty were born; on the other, the order of the 'preacher friars', born of Dominic of Guzmán (1170–1221),[9] later called Dominicans.

Unlike other personalities such as Peter Waldo (1140–1205), Francis did not challenge the Church's authority, but considered

---

7   'Evangelical' here refers to the quest for simplicity in lifestyle and radical discipleship based on the gospel that characterised dissenting movements in the Middle Ages. For an overview, see J. B. Russell, *Dissent and Reform in the Early Middle Ages* (Eugene, OR: Wipf and Stock, 2005).

8   The literature on Francis of Assisi is immense. A contemporary hagiography written in 1260 is by Saint Bonaventure, *The Life of St. Francis of Assisi* (Charlotte, NC: TAN Books, 2010). Modern interpretations of Francis include C. Frugoni, *Francis of Assisi: A Life* (London: Continuum, 1997) and A. Vauchez, *Francis of Assisi: The Life and Afterlife of a Medieval Saint* (New Haven, CT: Yale University Press, 2012).

9   D. J. Goergen, *St. Dominic: The Story of a Preaching Friar* (New York, NY: The Paulist Press, 2016). A history of the Dominican Order written from within the order is D. Penone, *I domenicani nei secoli: panorama storico dell'Ordine dei frati predicatori* (Bologna: Edizioni Studio Domenicano, 1998).

her as 'mother' and offered her sincere obedience. Francis was the figure who was seen by the established Church as being capable of channelling the anxieties and the need for participation of the humblest classes, without placing himself as an antagonist to the Church: not a dissenter but a promoter of the Church. On the other hand, the Dominican preachers, once their fidelity to the magisterium and the authorities of the Church had been ascertained, could be seen as an instrument for the catechisation of the masses in a turbulent time. If previous monastic orders wanted to bring the world into the cloister, the Franciscan and Dominican friars tried to reverse the movement, that is, to bring the cloister into the world through an itinerant action in support of the institutional Church's mission. Their tumultuous development gave rise to internal and external tensions. These tensions were resolved with the Second Council of Lyon (1274), which regulated these new orders and framed them definitively within the structures of the Church. The institutional Church recognised their value and used them as an instrument of pastoral and disciplinary control in a time marked by the diffusion of dissenting movements.

The Dominican and Franciscan movements also introduced particular emphases on medieval theology. It can be said that they began to form schools of thought or traditions within the practice of theology: the first marked by a 'scholastic' imprint, the second by a 'spiritual' tendency.[10] The Dominicans drew attention to the primacy of the intellect over will in the intellectual/spiritual life of human beings. For the Dominicans, the supreme goal is 'to see God', while for the Franciscans, the ultimate goal is 'to love God'. For the former, what is higher is 'the true', while for the latter, it is 'the good'. For both traditions, 'the true' is also 'the good', and 'the good' is also 'the true'. It was a question of different accents and different theological styles: a sort of ellipse held together by the 'catholic' embracement of the institutional Church.

The Dominicans dedicated themselves to preaching the doctrine

10 I borrow these categories from S. Ozment, *The Age of Reform, 1250–1550: An Intellectual and Religious History of Late Medieval and Reformation Europe* (New Haven, CT: Yale University Press, 1980), pp. 22–72 (on the scholastic tradition) and pp. 73–134 (on the spiritual tradition).

of the Roman Church (hence their name of *Ordo Praedicatorum*, literally 'The Order of Preachers') to contribute to the correction of many deviant movements of the time. To represent a pauperistic alternative faithful within the official Church, the Franciscans worked to highlight the Church's openness to radical forms of spirituality. In one direction and the other, the Roman Catholic system emerged strengthened, having covered two critical sides which the widespread dissidence had opened. Another feature was the focus of Dominican activity on devoting themselves to study and preaching, which took place in the cities and university centres of the time: above all, Bologna (the Dominicans settled there as early as 1217) and Paris. The Franciscans, for their part, acted mainly (although not exclusively) in the suburbs and in the countryside. Both orders founded their houses of study in the main convents and established close relationships with the universities, soon becoming an important institutional component of the academic world.[11] Theology, already taught in universities by regular priests, also used the presence and contribution of Dominican and Franciscan theologians dedicated to theological training. Their presence was not always welcomed by the theologians of the regular clergy who already taught in universities and Thomas became involved in the controversy, especially during his two Parisian sojourns. The Second Council of Lyon (1274) established the right of Dominican and Franciscan theologians to teach in universities.

Two giants of the thirteenth century: Thomas Aquinas and Bonaventure of Bagnoregio

Thirteenth-century Western theology was dominated by two towering figures: Thomas Aquinas and Bonaventure of Bagnoregio (1221–74). The former belonged to the Dominican Order, the latter to the Franciscan Order. Both were born in Italy; both became professors in Paris at the theological centres of their respective

---

11 Cf. L. Pellegrini, *L'incontro di due 'invenzioni' medievali: università e ordini mendicanti* (Naples: Liguori Editore, 2005).

orders in the university city *par excellence* of the Middle Ages.[12] In this period, the mendicant orders became the contexts in which theology developed and flourished, while scholasticism was the mode of theologising of the time and the university was the place where theological reflection had to come to terms with the growing role of Aristotelian philosophy.

Roman Catholic hagiography has equated Thomas and Bonaventure to the 'two candlesticks, standing before the God of the earth', of Revelation 11:4, jointly considering them as the heroes of Roman Catholic thought.[13] Even before the formal recognition given by ecclesiastical authorities, it was Dante who placed Thomas and Bonaventure together in *Paradise* (canto X), evidently perceiving the role of both of them as outstanding.[14] The continuity and connections between the two main thirteenth-century theologians cannot be overlooked, but their profound differences must not be underestimated either. Some have spoken of a 'discordant harmony' between the two, in the sense that Thomas would have given primacy to intellect and speculation, Bonaventure to affection and wisdom.[15] Furthermore, while Thomas focused on the critical assimilation of Aristotelianism into Christian thought from a Dominican point of view, Bonaventure reworked the Augustinian legacy through Franciscan lenses.

In summary, medieval religious orders went beyond the previous Benedictine tradition, stemming from Benedict of Nursia (480–548) and based on the discipline of prayer and work. They elaborated new forms of religious life that updated the medieval

---

12 Cf. R. B. Smith, *Aquinas, Bonaventure, and the Scholastic Culture of Medieval Paris: Preaching, Prologues, and Biblical Commentaries* (Cambridge: Cambridge University Press, 2021).

13 Di Maio cites the bull *Triumphantis Hierusalem* by Pope Sixtus V (1558) and the letter by Leo XIII to the minister of the Ordo Fratrum Minorum (1885) in which Aquinas and Bonaventure are presented together as champions of the Roman Catholic faith: A. Di Maio, *Piccolo glossario bonaventuriano: prima introduzione al pensiero e al lessico di Bonaventura da Bagnoregio* (Rome: Aracne, 2008), p. 21.

14 The doctrinal scaffolding of the *Divine Comedy* is largely dependent on the thought of Thomas Aquinas, especially his *Summa Theologiae*. This is not the only direct reference to Thomas found in the *Paradise* canticle, but the influence of Thomas is pervasive throughout the *Comedy*.

15 Di Maio, *Piccolo glossario bonaventuriano*, pp. 31–32.

Church's ability to renew itself from within without changing the supporting structures of the hierarchical Church and its theological self-understanding.[16] The full ecclesiastical integration of these new orders bears witness to the flexibility of the Roman Catholic system, which could absorb calls and expectations for renewal as long as they were compatible with the traditional claims of the Church and submitted to its authority. Thomas's biography exemplifies the spiritual and intellectual life the Dominican Order sought to infuse in the wider Church.

The 'dumb ox' whose bellow resounded throughout the world

The biography of Thomas that accompanied the process leading to his canonisation in 1323 describes him as a 'silent man, assiduous in study and devout in prayer'.[17] From this, the Dominican brothers of Thomas began to call him the 'dumb ox' (*bovem mutum*). The nickname suggests a certain body corpulence (*magnus in corpore* as his contemporary biographer William of Tocco would say), and a well-balanced temperament and countenance: simultaneously a robust and delicate person. In any case, when Albert the Great, his master, came into direct contact with Thomas and recognised in him some extraordinary intellectual abilities, he exclaimed: 'We call him the dumb ox, but he will make resound in his doctrine such a bellowing that it will echo throughout the entire world.'[18] Indeed, from Thomas's placid disposition a movement of thought was born which has reverberated over the centuries and is still flourishing.

There is uncertainty over his exact birthdate, and the only objective reference point that we have is that he died on 7 March 1274

---

16 Cf. G. Melville, *The World of Medieval Monasticism: Its History and Forms of Life* (Collegeville, MN: Liturgical Press, 2016), pp. 206–48.

17 William of Tocco, *The Life of St. Thomas Aquinas* [1323] (Saint Marys, KS: Angelus Press, 2023). Otherwise available here: https://ia600905.us.archive.org/31/items/lifeofangelicdoc00cavauoft/lifeofangelicdoc00cavauoft.pdf (accessed 24 January 2024).

18 William of Tocco, *The Life of St. Thomas Aquinas*, p. 53.

at the age of 49. Therefore, the inferred date of birth is 1224. His family (D'Aquino) was of aristocratic descent and had a domain at the border of the states of the pope and the emperor. The two authorities always contested the influence over the nearby monastery of Monte Cassino. Thomas was the youngest of nine children (five girls and four boys) born to his parents: Landolfo and Theodora. Thomas's major modern biographer speaks of the beginning of his life as an 'eventful youth'.[19]

Indeed, after being born in Roccasecca (in the current province of Frosinone, almost halfway between Rome and Naples) in 1224 and having taken his first steps in his studies at the abbey of Monte Cassino, the young Tommaso studied in Naples at the local university founded by Frederick II. As he was the youngest son, the custom of the time prescribed that he be destined for the Church. He arrived in Naples in 1239 and had his first encounter with the texts of Aristotle in Latin translation (natural philosophy and metaphysics) and his Arabic commentators. In Naples, he encountered the Dominican Order (preaching friars) to which he felt he must belong despite the opposition of family members who even, in vain, imprisoned him to prevent him from joining. The family opposed Thomas's decision because the Dominicans were a recently established and mendicant order with little social power. Moreover, their wish for the youngest and most brilliant member to become the future abbot of Monte Cassino would be compromised. However, the young Aquinas was attracted by the intellectual and spiritual ideal of the Dominican friars intertwined around the disciplines of study, teaching and preaching. Later in life he would describe the religious life dedicated to teaching and preaching as having the 'highest place' (*summum gradum*, ST II–II, q. 188, a. 6). Thomas perceived that his inclination towards study and poverty could be accomplished in the Dominican Order.

---

19 J.-P. Torrell, *Saint Thomas Aquinas, vol. 1: The Person and His Work*, tr. Robert Royal (Washington, DC: Catholic University of America Press, 1996; rev. edn 2005), pp. 1–17. The other modern biography to be consulted is J. A. Weisheipl, *Friar Thomas d'Aquino: His Life, Thought and Work* (New York, NY: Doubleday, 1983).

The stubborn opposition of his family went as far as physically stopping him in a kind of house arrest. Thomas did not give up and maintained good relationships with his relatives. After receiving the Dominican habit in 1244, he moved to the Dominican convent in Paris (Saint-Jacques) in 1245, where he attended the lectures of Albert the Great (1200–80). Paris was the intellectual capital of Western Christianity at the time. In that intellectually stimulating environment, he familiarised himself with Aristotle's ethics and the work of Dionysius the Areopagite. When Albert moved to Cologne to teach there, Thomas followed him to complete his training (1248–52), being deeply impacted by him, especially in his reading of Dionysius's *Divine Names* and Aristotle's *Nicomachean Ethics*. In Cologne, Thomas taught introductory courses on biblical books such as Jeremiah, Lamentations and parts of Isaiah. With Albert's commendation and support, in 1253 he returned to Paris to begin his academic career in the theological department of the university, commenting on the Bible and the *Sentences* of Peter Lombard. The fruit of these lectures on Peter Lombard is contained in the *Scriptum super Sententiis*. In his second Parisian sojourn in Paris, Thomas also wrote his commentaries on Boethius's *De Trinitate* and began to draft the *Summa against the Gentiles*. In 1257 he was appointed as master (*magister*). The Parisian university was at the centre of a debate on the role of subscribing to the teaching of Aristotle. Thomas was caught in the middle of these discussions, trying to argue the necessity of avoiding the rejection of Aristotle while maintaining the Augustinian legacy. There was another quarrel going on in Paris: the role of the mendicant religious orders came under attack by the regular priests, who questioned the legitimacy of the religious orders to teach and to belong to the professorial body. Thomas defended both the spiritual ideals of mendicant life and the right for the mendicant religious orders to be dedicated to teaching in the university context.

After the first three years of teaching (1257–59) in Paris, Thomas taught for the following decade in various study centres in Italy. After stopping by Naples, he resided in Orvieto (1261–65), where he concluded the *Summa against the Gentiles* and wrote his *Commentary on Job*. In this work he dealt extensively with the metaphysical problem of providence rather than focusing on the exhortation to patience during trials. In Orvieto, he also composed the *Contra errores Graecorum* (*Against the errors of the Greeks*) where, unlike the impression given by the apologetic title, he irenically examined a collection of texts from the Greek Fathers, including his comments on disputed matters such as the *Filioque* – the trinitarian controversy between Eastern and Western Christianity over the procession of the Spirit that caused a schism in 1054. This was also when he began to write the *Catena Aurea* (*Golden Chain*), a commentary on the four Evangelists through a series of quotations from the Church Fathers. Besides theological and exegetical works, Thomas also composed the *Officium de Festo Corporis Christi*, a liturgical text that would be used to celebrate the feast of the *Corpus Christi* focused solely on the Eucharist, emphasising the joy of the Eucharist being the body and blood, soul and divinity of Jesus Christ.

After his productive and rather peaceful years in Orvieto, Thomas was sent by the Dominican Order to Rome to establish a study centre to educate men from the region to become friars. It was in Rome (1265–68) that he began writing the *Summa Theologiae* as a comprehensive manual for teaching the students. He also began the *Compendium Theologiae* (*Compendium of Theology*), a relatively brief treatment of Christian doctrine built on the three theological virtues of faith, hope and love.

After Rome, he resumed teaching in Paris (1269–72) and finally in Naples (1272–74). During his second stay in Paris, Thomas again found himself involved in the ongoing controversies over the dangers of Aristotelianism in teaching theology and the age-old dispute on the conditions of teaching for teachers belonging to the secular clergy and mendicant orders. Thomas defended the plausibility of using Aristotle while exposing the dangers of some Averroist interpretations of the Stagirite Philosopher concerning the unicity of the intellectual soul of all human beings. As he had already done in his second Parisian sojourn, the first as a teacher, he also strenuously advocated for the legitimacy of mendicant orders to teach theology in the university. While engaged in these controversies, Thomas wrote his commentary on John's Gospel and various shorter writings on philosophical and theological issues.

After Paris, it was time for Thomas to return to Naples to teach at the Dominican study centre there, where he concentrated on courses on Paul's letters and the Psalms, simultaneously writing the remaining parts of the *Summa Theologiae*. According to Torrell, this period of his life is 'the one from which we have the greatest amount of concrete data'.[20] The main reason for this is because some of the witnesses to his later canonisation (1323) were confreres, friends and family members who had been acquainted with Thomas during the last months of his life in Naples. In this period, it is reported that he had prolonged ecstasies and absent-mindedness. While in Naples, on 6 December 1273, Thomas, following an astounding experience during the celebration of the Mass, interrupted the dictation of his works by saying to his disciple Reginald of Piperno: 'I cannot do any more. Everything I have written seems as straw in comparison with what I have seen' (*omnia quae scripsi videntur michi palee*).[21] This mystical experience further accentuated the *abstractio mentis* he was already used to, perhaps fostering a near total detachment from his work. Weisheipl prefers to speak of a physical and psychological breakdown resulting from the overwork that Thomas had imposed on himself for such a long time.[22]

After that event, Thomas's appearance profoundly changed. Not knowing what was happening to him and trusting the theological expertise that Thomas had shown in the *Contra errores Graecorum*, Pope Gregory X ordered him to go to Lyon to participate in the Council convened to promote reconciliation between the Latin and Greek Churches. However, he did not join in that Council. In fact, during the journey, in a place close to Teano, he struck his head against a branch of a fallen tree that he had failed to notice. An internal haemorrhage may have taken place as a result.[23] We know that shortly after, on 7 March 1274, Thomas died in the Cistercian

---

20 Torrell, *Saint Thomas Aquinas, vol. 1*, p. 267.

21 Torrell, *Saint Thomas Aquinas, vol. 1*, p. 289.

22 Weisheipl, *Friar Thomas d'Aquino*, pp. 320–23.

23 Weisheipl, *Friar Thomas d'Aquino*, p. 328.

abbey of Fossanova (near Latina), only 40 miles (66 km) from where he was born. After travelling up and down the peninsula from Naples to Paris, to Cologne, back to Orvieto and Rome, up to Paris again and then down to Naples, while he was travelling again to reach a destination above the Alps, Thomas's life ended very close to where it all had begun.

A most impressive work

The life of Thomas cannot be thought of separately from his massive body of writings. Scholars have calculated that his works are composed of a total of 8 million words: 2 million in commentaries on the Bible, 1 million in discussions around Aristotle, and the others employed in his numerous books, disputations, treatises, etc.[24] Thomas had the habit of writing at a fast speed and correcting his writing on the way. He also dictated to his secretaries consecutively, with more than one of them assisting him. Occasionally his listeners would write down his lectures (especially on the biblical books) or his sermons. His style was precise, with no repetition and careful nuancing of his arguments. His works reflect his richness, vitality and complexity of thought.

The publication of the critical edition of the complete works of Thomas (in Latin) is still in progress under the auspices of the Leonine Commission. It was Pope Leo XIII who instituted this work in 1879 and entrusted it to the Dominicans. The series will comprise fifty volumes and has become the standard reference point for scholars and translators into modern languages.[25] Of course, Thomas's work is available in most languages, and most of it is also freely accessible online.[26]

Although such a massive body of literature is difficult to map out, Thomas's impressive work is catalogued by Weisheipl in the

24 Kerr, *Thomas Aquinas: A Very Short Introduction*, p. 20.

25 C. Luna, 'L'édition léonine de saint Thomas d'Aquin', *Revue des sciences philosophiques et théologiques* 89:1 (2005), pp. 31–110.

26 Details on the English translations that will be used in this book will be given in the Bibliography.

following way: 1. Theological syntheses; 2. Scholarly disputes or debated questions; 3. Commentaries on sacred Scripture; 4. Commentaries on Aristotle; 5. Other commentaries; 6. Polemical writings; 7. Treatises on special topics; 8. Letters and requests for expert opinion; 9. Liturgical writings and sermons; 10. Works of dubious authenticity.[27] What follows is an annotated list of the main works for each collection. Next to the titles of the main works, the places and the dates of their composition will be indicated and a short description of their contents will follow.

1. Theological syntheses

– *Commentary on the Sentences* of Peter Lombard (Paris, 1252–56)
Thomas discusses the famous work of Peter Lombard, divided into four books (1. God; 2. Creation; 3. Christ; 4: The Christian life and the sacraments). The *Sentences* were the standard theological reference point for the teaching of theology in the Middle Ages. Though always referring to Peter Lombard, Thomas would build his own main works (the two *Summae*), no longer following the fourfold structure of the *Sentences* but around the *exitus–reditus* (procession–return) motif.

– *Summa contra Gentiles* [*Summa against the Gentiles*] (Paris, Naples and Orvieto, 1258–64)
A philosophical and theological synthesis that examines what can be known of God both by reason (shared with Gentiles, e.g. Jews and Muslims) and by divine revelation (accepted by Christians only).

– *Summa Theologiae* (Rome, Paris and Naples, 1266–72)
One of the most influential treatises on Christian theology ever written, divided into three parts. To help students become acquainted with the basics of a theological vision, Thomas displays his outstanding ability to blend biblical exegesis, the legacy of the

---

27 Weisheipl, *Friar Thomas d'Aquino*, pp. 355–405. See also Torrell, *Saint Thomas Aquinas*, vol. 1, pp. 330–61.

Church Fathers and philosophical insights in this *chef d'oeuvre* of scholastic theology. Left incomplete by Thomas, his disciples subsequently finished it with various *Supplements* based on the teaching of their master.

2. Scholarly disputes

These writings are called *Quaestiones Disputatae*, i.e. disputed questions, and *Quaestiones Quodlibetales*, i.e. questions on any subject. As a university teacher, Thomas deals with topics and issues suggested by students and assistants. Among the most important ones, the following *Quaestiones* need to be highlighted:

– *De veritate* (Paris, 1256–59)
On truth (*verum*), goodness (*bonum*) and the natural human appetite for both. The human will has a natural inclination towards the good.

– *De potentia* (Rome, 1265–66)
Thomas discusses what it means for God to be powerful, the role of secondary causes and the function of miracles.

– *De malo* (Rome, 1266–67)
The issues of evil, sin and its causes, original sin and its consequences, venial and capital sins, and the devil are central to this discussion. In a Neoplatonic way, evil is interpreted as privation whereas sin is seen as both violation of a rule and deviation from a target. Original sin is viewed in Augustinian terms; one of its consequences is the subtraction of the lower human faculties from the dominion of reason.

– *De anima* (Paris, 1269)
Here we find some important elements of Thomas's anthropology with special reference to the soul. A human being is not a disembodied soul, but always the union between soul and body. Having said that, the soul presupposes the body but can live independently from it.

3. Commentaries on sacred Scripture

Commentary on Isaiah (Cologne, 1249–52); Commentary on the Gospel according to Matthew (Paris, 1256–59); Commentaries on the letters of Paul, including Romans (1259–65, 1272–73); *Catena Aurea* (Golden Chain) or *Glossa* on the Four Gospels (Orvieto and Rome, 1262–67); Commentary on the Gospel according to John (Paris, 1269–72).

4. Commentaries on Aristotle

– Commentary on *Metaphysics* (Paris and Naples, 1269–72)
A discussion on what is universal and what is first and the notion of causality.

– Commentary on *Politics* (Paris, 1269–72)
Thomas endorses Aristotle's view of the human being as *animal sociale, animal civile* and *animal politicum*, although his political views are better expressed in the treatise *De regno*.

– Commentary on *Peri Hermeneias* (Paris, 1270–71)
On the issue of interpretation and the way the intellect apprehends.

– Commentary on the *Nicomachean Ethics* (Paris, 1271)
Thomas endorses Aristotle's view of ethics as the science of the good for human life, that which is the end or goal at which all our actions aim.

– Commentary on the *Posterior Analytics* (1271–72)
The focus is on the nature of demonstration and scientific knowledge.

5. Other commentaries

– On Boethius's *De Trinitate* (Paris, 1252–59)
An exposition of Boethius's treatise on the Trinity and a detailed examination of its emerging issues. Thomas elaborates on the scientific nature of theology, the knowability of God and the distinction between rational enquiry and faith.

– On the *Divine Names* of Dionysius the Areopagite (Rome, 1265–67)
Commenting on this work allows Thomas to deal with the Neoplatonic tradition and apophatic theology.

– On *Liber de Causis* (Paris, 1271–72)
Another exposure to the Neoplatonic tradition with special reference to the issue of causality with the different mediations between remote and proximate causes.

6. Polemical writings

– Against opponents of religious life (Paris, 1256) and on the perfection of the spiritual life (Paris, 1269–70)
The defence of the contemplative life as practised by the mendicant orders is also an argument to support the prerogatives of the religious orders to teach (*docere*), including the possibility to study and research.

– On the unity of the intellect (Paris, 1270)
Against Averroist speculations on the unicity of the human intellect.

7. Treatises on special topics

– *De ente et essentia* (Paris, 1252–56)
Thomas defines the terms 'being' and 'essence' as the primary notions the intellect acquires. They provide the basic metaphysical lexicon of his philosophical work. Being is the truth of what is; essence is what constitutes its being (its *quidditas*).

– *De regno* (Rome, 1265–67)
Dedicated to the king of Cyprus, the treatise investigates the monarchy's origin and the king's duties following three steps: the authority of Scripture, philosophical doctrines and the example of illustrious princes.

– *Compendium of Theology* (Paris or Naples, 1269–73)
An incomplete but profound synthesis of the Christian faith dedicated to Reginald of Piperno, Thomas's faithful secretary.

8. Letters and requests for expert opinion

– *Against the errors of the Greeks* (Orvieto, 1263)
At the request of Pope Urban IV, Thomas argues that the Greek Fathers, if properly understood, support the procession of the Spirit from the Father and the Son, the primacy of papal authority and even the existence of purgatory.

9. Liturgical writings and sermons

Of particular importance are the liturgy for the *Corpus Christi* feast, which shows Thomas's eucharistic theology as it shapes devotional practices that he fully endorsed, and his Lent sermons on the Apostles' Creed (*Collationes in Symbolum Apostolorum*, Naples, 1273).

10. Works of dubious authenticity

Several short writings on philosophical and theological issues whose attribution to Thomas is debated among scholars.

As indicated previously, Thomas's work is an almost boundless theological, philosophical, exegetical and spiritual universe with monumental proportions. To put it in context, the book you are now reading is around 80,000 words, and took around a year to write after years of regular research. Aquinas's output would be equal to 100 books of this size! Its significance moves way beyond medieval culture and even beyond Christian theology, strictly speaking. It is time to look at its sources and its syntheses more carefully.

2

Sources and synthesis of Thomas Aquinas's thought

The biography of a theologian provides a valuable interpretative key to access their work. It is now time to delve into the sources and the outcomes of Thomas's thought. His theology has been rightly described as 'a great river' into which a 'multitude of tributaries' flow.[1] The metaphor is effective in rendering the idea both of the grandeur of his thought and of the multiple currents which, mixing, contribute to characterising it for what it is. At least three main sources must be considered as entering Thomas's thought, each on its terms and intertwining with the others. Thomas was a great scholar of ancient and contemporary texts, a fruitful commentator and assimilator of different thoughts, and a skilled teacher who reworked the amount of knowledge he examined into an 'original synthesis'[2] of his own, which became Thomism.

In this chapter, the three main sources will be briefly examined before approaching the task of critically evaluating how Thomas makes his synthesis, taking the *Summa Theologiae* as the main reference point of the investigation. For each source, a case study will illustrate how Thomas used these sources and applied them

---

1 The metaphor is used by J.-P. Torrell, *La 'somme' de saint Thomas* (Paris: Cerf, 2011), p. 8. On the sources of Thomas's thought, see pp. 102–20, and by the same Torrell, *Saint Thomas Aquinas, vol. 2: Spiritual Master*, tr. Robert Royal (Washington, DC: Catholic University of America Press, 2003), pp. 376–84, and 'Saint Thomas and His Sources' in M. Levering and M. Plested (eds), *The Oxford Handbook of the Reception of Aquinas* (Oxford: Oxford University Press, 2021), pp. 1–20. See also C. Pera, *Le fonti del pensiero di S. Tommaso d'Aquino nella Somma teologica* (Turin: Marietti Editore, 1979).

2 Again Torrell, *La 'somme' de saint Thomas*, p. 119. For Torrell it is 'original' because, while absorbing various contributions, Thomas's doctrine is neither Platonic, nor Aristotelian, not even Averroist: it is simply 'Christian', although not simplistically so. This evaluation is, of course, subject to objections, as will be indicated later.

in specific works or themes of particular importance for an evangelical evaluation of his thought.

Aristotle and philosophical thought

Thomas lived in a historical phase in which Aristotle's works were in the early stages of the university teaching culture of the time. Thomas's teacher, Albert the Great, set out to make Greek science and reason comprehensible to the medieval Latin world and compatible with the Christian tradition, as personified by the then recently rediscovered Aristotle. During his studies, while training to become a teacher, Thomas decided to comment analytically on Aristotle's works to equip himself with a 'scientific' basis that would accompany him throughout his life's work. This practice punctuates his intellectual biography. In fact, until the last months of his life, Thomas did not stop reading and commenting on the works of Aristotle.[3]

As a theology teacher, Thomas did not have to comment on Aristotle as this was not his professional duty. His reason for dealing with the Stagirite Philosopher was his awareness that his theological work should interact with the 'science' of the day. For him, a good theologian must be someone educated in science, and Aristotle's thought was the body of science that was increasingly accepted in university circles.[4]

From Aristotle, Thomas learned to use the fundamental categories of form and matter, sensible and intelligible, actuality and potentiality, substance and accident, genus and species. Thomas regarded Aristotle as a *generally* reliable guide for philosophical investigation based on natural facts. From Aristotle, he drew answers to traditional philosophical questions on the role of reason, the nature of human beings, the function of language in

---

3 The 'philosophical' contribution of Thomas in which the influence of Aristotle (among others) is aptly presented can be found in P. Porro, *Tommaso d'Aquino: un profilo storico-filosofico* (Rome: Carocci Editore, 2019; repr. 2021).

4 Cf. J. Owen, 'Aristotle and Aquinas' in N. Kretzmann and E. Stump (eds), *The Cambridge Companion to Aquinas* (Cambridge: Cambridge University Press, 1993), pp. 38–59.

speaking of God, and the impediments and encouragements for acting virtuously. In the words of Davies, Fordham University professor, Aquinas 'believes that he can go a long way to defending these answers without invoking the articles of faith as premises in his arguments'.[5] From Aristotle he accepted (even if not passively) the metaphysics that theology must investigate and the logic that underlies theological research. He also borrowed from his psychology and ethics. In this respect, Torrell points out the fact that Thomas intended to 'extend' the Philosopher, drawing from him as far as the basic framework of a scientific world view was concerned and stretching his thought to make it compatible with Christian categories where the paganism of Aristotle could not be received, as can be seen with his view of the eternity of the world.[6]

As explained in his commentary on Boethius's *De Trinitate*, Thomas believed that Aristotle (and, by extension, 'philosophy' as the two are deeply intertwined in his thought) is necessary to demonstrate the *praeambula fidei* (preambles of faith) such as the existence and the unicity of God which are accessible to natural reason; to illustrate, through the use of similitudes and comparisons, some truths of faith that are otherwise difficult to understand and to communicate; and to refute objections to the faith rationally. Especially on the first point, legitimate questions about Thomas's overall moderate dependence on Aristotle can be asked. Thomas did not follow Aristotle because of an academic trend but more simply because he believed that his philosophy was *true* as far as it goes. It was Aristotle who opened eyes to discover the truth of the divine mysteries that is accessible by faith.

Was Thomas's use of Aristotle a theologically compromised use of the Christian faith? Certainly, Thomas rejected Aristotle's polytheism in favour of trinitarian monotheism, just as his doctrine of creation in time owes little or nothing to Aristotelian cosmogony. That said, the profound affinities between the *De anima* of the Greek philosopher and the psychological section of the *Summa*

---

5 B. Davies, *Thomas Aquinas's Summa Contra Gentiles: A Guide and Commentary* (Oxford: Oxford University Press, 2016), p. 7.

6 Torrell, *Saint Thomas Aquinas, vol. 1*, p. 236.

Theologiae, and between the *Nicomachean Ethics* and the part of the *Summa* dedicated to morality, should also be noted. Thomas's epistemology also proposes Aristotelian theory of knowledge with some revisions which do not alter their fundamental orientation.

In his appropriation of Aristotle, Thomas achieved a great 'harmony' for Roman Catholic theology. He operated a virtuous 'synthesis' between philosophy and theology, Christianity and Aristotelianism, faith and rational thought.[7] In the words of Benedict XVI, 'Thomas Aquinas showed that a natural harmony exists between Christian faith and reason. And this was the great achievement of Thomas who, at that time of clashes between two cultures[,] that time when it seemed that faith would have to give in to reason[,] showed that they go hand in hand, that insofar as reason appeared incompatible with faith it was not reason, and so what appeared to be faith was not faith, since it was in opposition to true rationality; thus he created a new synthesis which formed the culture of the centuries to come.'[8] It is evident that the assimilatory approach suits the very nature of Roman Catholicism, which, not surprisingly, considers Thomas the theologian who has reached the highest point of integration (synthesis) between Judeo-Christian roots and Greek thought,[9] thus completing the process by which Hellenism was eventually Christianised.

For a Reformed critic like Cornelius Van Til, the evaluation is similar in recording Thomas's ability to operate a 'synthesis', but radically different in assessing its impact on the integrity of the faith. For Van Til, Thomas imposed 'the Christian worldview on

---

7   Cf. R. Garrigou-Lagrange, *La sintesi tomistica* [1950] (Italian edition, Verona: Fede & Cultura, 2015), where the word 'synthesis' is used to capture the heart of Thomas's thought.

8   Benedict XVI, *General Audience* (2 June 2010): https://www.vatican.va/content/benedict-xvi/en/audiences/2010/documents/hf_ben-xvi_aud_20100602.html (accessed 12 May 2023).

9   On the 'synthesis' between the Greek spirit and the Christian spirit, Benedict XVI came back in his famous (and hotly debated!) speech 'Faith, Reason and the University' given in Regensburg in 2006. Cf. Benedict XVI, *Lecture of the Holy Father* (12 September 2006): https://www.vatican.va/content/benedict-xvi/en/speeches/2006/september/documents/hf_ben-xvi_spe_20060912_university-regensburg.html (accessed 12 May 2023). In this speech, Pope Benedict does not explicitly refer to Thomas but it is clear that the acclaimed 'synthesis' has a Thomistic flavour.

top of Aristotle's scheme of abstract form and chaotic matter'.[10] Nature is thought of in Aristotelian categories, while grace in Christian terms is *supra naturam* (above nature). Their relationship is one of juxtaposition, thanks to which each maintains its autonomy. At most, grace elevates nature but does not predefine or redefine it altogether. For Van Til, the kind of Christianity shaped by Thomas is the 'synthesis of Aristotle plus Christ',[11] that is the 'Aristotle-Christ',[12] and this represents something *other* than the biblical Christ: the hellenisation of Christianity.

When Thomas quotes or interacts with the 'philosophers' he has Greek and Arab thinkers in mind, i.e. Aristotle and the Arab commentators Avicenna (970–1037) and Averroes (1126–98). An Arab philosopher and physician whose *Metaphysics* circulated from the second half of the twelfth century, Avicenna was taken as an interlocutor in some treatises such as *De ente et essentia* (*On Being and Essence*), or cited extensively in the *Commentary on the Sentences* of Peter Lombard or in the *Disputed Questions on Truth*. Thomas distances himself from Avicenna's doctrine of eternal creation, of the separation of the intellect, and of the denial of the resurrection of the body. Averroes is an Arab commentator on Aristotle and was taken seriously by Thomas in the *Commentary on the Sentences* and in the *Summa contra Gentiles*. Thomas favourably quoted Averroes on 'natural' philosophy topics such as the conception of infinity, time, numbers, movement and matter. He dismissed Averroes as 'depraving' Aristotle about the unity of the intellect,[13] describing him as the *depravator* (detractor) and *perversor* (perverter) of Aristotle's thought. In addition to the two Arab philosophers, Thomas conversed with Maimonides

10 J. M. Frame, *Cornelius Van Til: An Analysis of His Thought* (Phillipsburg, NJ: P & R Publishing, 1995), p. 267.

11 C. Van Til, *A Christian Theory of Knowledge* (Phillipsburg, NJ: P & R Publishing, 1969), p. 175.

12 Van Til, *A Christian Theory of Knowledge*, p. 185. On the merits and limits of Van Til's analysis, see my '"The Clay of Paganism with the Iron of Christianity": Cornelius Van Til's Critique of Roman Catholicism' in J. Eglinton and G. Harinck (eds), *Neo-Calvinism and Roman Catholicism* (Leiden, the Netherlands: Brill, 2023), pp. 249–62.

13 *De unitate intellectus contra Averroistas*. Thomas's master, Albert the Great, had already written on the subject and against Averroes in his 1263–64 *De unitate intellectus contra Averroistas*, being asked to do so by Pope Alexander IV.

(1135–1204), a Judeo-Hispanic Arabic-speaking thinker often regarded as an adversary and as an interpreter of Jewish objections to Christianity.

A case study on the *Summa against the Gentiles*

The comparison between Christianity and the Greek–Arab culture, in addition to obvious scientific interests and its use in university studies, also involves some apologetic concerns. This was the context in which Thomas penned the *Summa against the Gentiles* (1258–64). The perception of medieval culture that Thomas made his own was that the traditional Christian theology grounded on Augustinian foundations was losing ground in comparison with the philosophical trends championed by Aristotle and his commentators. The need, then, was for a work that refuted the errors of a whole range of 'Gentiles' or wanderers, such as Muslims, Jews and various heretics present both outside the geographical borders of Christianity and in its cultural institutions, i.e. the universities. In the words of Dulles, the Jesuit theologian who was created cardinal by John Paul II in 2001, 'The *Summa* is an all-embracing apologetical theology drawn up with an eye to the new challenge of the scientific Greco-Arabic worldview.'[14] It was not so much the missionary intent to refute the Qur'an or Jewish theology that drove Thomas; rather, the cultural concern arising in one who critically read Avicenna and Averroes prompted him to write the work. It was not so much the contemporary unfaithful or pagans to be converted who were in sight. It was the ancient Greek and Arab philosophers who were dead, but whose thought was becoming increasingly influential.

The cultural strategy was to integrate parts of what pagan philosophy stands for and to reject the residual errors on the premise that reason is the same for Christians and pagans. In the *Summa*,

---

14 A. Dulles, *A History of Apologetics* (San Francisco, CA: Ignatius Press, 2005), p. 114. A very useful introduction to the *Summa* is 'Una introduzione alla *Summa contra Gentiles* di San Tommaso' in I. Biffi, *Sulle vie dell'Angelico: teologia, storia, contemplazione* (Milan: Jaca Book, 2009), pp. 385–404.

Aquinas tries to explain his views on what people, regardless of their faith commitments, can know about God and divine revelation. He tries to explain how a 'wise man', as Aristotle understood the phrase, can use his reason and end up believing in God. The assumption is that 'reason' is common to all: 'Some of them, as Mohammedans and Pagans, do not agree with us in recognising the authority of any Scripture, available for their conviction, as we can argue against the Jews from the Old Testament, and heretics from the New. But these receive neither: hence it is necessary to have recourse to natural reason, which all are obliged to assent to. But in the things of God, natural reason is often at a loss' (*SG* I, 1, 2).[15] Not everyone accepts Scripture as the revealed Word of God, but reason works in the same way for everyone, pagan and Christian alike. Therefore, reason must be appealed to. Here is a central point in Thomas's thought. As historical theologian Bray puts it, 'Scholastic theologians thought that by distinguishing reason from revelation and by subordinating the former to the latter, they could meet the challenge of pagan and Islamic science without surrendering the supremacy of the Christian gospel.'[16] Whether Thomas was able to preserve the integrity of the gospel in the process is discussed among scholars of different traditions, as we will see.

Given that for Thomas, some truths of faith are accessible to reason (e.g. God's existence and uniqueness) and others are inaccessible (e.g. the Trinity), the *Summa* sets out the demonstrative or probable reasons that make them acceptable to reason while clarifying the truths of faith with probable reasons, using analogies and similarities which would make them plausible at least. To reject errors, Thomas insisted on rationally demonstrating what is accessible to reason. This rational exercise is meant to show the likelihood of Christian truths. This explains why Thomas dedicated three of the four books of the *Summa* to arguing the defensibility of truths about God and the world without invoking Scripture and

---

15 The translation is taken from https://www3.nd.edu/~afreddos/courses/264/scgbk1chap1-9. htm (accessed 20 December 2023).

16 G. Bray, *God Has Spoken: A History of Christian Theology* (Wheaton, IL: Crossway, 2014), p. 554.

its authority, nor relying on the Church's creeds. Three-quarters of the *Summa* are, therefore, an exercise in 'natural theology' basically driven by what he calls 'philosophical insights', or 'philosophy', or just 'reason' to which all people are forced to give their assent.

After clarifying the difference between the two orders of truth (I, 1–9), the *Summa* presents the proofs of the existence of God *a posteriori* (since, contrary to Anselm, the existence of God is not known *a priori* and as a starting point). God is simple. Moreover, rational reflection can determine his perfections: goodness, unity, infinity, intelligence, truth, will, life and bliss. The second book deals with the derivation of all creatures from God, as God is understood to be the efficient cause of creation. What follows is the refutation of the theses concerning the uniqueness of the intellect of different individuals (73 onwards), and it is conducted through the analysis of the opinions of Averroes and Avicenna, among others. Book III deals with the order of creatures and the end God assigned to them. God is the ultimate end of all things; this implies that evil has a cause *per accidens* and that it is always, as such, *per accidens*, i.e. that there is no supreme evil, and that all beings are therefore ordered to good (4–17). Human intelligence tends to God as its end, beyond earthly life (45–48). God governs all things and orders both the project and the fulfilment of things through his general and particular providence. To fulfil the purpose to which creatures are called, God bestows his grace (147–63). Book IV expounds the central theological themes of the Christian faith such as the Trinity, the Incarnation, the sacraments and the resurrection of the body. These are truths that need divine revelation to be received and believed. Especially as far as the doctrine of God is concerned, the *Summa* contains *in nuce* a separation of headings that will have an enormous impact in subsequent Western theology: the distinction within theology proper between *de Deo uno* (the one God) and *de Deo trino* (the triune God). The former is contained in nature and accessible via reason; the latter is revealed in the Bible and appropriated by faith. Philosophical exercise is what is needed to come to the knowledge of God as one; biblical revelation is what is necessary to approach God as triune.

The division between the first three books and the last one has been depicted brilliantly by the late professor of philosophy at Cornell University, Kretzmann. According to him, in books I to III Thomas presents 'theology from the bottom up' because he talks about God 'without recourse to revelation' while in book IV he expounds a theology 'from the top down' since he reflects on God in the light of divine revelation.[17]

In essence, the subject of the first three books is 'the truths that find a foothold or intersection in Aristotle',[18] while the last book expounds the Christian truth accessible through Scripture. To simplify, one could say that the whole supporting scaffolding rests on Aristotle, while the Bible acts as an element that completes and finalises the argument. The structure of the *Summa* plastically depicts the architecture of Thomas's thought: at the foundation of reason, the level of faith which elevates and perfects it is added. According to Thomas, what reason can demonstrate cannot conflict with what God has revealed in Scripture as if reason is the faculty with contents and procedures that, even after the Fall and the impact of sin, can convey and lead to truth. Despite the thoroughness of the work, there is a lack of adequate attention to the theme of sin, which, although taken into account in the discussion, has an accidental rather than a structuring weight in the unfolding of the main argument of the *Summa*.

The 'sacred page' of Scripture

Having recognised Aristotle's undoubtable and extensive influence, we can consider another upstream source for Thomas's thought. As a *magister in sacra pagina* (master of the sacred page), the Bible and the study of biblical texts were equally impactful sources on Thomas's theological formation and, therefore, his work. Indeed, according to Chenu, in the thirteenth century 'the fruitful impulse

---

17 N. Kretzmann, *The Metaphysics of Theism: Aquinas's Natural Theology in Summa contra Gentiles 1* (Oxford: Clarendon Press, 1997), pp. 20–53.

18 Biffi, 'Una introduzione alla *Summa contra Gentiles* di San Tommaso', p. 401. At this point Biffi echoes and evaluates the interpretations of scholars like Gauthier, Lafont and others.

derives not from the discovery of Aristotle's texts, but from the reawakening of a faith nourished by the sacred texts'.[19] In this reading of Thomas, the Bible has a primary and coextensive role concerning the philosophy of Aristotle.

Indeed, Thomas wrote numerous commentaries on books of the Old Testament (from Job to Jeremiah) and the New Testament (from the Gospels to the letters of Paul), generally favouring the literal sense of the text and, as in the case of the *Catena Aurea* commentary on the Gospels, listening to the patristic interpretations (Thomas quotes fifty-seven Greek Fathers and twenty-two Latin Fathers). In his skills as a Bible commentator, Thomas followed his master Albert the Great, who was himself an outstanding exegete.[20] Thomas's exegetical studies must be coupled with sermons on biblical passages, mostly preached to theology students rather than to ordinary people.

Torrell summarises Thomas's approach to biblical exegesis in this sequence: *legere, disputare, praedicare* (read, dispute, preach).[21] The text reading is carried out as a scholastic practice leading to a set of arguments that feeds the responsibility of preaching.[22] In more detail, the reading exercise focused on grammatical and semantic questions to establish the meaning of words and sentences. This kind of reading of the text was followed by discussing the uncertain or particularly complex aspects left open in the enquiry. In principle, the contradictions were not attributable to Scripture and therefore it was necessary to work to resolve them on the side of the reader–interpreter. The discussion also included resolving conflicts of interpretation between the Church Fathers. Finally, the preaching of the biblical text received an impulse from the interpretative work and led to an exhortation to Christian

19 M.-D. Chenu, *Introduzione allo studio di S. Tommaso d'Aquino* (Florence: Libreria Editrice Fiorentina, 1953), p. 41.

20 See the essays edited by A. Colli, 'Albert the Great and Holy Scripture', *Divus Thomas* 122 (2019).

21 Torrell, *Saint Thomas Aquinas, vol. 1*, pp. 54–74. Cf. F. Santi, 'L'esegesi biblica di Tommaso d'Aquino nel contesto dell'esegesi biblica medievale', *Angelicum* 71:4 (1994), pp. 509–35.

22 On his preaching see R. B. Smith, *Reading the Sermons of Thomas Aquinas: A Beginner's Guide* (Steubenville, OH: Emmaus Academic, 2016).

perfection if it took place in a monastic context, or to moral teaching if it was carried out in a regular church context.[23]

Commenting on the second article of the Apostles' Creed, Thomas lists and commends five attitudes towards the Word of God that are typical of his approach: 1. Listening to it willingly; 2. Believing in it; 3. Meditating on it; 4. Communicating it to others in teaching, preaching and enkindling; 5. Completing it by being realisers of the Word and not forgetful listeners only (*Collationes in Symbolum Apostolorum*, Part 2). For a contemporary evangelical reader, it is interesting to read Thomas's commendation of Mary as the one who observed these attitudes and therefore deserves a *laus Mariae* (praise of Mary).

Furthermore, in the two *Summae*, there are 25,000 explicit citations from the Bible (out of a total of 38,000 from all sources; therefore, about two-thirds of the sources cited). This consistent reliance on Scripture and the widespread search for biblical justification means for Gilson that '[t]he whole theology of St. Thomas is a commentary on the Bible';[24] however, if this is a fair summary, it may be intriguing but it is clearly not the whole story. On the other hand, arguing as Oliphint, professor of apologetics at Westminster Theological Seminary (Philadelphia), does that, whatever his strengths, Thomas 'was no exegete' seems to be a one-sided argument that goes to the other extreme.[25] The reality is that Thomas's thought is, to take up the metaphor that was used at the beginning of this chapter, 'a great river with many tributaries'. The well-developed biblical insights and themes seem, if anything, to enter structures of thought that result from a complex process of integration between different factors. Chenu himself recognises that Thomas finds in Aristotle 'the means to ground himself in reason and in sound methodology in order to be able

23 G. Bray, *Biblical Interpretation: Past & Present* (Downers Grove, IL: IVP, 1996), pp. 150–51.

24 Quoted by Torrell, *La 'somme' de saint Thomas*, p. 103. Along the same interpretative line, Chenu argues that 'his *Summa Theologiae*, despite its technical methodology, can only be understood properly as a living emanation from the *pagina sacra* (the sacred page of the Bible)': M.-D. Chenu, *Aquinas and His Role in Theology* [1959] (Collegeville, MN: Liturgical Press, 2002), p. 21.

25 K. S. Oliphint, *Thomas Aquinas* (Phillipsburg, NJ: P & R Publishing, 2017), p. 121.

to construct a system'.[26] The Bible, so to speak, fills with bricks a structure of thought which, rather than depending on Scripture alone, seems to have been built on a framework which takes as its model, with modifications, that of natural reason as presented by the Philosopher. It is one thing to exegete Scripture and demonstrate some good biblical exegesis; it is quite another to build an entire system of thought that is biblically framed. Thomas perhaps excelled in the first activity, but his exegetical commitment did not translate into a necessary and comprehensive biblical integrity at a systemic level.

Thomas seems to have a high view of Scripture, which was shared by much of medieval theology. According to him, 'The author of Holy Writ is God' (*ST* I, q. 1, a. 10). In the *Summa Theologiae*, he also writes that 'the formal object of faith is the First Truth, as manifested in Holy Writ and the teaching of the Church, which proceeds from the First Truth. Consequently whoever does not adhere, as to an infallible and Divine rule, to the teaching of the Church, which proceeds from the First Truth manifested in Holy Writ, has not the habit of faith, but holds that which is of faith otherwise than by faith' (*ST* II–II, q. 5, a. 3) and, again, 'our faith receives its surety from Scripture' (*ST* III, q. 55, a. 4).[27] In his commentary on John 21:2, he peremptorily states: *sola scriptura canonica est regula fidei* (canonical Scripture alone is the rule of faith).[28] We find in Thomas a deferential respect for and a reverent listening to the Bible, which he considered the 'first truth' and 'rule of faith'. That this acknowledgment makes Thomas a forerunner of the Protestant 'Scripture alone' principle (as French scholar Gaboriau argues) is an anachronistic and even forced conclusion when one considers his work as a whole. As Thomas scholar

---

26 Chenu, *Aquinas and His Role in Theology*, p. 93.

27 The last two quotations are taken from https://www.newadvent.org/summa/3005.htm and https://www.newadvent.org/summa/4055.htm, respectively (accessed 20 December 2023).

28 A helpful study on the theology of Scripture in Thomas is F. Gaboriau, *L'Écriture seule?* (Paris: FAC-éditions, 1997). I thank Jean-Marc Berthoud for pointing out this book to me, although the author unwarrantedly wishes to make Thomas an advocate of the 'Scripture alone' principle. See also J. F. Boyle, *Aquinas on Scripture: A Primer* (Steubenville, OH: Emmaus Academic, 2023).

Torrell points out: 'The primacy he [Thomas] acknowledges in the scriptural argument has nothing to do with a defence of the Lutheran *sola Scriptura* before the name'.[29] As we have already seen, Thomas escapes simplistic readings that would make him entirely Aristotelian in the philosophical sense or entirely biblical in the Protestant sense. Just as he appears to be dedicated to adorning his work with biblical content, his theological project is also fuelled by the desire to conform to reason derived from Aristotelian philosophy as a co-structuring principle. Scripture is always in view, but the universe of Thomas is bigger and includes other reference points such as Aristotelian philosophy.

For Thomas, 'The apostles and prophets under divine inspiration have never said anything contrary to the dictates of natural reason. Nevertheless, they have said things which are beyond the comprehension of reason, and so to this extent seem to contradict reason, although they do not really oppose it' (*De veritate* 14,10). Scripture teaches something 'reasonable' according to the canons of natural reason, even if it goes beyond reason, without ever being against reason. It is evident that while formally recognising the authority of Scripture, Thomas interprets it within his harmonious vision of reason, which, however limited and in need of being elevated, is assumed as a structure of universal plausibility and a reference grid. On the contrary, the evangelical 'Scripture alone' principle confesses that Scripture is the ultimate authority and that reason is not only limited to creatures, but also flawed because of sin. The harmony between reason and faith was definitively disrupted with the breaking of the covenant and, while reason continues to function by virtue of common grace, it is no longer just limited and partial: it is corrupt and therefore in need of redemption. In Thomas, the primacy of Scripture is valid as an integration to reason for the purposes of its elevation, not in view of its reorientation. To affirm, as theologian Elliott does, that 'Scripture for Thomas was source and framework, not proof and garnish',[30]

---

29 Torrell, 'Saint Thomas and His Sources', p. 5.

30 M. W. Elliott, 'Thomas Aquinas' in B. G. Green (ed.), *Shapers of Christian Orthodoxy* (Downers Grove, IL: IVP Academic, 2010), p. 352.

means not moving beyond single statements Thomas made on the importance of the Bible and failing to grasp the very heart of his theology. Thomas has an eminent place for Scripture, but within a framework that goes beyond Scripture.

A case study on Thomas's use of Scripture in his doctrine of justification by faith

After surveying Thomas's approach to Scripture, it is useful to test his approach against the background of his views on justification. To start with, one obvious point should be made: Thomas's doctrine must be seen more as an instance of medieval discussions than one of post-Reformation controversies.[31] To approach them properly, the semi-Augustinian framework should be recognised. Justification is viewed as a process moved by God, who initiates a journey of transformation by infusing supernatural grace. Again, Duffy, late professor of systematic theology at Loyola University, aptly summarises Augustine's view when he argues that 'grace accomplishes a real change in the human being: rebirth, justification, adoption, divinization, participation in the divine life'.[32] Although distinguished, justification is not thought of in forensic or declarative terms only, but also in transformative terms. All of the steps require God's grace to occur, but they do impress a change that initiates a process. This process is guided by grace and made possible by the infusion of divine grace. The result is a journey of justification.[33] Both the event and the process are to be considered part of justification. Another feature of Augustine's doctrine of justification is his understanding of *iustitia Dei*. According to McGrath, in Augustine 'the righteousness of God is not that

---

31 For a useful overview, cf. N. Needham, 'The Evolution of Justification: Justification in the Medieval Traditions' in M. Barrett (ed.), *The Doctrine on Which the Church Stands or Falls: Justification in Biblical, Theological, Historical, and Pastoral Perspective* (Wheaton, IL: Crossway, 2019), pp. 587–622, and J. D. Kilcrease, *Justification by the Word: Restoring Sola Fide* (Bellingham, WA: Lexham Press, 2022), pp. 140–51.

32 S. J. Duffy, *The Dynamics of Grace: Perspectives in Theological Anthropology*, vol. 3 (Collegeville, MN: Liturgical Press, 1993), p. 79.

33 In my interpretation of Augustine at this point I am following V. Subilia, *La giustificazione per fede* (Brescia: Paideia, 1976), pp. 56–61.

righteousness by which he is himself righteous, but that by which he justifies sinners'.[34] In justification God makes us righteous.

A full treatment of the doctrine of justification, at least from the exegetical point of view, is to be found in Thomas's *Commentary to the Romans*.[35] This commentary belongs to the second period of teaching in Paris, and was completed around the same time as the dedicated section of the *Summa* (I–II) which expounds it systematically. According to Thomas, Romans explores grace 'as it is in itself' (1:1, p. 5).

In terms of the relationship between divine agency and human free will, for Thomas divine and human agencies are not to be seen in competition. In this sense, while adhering to the Augustinian affirmation of the primacy of grace, Thomas interprets it as softening the radical effects of sin on the mind and the will. If this position appears to be a milder form of Augustinianism, it is nonetheless stronger than it used to be in his previous works. In fact, in commenting on grace in Peter Lombard's *Sentences* between 1252 and 1256, Thomas had come close to embracing a 'quasi semi-Pelagian view that one may prepare oneself for grace by free will'.[36] The young Aquinas had argued that human beings ought to prepare themselves for salvific grace by acting in such a way as to merit grace, albeit imperfectly. The more mature Thomas argues that God, in his grace, has enabled human beings to receive the supernatural grace already bestowed at baptism. Evidently, from his *Commentary* on Peter Lombard to the one on Romans, there had been some developments in his thought regarding grace.

An important element in Thomas's account of justification is the use of participatory categories in expounding the relationship

---

34 A. E. McGrath, *Iustitia Dei: A History of the Christian Doctrine of Justification* (Cambridge: Cambridge University Press, 1986; 3rd edn 2005), p. 44.

35 *Commentary on the Letter of Saint Paul to the Romans*, ed. J. Mortensen and E. Alancórn (Lander, WY: Aquinas Institute, 2012). The page number after the quotation of Thomas's commentary will refer to this edition. A thorough study of the *Commentary* is M. Levering and M. Dauphinais (eds), *Reading Romans with St. Thomas Aquinas* (Washington, DC: Catholic University of America Press, 2012).

36 M. Horton, *Justification*, vol. 1 (Grand Rapids, MI: Zondervan, 2018), p. 113, where he refers to *Scriptum super libros sententiarum* II, 27, 1, 4. The same point is made by J. P. Wawrykow, *A–Z of Thomas Aquinas* (London: SCM Press, 2005), pp. 67–68.

between Christ, who is the Son of God by nature, and human beings, who are sons of God in an adoptive sense (1:3, p. 13). The participation of the justified is in the latter sense but nonetheless thought of in these terms.

Paul's statement that 'there is no one righteous' is understood to mean that 'no one is just within himself and of himself, but of himself everyone is a sinner' (3:2, p. 95). The presence of sin is not as corruptive as one could imagine. Everyone 'has some sin' and this condition does not agree with the later Protestant understanding of total depravity caused by sin. The principal effect of sin is on the higher soul (the mind) that loses control over the lower soul that governs the body and one's own passions. After the mind was turned away from God by sin, human beings lost control of the lower powers (5:3, p. 141). Grace as *donum superadditum*, which humankind had at creation, was lost but is infused with justification. There is no sense of justification meaning the imputation of Christ's righteousness to the sinner. Even when Thomas deals with Romans 4 and the story of Abraham with its language of 'reckoning', justification is primarily seen as 'complete cleansing' (5:5, p. 149).[37]

As for the nature of justifying faith, according to the reading of Thomas by Horton, professor of systematic theology at Westminster Theological Seminary (California), 'faith justifies because it is an inherent virtue caused by the infusion of grace',[38] and again, 'faith justifies not because it embraces Christ's alien righteousness as one's own . . . but because it is the beginning of sanctification'.[39] The categories of the Reformation (e.g. imputation, alien righteousness) cannot be found in Thomas, nor can they be projected backwards. Thomas simply does not have them in their forensic and covenantal meaning. Thomas hints at aspects of them but places them in a transformative journey: 'justification is a process

---

37 See B. Marshall, 'Beatus Vir: Aquinas, Romans 4, and the Role of "Reckoning" in Justification' in Levering and Dauphinais (eds), *Reading Romans with St. Thomas Aquinas*, pp. 219–31. Marshall points out that Thomas never understood Paul's language as purely forensic but interpreted it in transformational terms.

38 Horton, *Justification*, vol. 1, p. 107.

39 Horton, *Justification*, vol. 1, p. 108.

of becoming holy through infused grace and . . . grace-inspired merits are means to that end'.[40] While the first grace of justification is not merited even by faith, in order to bring complete justification (i.e. sanctification), faith must become love and meritorious works.

To summarise, in Thomas's *Commentary on Romans,* justification is the movement of a sinner from a state of interior injustice known as sin to a state of interior justice that expels such sin. This happens instantaneously when the grace of God is infused and causes the sinner to accept grace by their free will. The sinner then freely despises sin and turns from loving sin towards God with new love for him. The justice brought about by this grace in the interior of a human soul is such that the human intellect or reason is directed towards God, instructing the human will to submit to the human intellect and, therefore, love God as the final or ultimate good. Justification is by faith, because faith has a structural priority over charity (love for God) and the intellect has a structural priority over the will. Though justification is brought about by faith and is the sinner's first movement towards God, it especially exists in charity because justice is especially concerned with the good.

The issue regarding the justification of the sinner (*iustificatio impii*) is dealt with in *Summa Theologiae* I–II, q. 113. It was written around the same time as the *Commentary on Romans* in the context of Thomas's exposition of the doctrine of grace, and towards the end of the writing of the latter. In this section we find some themes already dealt with in the *Commentary on Romans,* but with an even more pronounced scholastic argumentative structure. According to Pesch, this section of the *Summa* is 'replete with Aristotelian concepts, yet its outcomes reflect the purest Augustinian spirit'.[41] While certainly present, the association with Augustine's view of justification seems overstated. Thomas is closer to the medieval readings of Augustine with their blurred line on the divine agency/free will relationship and their more pronounced emphasis on the sacramental mechanism of grace than to Augustine himself.

---

40 Horton, *Justification*, vol. 1, p. 108.

41 O. H. Pesch, *Tommaso d'Aquino: limiti e grandezza della teologia medievale. Una introduzione* (Brescia: Queriniana, 1994), p. 172.

Thomas's is an interpretation of Augustine which contains some resemblances to him and some points of departure from him. What is most impressive is Thomas's reliance on Aristotle's physics in his account of justification: it is the infusion of grace that moves the mind and the will towards God and away from sin, leading to forgiveness. The act of freedom is necessary for justification because justifying grace cannot be given if he who receives it is not prepared for it. According to Aristotelian philosophy, no form is communicated if 'matter' is not disposed to it.

In a nutshell, here is how Thomas summarises his view of justification: 'the justification of the ungodly is a certain movement whereby the human mind is moved by God from the state of sin to the state of justice' (*ST* I–II, q. 113, a. 5).[42] In this definition we find the characteristic features of Thomas's view: the understanding of justification as *motus* (a movement), the primacy of the mind, the role of grace as elevating and healing the disorder in the soul, and the transition from the state of sin to the state of justice. Thomas gives voice to an intellectualist understanding of human nature whereby if the higher nature (the mind) is subject to God, then the lower nature (will, affections, etc.) will be governed by it.

It is in question 113 that Thomas deals with the effects of grace with special reference to justification. Against the background of Aristotle's *Physics*, Thomas sees justification as a movement from injustice to justice. Thomas understands justification as a process (transmutation) of becoming righteous. It is true that justification is through faith; however, 'the movement of faith is not perfect unless it is quickened by charity; hence in the justification of the ungodly, a movement of charity is infused together with the movement of faith' (*ST* I–II, q. 113, a. 4).

The movement is brought about by four steps: 1. The infusion of grace; 2. The movement of the free will towards God by faith; 3. The movement of the free will away from sin; 4. The remission of sin (*ST* I–II, q. 113, a. 6.). Step number 2 equates to conversion to God,

---

42 A summary of this section is given by P. Leithart, 'Aquinas on Justification' (28 April 2005): https://theopolisinstitute.com/leithart_post/aquinas-on-justification (accessed 7 April 2023). See also Bray, *God Has Spoken*, pp. 515–18.

whereas step number 3 talks about moving away from sin. They all happen simultaneously, although there is a logical order to be recognised. The entire process is thought of as being characterised by an infusion of grace, and the remission of sin is the goal, not the beginning of the process.

In Horton's helpful summary, in the account of justification seen in the work of Thomas 'there are two types of grace (operating and cooperating), five effects (healing the soul, movement of the will to the good, good acts, perseverance and attaining glory) and four requirements of justification (infusion of grace, faith, repentance and forgiveness)'.[43]

While coming close to certain aspects of a forensic doctrine of justification when dealing with the language of Romans concerning 'reckoning', it is Aristotle's view of motion that is of paramount importance in accounting for it. While there is some propensity to consider the legal interpretation of the Greek verb *dikaioō* (to justify) and cognate words, it is the transformative interpretation of the Latin *iustificare* that prevails. According to Thomas, justification is a gift that can be increased by cooperation with no assurance of the end results. Thomas's reading of justification starts with an Augustinian foundation, albeit revised in terms of the medieval semi-Augustinian appropriations of Augustine, then adds biblical contents especially derived from the letter to the Romans but significantly driven by Aristotelian categories and couched in medieval accounts of salvation marked by baptismal regeneration, justification by infusion, acts of penance and indulgences.[44]

Horton is again helpful in providing a careful interpretation of the overall trajectory: 'Justification for Thomas Aquinas includes forgiveness and renewal. It is both an event (the first justification

---

43 Horton, *Justification*, vol. 1, p. 122.

44 O. Strachan, 'Did Thomas Teach the Biblical God of Monergistic Salvation?', *Pro Pastor* 1:1 (2022), pp. 33–40. These are the four central tenets of Aquinas's doctrine of salvation, although this account fails to do justice to Aquinas's hints towards forensic dimensions of salvation and his embrace of a version of the doctrine of predestination. A contemporary Thomistic account of Thomas's view of salvation is contained in the thirteen papers included in 'San Tommaso e la salvezza', ed. S.-T. Bonino and G. Mazzotta, *Doctor Communis* 4 (2020).

or regeneration in baptism) and a process (sanctification). In other words, justification is an all-inclusive term for "salvation."[45] This is the reason why what Beckwith writes after surveying Thomas's doctrine of justification is fitting as a conclusion: 'It is abundantly clear that Aquinas was more a Proto-Tridentine Catholic than a Proto-Protestant.'[46] While careful and respectful, his reading of Scripture as it is exemplified in his doctrine of justification by faith is influenced by Aristotelian categories and semi-Augustinian interpretations of Augustine. Scripture is a significant component of Thomas's theology, but not the paramount nor the ultimate influence in terms of his epistemology and authority framework.

The Church Fathers and patristic traditions

In addition to Greek and Arab philosophers and to Scripture, Thomas elaborated his theology in constant conversation with the Church Fathers, both ancient (e.g. Jerome, Hilary of Poitiers, Ambrose, Augustine, Gregory the Great), Greek (e.g. Origen, Basil, Maximus the Confessor, John Chrysostom, Dionysius the Areopagite) and medieval ones (e.g. Boethius, Bernard of Clairvaux, Anselm and Peter Lombard). In the two *Summae*, out

---

45 Horton, *Justification*, vol. 1, p. 125. On the relationship between justification and sanctification in Thomas, see D. A. Keating, 'Justification, Sanctification, and Divinization in Thomas Aquinas' in T. G. Weinandy, D. A. Keating and J. P. Yocum (eds), *Aquinas on Doctrine: A Critical Introduction* (New York, NY: T&T Clark, 2004), pp. 117–58.

46 F. J. Beckwith, *Never Doubt Thomas: The Catholic Aquinas as Evangelical and Protestant* (Waco, TX: Baylor University Press, 2019), p. 104. On the relationship between Luther's and Aquinas's accounts of justification see also O. H. Pesch, *Theologie der Rechtfertigung bei Martin Luther und Thomas von Aquin* (Mainz: Matthias-Grünewald-Verlag, 1967). Pesch's conclusions are centred on three fundamental theses: 1. Between Aquinas and Luther there is no contradiction on justification; 2. The difference between the two lies in their different ways of doing theology: Luther's theology is existential and relational, Thomas's is sapiential and ontological; 3. The starting point of Thomas's soteriology is creation, on top of which he elaborates his anthropology and view of salvation history, whereas for Luther, his theology of the cross becomes the starting point. For another perspective, see L. Steffensmeier, 'Revisiting the Reformation: Aquinas and Luther on Justification' (2017), *Celebrating Scholarship & Creativity Day*, 136; https://digitalcommons.csbsju.edu/elce_cscday/136 (accessed 7 April 2023).

of a total of 38,000 citations from different authors, 8,000 come from the Church Fathers. Evidently Thomas considered himself the interpreter of a long and composite tradition of thought inherited from the Church.

Of particular importance is the uninterrupted dialogue with Augustine. Examining the *Summa Theologiae* alone turns up 2,000 quotations from him. Some scholars go so far as to classify Thomas's theological personality as that of an 'Augustinian', and even view him as the most illustrious disciple of Augustine.[47] Scholars like Pera, while acknowledging the profound proximity between the two, warn against considering Thomas as belonging to the medieval stream of thought referred to as Augustinianism.[48] Again, Thomas challenges excessive simplifications that tend to isolate one element to the detriment of others. A more balanced assessment is offered by Dulles when he argues that where 'Augustine used Neoplatonism, Thomas has recourse to Aristotle. Where Augustine argued through the interpretation of history, Thomas depends primarily on metaphysics. Where Augustine uses the persuasion of rhetoric, Thomas uses careful and dispassionate reasoning.'[49] Theirs are two different worlds and the features of their theologies do not overlap, especially in their respective doctrines of sin. Even if rightly pinpointing the importance of sin, Elliott's assessment that 'Aquinas remains a bit more optimistic than Augustine about the natural capacity of humans for virtue' appears to be underestimated.[50] Indeed, Augustine has a biblically realistic and therefore tragic theology of sin which is almost entirely absent in Thomas. The latter adopts a lighter version of it. The 'light' conception of sin not only gives him a tone that is 'a bit more optimistic' but makes

47 For example, M. Dauphinais, B. David and M. Levering (eds), *Aquinas the Augustinian* (Washington, DC: Catholic University of America Press, 2007). The relationship between Thomas and scholastic Augustinianism is explored by Weisheipl, *Friar Thomas d'Aquino*, pp. 289–92.

48 Pera, *Le fonti del pensiero di S. Tommaso d'Aquino nella Somma teologica*, p. 49.

49 Dulles, *A History of Apologetics*, p. 120.

50 Elliott, 'Thomas Aquinas', p. 357. Later on Elliott acknowledges that 'the difference from Augustine is that Thomas plays down the role of original sin' (p. 359), but underestimates the theological weight of such a statement and treats it as if it were a matter of detail.

it possible for Thomas to build a thought-system that sees nature, albeit fallen, as always 'open' to grace and capable of being raised in its entirety.

In addition to the Latin Church Fathers, the Greek tradition also exercised a certain influence on Thomas. In the *Catena Aurea*, a voluminous commentary on the Gospels, Thomas included numerous references to the Eastern Fathers and valued their biblical insights. It is not surprising that departing from Augustine on the effects of sin, he instead followed the line of the theology of free will of John of Damascus, therefore embracing a milder doctrine of sin. In so doing he was able to find a way to harmonise the Christian faith with Aristotelian and Neoplatonic philosophy.

Having said that, Dionysius the Areopagite is the Greek Father to whom Thomas dedicated much attention in his commentary on the *Divine Names* and who is explicitly mentioned 702 times in the *Summa Theologiae* alone. Beyond numbers, it is the substantial influences of Dionysius's apophatic and mystical thought that count. In the commentary on the *Divine Names*, Thomas comes into contact with the Neoplatonic tradition, which would become another significant source of his work.[51] According to Pera, it is Dionysius, who shares with Augustine a Neoplatonic inspiration but also embraces elements of Aristotelian provenance, who is the bridge that allows Thomas to move between the two sides of medieval thought.[52] The hierarchical vision of the universe and his angelology are of Neoplatonic origin. Furthermore, much of Thomas's doctrine of God depends on the *Divine Names*, especially the traces of apophaticism and the elaboration of the doctrine of analogy.[53] In addition, the Neoplatonic concepts of *exitus* and *reditus* (procession and return), which would become so

---

51 See Porro, *Tommaso d'Aquino*, pp. 231–48.

52 Pera, *Le fonti del pensiero di S. Tommaso d'Aquino nella Summa teologica*, p. 54.

53 On the influence of the *Divine Names* on the theology of Thomas, see A. Ghisalberti, 'Dio come essere e Dio come uno: la sintesi di Tommaso d'Aquino' in *Medioevo teologico: categorie della teologia razionale nel Medioevo* (Rome-Bari: Laterza, 1990), pp. 85–112.

influential in the construction of the *Summa*, are borrowed from the Neoplatonic book *Liber de Causis*.[54]

Of the medieval Fathers, Thomas was influenced above all by Boethius and Peter Lombard. As far as Boethius is concerned, Thomas commented on parts of the *De Trinitate* in which he refined his distinction between metaphysics and theology, and on the *Book on the Hebdomades* (axioms) in which, in distinguishing between *esse* (being) and *id quod est* (what is), he laid the foundations of his doctrine of participation: God is *being*, as such; the rest *is*, insofar as it participates in the being of God in various ways.[55]

In terms of the relationship with the theology of Peter Lombard, all medieval theology students had to study Peter Lombard's *Sentences*. In his training to become *magister*, Thomas had to comment on the *Sentences*, which were considered the manual for the study of theology. His *Commentary on the Sentences* (*Scriptum super Sententiis*) can be compared to a modern doctoral thesis. In it we find a Thomas who, even if he had already outlined the main framework of his thought, was still in progress and less settled than he would become in subsequent years.[56] Beyond the specific contents of the *Sentences*, the overall structure that Thomas gives to his exposition deserves to be understood clearly. Peter Lombard divided his *Sentences* into four books: 1. The triune God; 2. Creation; 3. Christ; and 4. The sacraments. In this macro-structure, sin was not recognised as a crucial disruption in his theology. Inheriting this underestimation of the effects of sin, Thomas reiterates it and, if anything, reinterprets the scheme of the *Sentences* in the Neoplatonic movement of *exitus* and *reditus*:[57] for him, the first two books (on God and creation) deal with emanation (*exitus*) of everything from God, the other two (on Christ and the sacraments) focus on the return (*reditus*) of everything to God. It is curious to note that, in university theological training, the *Summa Theologiae*

---

54 Porro, *Tommaso d'Aquino*, pp. 403–08.

55 See Vanni Rovighi, *Introduzione a Tommaso d'Aquino*, pp. 52–53.

56 For a thorough study on Thomas's *Commentary on the Sentences*, see I. Biffi, 'Il commento alle Sentenze' in *Alla scuola di Tommaso* (Milan: Jaca Book, 2007), pp. 1–80.

57 So it is argued by Weisheipl, *Friar Thomas d'Aquino*, p. 75.

by Thomas, who had commented on the *Sentences* and reiterated its structure, would replace Lombard's book as the standard theology manual from the sixteenth century. In both cases, a fully Augustinian doctrine of sin was expunged from theology and was replaced by an increasingly bland version of semi-Augustinianism.

A case study on the *exitus–reditus* motif

One way of testing the impact of streams of Neoplatonic patristic traditions on Thomas is to look at the *exitus–reditus* motif. In presenting the plan of the *Summa Theologiae*, it is Thomas himself who indicates the theological trajectory of the work: 'In our endeavor to expound this science, we shall treat: (1) Of God; (2) Of the rational creature's advance towards God; (3) Of Christ, Who as man, is our way to God' (*ST* I, q. 2). This threefold movement reflects the flowing of all things from God and their return to God, Christ being the medium of the return.[58] To understand the heart of Thomas's theology, it is important to come to terms with the movement that drives the whole of the *Summa*, although it should not be taken as a 'fixed schema' in his mind.[59] The project is based on the paired words *exitus–reditus*: exit and return. The trend is the exit from God towards creatures and their return to God. This is the macro-structure of the *Summa*, already used in the *Commentary on the Sentences* of Peter Lombard and, to a less evident extent, in the *Summa against the Gentiles* (e.g. *SG* I,9; II,1; III,1 and IV,1).[60] The circular dynamic starts from God himself, unfolds in the procession of the world and ends in its return to God from whom all began. This is a Christianised version of the emanationist motif of Neoplatonism, purged of its pantheistic element

---

58 M.-D. Chenu, 'Le plan de la Somme théologique de Saint Thomas', *Revue Thomiste* 47 (1939), pp. 93–107, reprised in *Introduction à l'étude de Saint Thomas d'Aquin* (Montreal: Institut d'études médiévals, 1954), pp. 255–76.

59 B. Davies, *Thomas Aquinas's Summa Theologiae: A Guide and Commentary* (Oxford: Oxford University Press, 2014), p. 15. Recent discussions on *exitus–reditus* include Torrell, *Saint Thomas Aquinas, vol. 1*, pp. 150–53, and B. Johnstone, 'The Debate on the Structure of the *Summa Theologiae*: From Chenu (1939) to Metz (1998)' in P. van Geest, H. Goris and C. Leget (eds), *Aquinas as Authority* (Leuven, Belgium: Peters, 2002), pp. 187–200.

60 For references to other works by Thomas where the *exitus–reditus* theme occurs, see McGinn, *Thomas Aquinas's Summa Theologiae*, pp. 68–71.

and qualified in a creationist sense. Neoplatonism had a cyclical conception of causality, and Thomas reworks it in the sense that God creates the movement out of God, and everything, in Christ, returns to God.

Beyond the always problematic retrieval and use of pagan motifs that are clothed with Christian meanings, in this Thomistic account of the *exitus–reditus*, at least two major problems must be mentioned. The first is the circular rather than linear progression of salvation history: the Bible presents a plot not of returning to the starting point, but of arriving at a goal that is no longer the starting point. The New Jerusalem is not the initial garden; the eschaton is no longer the beginning in Genesis. The new creation is not the reproduction of the original creation. In the biblical plot, there is historical–redemptive progress, rather than a return to square one. The gap between the circular and the linear motif is not a difference of mere aesthetic value. What is at stake is an underestimation of the tragedy of sin and an overestimation of nature's ability to be involved in a return flow. Considering this, Elliott's comment that the *Summa* is nothing but 'biblical theology'[61] is surprising. It contains many elements derived from biblical revelation, but the movement that supports it is not.

The second problem is that in the Thomistic scheme of *exitus–reditus* there is no breaking of the covenant between God and humanity. There is God's creation and Christ's redemption, but sin is missing in its radical disruption. Obviously, Thomas has a theology of sin, but it does not have an 'architectural' importance in constructing his thought.[62] Sin is swallowed up in the back-and-forth movement, without bringing about a change of direction. In the general outline of *Summa Theologiae*, sin does not have its section, but falls within the doctrine of human acts relating to vices and sins (*ST* I–II, qq. 71–89), while the commentary on the fall of Adam and Eve is a subsection of the treatise on the virtue of temperance (*ST* II–II, qq. 163–65). These comprise only 21

---

61 Elliott, 'Thomas Aquinas', p. 354.

62 See F. C. Bauerschmidt, 'Thomas Aquinas' in K. L. Johnson and D. Lauber (eds), *T&T Clark Companion to the Doctrine of Sin* (London: Bloomsbury T&T Clark, 2016), pp. 199–216.

questions out of 512, statistically just over 4% of the entire *Summa*. It is not so much the numerical data as the rather marginal overall theological weight of sin that constitutes a distinctive element of Thomas's thought.[63]

The 'cathedral of medieval theology': the *Summa Theologiae*

As mentioned, Thomas's work is vast and complex, with over 100 writings of the highest profile attributed to him. There is no doubt, however, that the *Summa Theologiae*, which he started writing in Rome in 1266 and which was left incomplete at his death, is the best-known and most important work, his masterpiece, and not only for being composed of a million and a half words: 512 questions and 2,668 articles. The *Summa* has had more than a thousand commentaries in history (only the Bible has received more), thus becoming a thought generator over the centuries. Due to its monumental grandeur, the Canadian Jesuit theologian Lonergan defined it as a 'a mighty contribution towards the medieval cultural synthesis'.[64] Changing metaphors, due to its imposing and refined construction, this work was also compared to the 'cathedral' of medieval thought.[65]

Thomas conceived it to help 'beginners' (*proemio*) in theological studies to have a reference work that would guide their first steps in acquiring the skills in the *sacra doctrina* ('sacred doctrine': I, q. 1), i.e. what the Church believes and teaches. The pedagogical intent is explicit: for Thomas, it is a question not only of exposing the contents of the doctrine but also of enabling those who acquire

---

63 Other than in the *Summa*, Thomas's theology of sin can be found in his *Commentary on the Sentences* of Peter Lombard (book 2, distinctions 30–44), in the *Summa against the Gentiles* (sundry comments in books III and IV, chapters 50–52) and in *Quaestiones disputate de malo*.

64 Quoted by McGinn, *Thomas Aquinas's Summa Theologiae*, p. 7. Important monographs on the *Summa* are Torrell, *La 'somme' de saint Thomas* and Davies, *Thomas Aquinas's Summa Theologiae*. A reliable summary of the *Summa* is given by M. Reeves, *Introducing Major Theologians* (Nottingham: IVP, 2015), pp. 133–52, while a more superficial and theologically naive reading is by G. W. Bromiley, *Historical Theology: An Introduction* (Grand Rapids, MI: Eerdmans, 1978), pp. 196–209.

65 Torrell, *La 'somme' de saint Thomas*, p. 31.

them to teach them in turn (*ST* I, q. 103, a. 6). The *Summa* was then thought of as a manual for teachers and a work to be read and commented on in the classroom.

For Thomas, *sacra doctrina* is a science insofar as it rests on principles known in the light of revelation. In the *Posterior Analytics*, a work by Aristotle that Thomas had extensively commented on, the Philosopher had argued that science was 'certain knowledge through causes': to do science, it was necessary to develop knowledge based on indisputable principles which, through syllogistic reasoning, would lead to necessary conclusions. Placing himself in these Aristotelian categories, for Thomas the *scientia divina* is indeed a science, but of two types: one, metaphysics, based on principles accessible to reason (Aristotelian); the other, *theologia christiana*, based on revelation, from which *sacra doctrina* derives. The peculiarity of Thomas's conception of theology is that it retains many of the characteristics attributed by Aristotle to philosophy but has a superior, elevated, additional meaning of theology with respect to philosophy. In commenting on Boethius's *De Trinitate*, Thomas wrote that 'it must be said that gifts of grace are added to those of nature in such a way that they do not destroy the latter, but rather perfect them; wherefore also the light of faith, which is gratuitously infused into our minds, does not destroy the natural light of cognition, which is in us by nature' (*Commentary on Boethius's De Trinitate* 1, q. 1, a. 3).

There are two modes of truth about God: natural and revelational. In this respect, what is argued in the *Summa Theologiae* was previously explained in the *Summa against the Gentiles*: 'Some truths about God exceed all the ability of the human reason. Such is the truth that God is triune. But there are some truths which the natural reason also can reach. Such are that God exists, He is one, and the like. Such truths about God have been proven demonstratively by the philosophers, guided by the light of the natural reason' (*SG* I, 1, 3). Aquinas believed that reason without revelation can arrive at the truth about God. In his refined scholastic style, Thomas's connection between the two has caused discussion and continues to be debated.

For some contemporary interpreters of Thomas (Catholics and evangelicals),[66] we are dealing with two autonomous orders of truth that are different from each other, juxtaposed and functioning separately. For other interpreters (Catholics and evangelicals),[67] these are two ways of the one truth that must be distinguished but not separated, harmoniously intertwined even if never disjoined. In the *Summa against the Gentiles*, Thomas uses both languages. While, on the one hand, he speaks of 'the twofold truth of divine things', on the other he underlines that 'I am speaking of a "twofold truth of divine things," not on the part of God Himself, Who is truth one and simple, but from the point of view of our knowledge, which is variously related to the knowledge of divine things' (*SG* I, 1, 9). Dante captures the centre of Thomas's thought when he places these lines into his mouth:

> Ope now thine eyes to what I answer thee;
> and thou'lt see that my words and thy belief
> grow one in truth, as in a ring its center.
> That which dies not, and that which mortal is,
> are naught but that Idea's reflected light,
> to which our Sire, by loving, giveth birth.
> (*Paradise* XIII, 49–54)[68]

---

66 Catholics: S. A. Long, *Natura Pura: On the Recovery of Nature in the Doctrine of Grace* (New York, NY: Fordham University Press, 2010) and R. McInerny, *Praeambula Fidei: Thomism and the God of the Philosophers* (Washington, DC: Catholic University of America Press, 2006).
　　Evangelicals: for example, Oliphint, *Thomas Aquinas*, especially pp. 11–53. Paradoxically, at least to a certain point, even an evangelical 'Thomist' such as Norman Geisler distinguishes Thomas's philosophy from his theology, thinking that he can embrace the former without subscribing to the latter: see N. Geisler, 'A New Look at the Relevance of Thomism for Evangelical Apologetics', *Christian Scholar's Review* 4:3 (1975), pp. 189–200.

67 Catholics: for example, E. Gilson, H. de Lubac, M.-D. Chenu and others; see Oliphint, *Thomas Aquinas*, p. 26.
　　Evangelicals: R. A. Muller, 'Aquinas Reconsidered', *Reformation21* (19 February 2018) is a very critical review of Oliphint's book and is available here: https://byk2739.tistory.com/712 (accessed 17 May 2023). Also worth reading by Muller is the essay 'Reading Aquinas from a Reformed Perspective: A Review Essay', *Calvin Theological Journal* 53:2 (2018), pp. 255–88.

68 Translated by Henry Wadsworth Longfellow (1867): http://dantelab.dartmouth.edu/reader?reader%5Bcantica%5D=3&reader%5Bcanto%5D=13 (accessed 20 December 2023).

The mortal and the immortal (and by extension reason and faith), however distinct, are both reflections of the same 'idea' (the Son) that the Father generated out of love.

A point where this conflict of interpretations becomes apparent is with the *praeambula fidei*, that is, those truths about God, including his existence, that can be known by natural reason. Thomas writes: 'The existence of God and other like truths about God, which can be known by natural reason, are not articles of faith, but are preambles to the articles; for faith presupposes natural knowledge, even as grace presupposes nature, and perfection supposes something that can be perfected' (*ST* I, q. 2, a. 2).[69] Does the 'preliminary' character mean the autonomous and parallel functioning of reason or does it mean that revelation elevates reason without necessarily reforming it? This debate mirrors Thomas's nuanced complexity, which has been read and is still read at times by underlining the differences until they become separations, other times insisting on the connections until they become organic relationships.

No doubt the *pax Thomistica* between theology and philosophy seems to be the elastic framework that best reflects Aquinas's thought. In Farrow's words, 'philosophy *qua* philosophy and theology qua theology reason together, each respectful of the other'.[70] Thomism knows how to hold the relation between philosophy and theology in a relaxed, or tense way, but always at peace. The bottom line is their friendly connection. In Western collective imagination, as it is colourfully depicted in the lively portrait given by G. K. Chesterton, Thomas 'knew how to reconcile Religion with Reason' or, in the words of John Paul II, he was a master at harmonising *fides et ratio* (faith and reason).

---

69 For a contemporary Roman Catholic reflection on the *praeambula*, see '"Praeambula fidei" e nuova apologetica', *Doctor Communis* 1–2 (2008), available here: https://www.vatican.va/roman_curia/pontifical_academies/san-tommaso/publications/dc10.pdf (accessed 17 May 2023). On this debate see also D. VanDrunen, 'The Contemporary Reception of Aquinas on the Natural Knowledge of God' in Levering and Plested (eds), *The Oxford Handbook of the Reception of Aquinas*, pp. 596–611.

70 D. Farrow, 'Theology and Philosophy: Recovering the Pax Thomistica' in *Theological Negotiations: Proposals in Soteriology and Anthropology* (Grand Rapids, MI: Baker, 2018), p. 18. According to Farrow the *pax Thomistica* was broken first by the Kantian critique and then by the rejection of natural theology by Karl Barth.

Still following Aristotle, according to whom the sciences could be speculative or practical, Thomas holds that sacred doctrine is simultaneously speculative (contemplative) and practical (action-oriented). The specificity of *sacra doctrina* as a speculative and practical science is that it is *sapientia*. Some scholars such as Otto Pesch consider wisdom and therefore the 'sapiential' character of theology the fundamental trait of Thomas's theology, distinguishing it from the 'existential' one of Luther and the Protestant Reformation.[71]

In the epistemological movement of the *scientia divina*, Thomas's thought references a kind of circular motion (or rather: spiral). The theologian gains a deeper understanding of the principles by starting with principles and arriving at conclusions through the scholastic argument. At the same time, taking up the apophatic tradition mediated by Dionysius the Areopagite, Thomas underlines the negative character of our knowledge of God: 'For what He is not is clearer to us than what He is' (*ST* I, q. 1, a. 9). Theological wisdom is therefore knowing that you do not know. The framework of the discourse is represented by two movements: one upwards in which human beings strive to know God by discovering the negative way; the other downwards in which God fulfils this desire through love. To understand these movements, we must enter Thomas's anthropology inspired by a certain understanding of the relationship between nature and grace. Human beings are structurally open to God, capable of God and oriented towards him. They have built-in limits that grace supernaturally overcomes so that they can access higher knowledge. According to Sarmenghi, for Thomas, 'the aspiration to the supernatural is already inscribed in the very nature of man'[72] and is depicted as the 'natural light' of reason. The 'light of grace' is added to nature. This 'addition' has a double purpose: it elevates nature beyond its limits and purifies it from sin. The

---

71 Pesch, *Theologie der Rechtfertigung bei Martin Luther und Thomas von Aquin*. Pesch has updated his thesis in his volume on Luther: *Hinführung zu Luther* (Mainz: Matthias-Grünewald-Verlag, 2004). See also I. Biffi, 'Una teologia sapienziale' in *Alla scuola di Tommaso* (Milan: Jaca Book, 2007), pp. 81–97.

72 A. Sarmenghi, *Rimuovere l'oscurità: conoscenza e amore nella Somma di Teologia di Tommaso d'Aquino* (Rome: Città Nuova, 2021), p. 165.

addition of grace occurs with faith, which is intensified by a mystical experience to be fulfilled in the final beatific vision.

Using the scholastic method, in the *Summa* Thomas poses the question to be examined, presents a series of arguments against the thesis he intends to support, cites a text from an authoritative source (Scripture and/or the Church Fathers) in favour of it, argues it and, finally, replies to the objections. The *Summa* is divided into three parts:

I. The *Prima Pars* (written between 1266 and 1268) deals with God and creation (119 questions and 584 articles). For Thomas, the existence of God and other truths about God can be known by natural reason. Moving away from Anselm, according to whom the fact that God exists is deducible from reason, Thomas believed that the existence of God can be deduced by looking at the effects of his work. Simplifying, we can say that while for Anselm the existence of God is given *a priori*, for Thomas it is to be argued for *a posteriori*. In particular, there are five ways of proving the existence of God (*ST* I, q. 2, a. 3): 1. From the motion or change of things one must deduce that they were moved by something and, backwards, by a 'prime mover that is not moved by others'; 2. From the effect of things to the efficient cause; 3. From things that may or may not be to the existence of a being that is necessary; 4. From the greater or lesser gradation of things to a supreme or absolute entity; 5. From the design of things to an 'intelligent being from whom all natural things are ordered to an end'. Except for the third way, which comes from Avicenna, these are all Aristotelian arguments. Thomas concludes that they lead to God. For each of the proofs provided, who or what is proven (first cause, motor, necessary, perfect and intelligent entity) is God: 'and this everyone understands to be God', 'to which everyone gives the name of God', 'This all men speak of as God', 'this being we call God'.[73] To the teaching on the existence

---

73 For an introductory reading on the 'five ways' of Thomas, see T. Pawl, 'The Five Ways' in B. Davies and E. Stump (eds), *The Oxford Handbook of Aquinas* (Oxford: Oxford University Press, 2012), pp. 115–34, and E. Berti, *Le prove dell'esistenza di Dio nella filosofia* (Brescia: Morcelliana, 2022), pp. 51–88.

of God, Thomas adds the teaching on how he should be: simple, perfect, infinite, immutable, one. Questions follow on the names of God, his intellect, his will, and his power. In line with Anselm's procedure in the *Monologion*, from the unity of God we pass to his Trinity: in fact, the following section is dedicated to the Trinity of the divine Persons (qq. 27–43) and another to the derivation of creatures from God (qq. 44–119). In Poythress's view, in Thomas's trinitarian theology there is 'repeated strain' because he 'must work in tension with the Aristotelian categories that he himself employs. He may succeed at many points in making distinctions in such a way as to show his readers a certain kind of rational resolution of difficulties . . . Aquinas must frequently postulate differences in the way things are for the Creator in order to keep in line with orthodox doctrine. Yet he continues to use the Aristotelian categories as though they were unproblematic'.[74] Even in this section which deals with trinitarian theology, the metaphysics of being and acting, the epistemology and logic employed are Aristotelian.[75] Of particular interest here is the anthropology presented: Thomas opposes any dualism between soul and body and teaches that the soul is the principle of life that animates human life. For this reason, it can survive the body but cannot exist eternally without a body.

II. The *Secunda Pars* (written between 1268 and 1272) is divided into two subparts (the *Prima secundae*: 114 questions and 619 articles and the *Secunda secundae* of 189 questions and 916 articles) and focuses on the role of human acts in achieving bliss. The goal of human life is happiness, which is approached with good habits (virtues) and destroyed by bad ones (vices). The virtues are pursued through the observance of the law (eternal, natural, human and the

---

74 V. S. Poythress, *The Mystery of the Trinity: A Trinitarian Approach to the Attributes of God* (Phillipsburg, NJ: P & R Publishing, 2020), p. 328. The heavy dependence of Thomas on Aristotle in the way he constructs and expounds trinitarian doctrine is thoroughly analysed on pp. 197–338.

75 G. Emery, 'Central Aristotelian Themes in Aquinas's Trinitarian Theology' in G. Emery and M. Levering (eds), *Aristotle in Aquinas's Theology* (Oxford: Oxford University Press, 2015), pp. 1–28.

new law) and grace. At question 113 we find Thomas's position on justification which will be a breaking point brought about by the Reformation. For Aquinas the grace of God must make us virtuous and capable of deserving eternal life, cooperating with it in the freedom of our will. In addition to a conception of sin not as total corruption, there is little trace of a forensic view of justification. In the *Secunda secundae*, the most extensive section of the *Summa*, Thomas deals with the theological virtues supernaturally infused by grace (faith, hope, charity) and with the cardinal virtues inherent in nature (prudence, justice, fortitude, temperance). He also touches on charisms, on the distinction between active and contemplative, and the characteristics of religious life.

III. The unfinished *Tertia Pars* (written between 1272 and 1273) deals with Christology and most sacraments (90 questions and 549 articles). Thomas addresses the person and work of Christ (qq. 1–59), the sacraments by which his work is extended and applied (qq. 60–90), and the final resurrection and the last things (*Supplements* 1–99). The mystery of the Incarnation offers Thomas the opportunity to present Christ as the personification of the standards of virtue outlined in Part II. Mary was not conceived immaculately but sanctified in her mother's womb to the point of not committing any sin in life (q. 27). On understanding Jesus' passion and death on the cross (qq. 46–49), Thomas follows Anselm, who considered the cross as 'satisfaction', but also, beyond Anselm, as the acquisition of merits for us. On the sacraments, Thomas believed that the Word-made-*flesh* requires that salvation come through *physical* objects. Grace can be found in his flesh, not just in the signs of his grace. The sacraments, therefore, are 'necessary for salvation' (q. 61) and extensions of the incarnation of Christ. The sacraments are seven (baptism, confirmation, eucharist, penance, extreme unction, holy orders, marriage). The Eucharist is the sacrament *par excellence* because it 'contains something which is sacred absolutely, namely, Christ's own body' (*ST* q. 73, a. 1) by transubstantiation of the bread and wine into the body and blood of Christ (*ST* q. 75, a. 4). As Reeves points out, it is a strange irony to reflect that, at the height of Thomas's theological construction, one does not have the grace that perfects nature by presupposing it, but the grace that transmutes nature by modifying its substance.[76] In the Eucharist, created nature is replaced by another nature made of supernatural substance and remains only in an accidental way. Thomas wrote up to the sacrament of penance, which was left unfinished. His students, possibly Reginald of Piperno (1230–90) having a central role in it, completed the missing parts (on penance, extreme unction, holy orders, and marriage) and the last things (including purgatory)[77] with the *Supplements* (99 questions and 443 articles out of the 612 questions and 2,699 articles in total), relying on other writings by Thomas on these topics.

Here is how Letham summarises Thomas's sacramental theology: 'We note two important points: (1) the materialising of grace – grace is contained in the material elements, and (2) a hierarchical concept of the church – the sacraments are constituted by the priests who administer them. This stress on the sacraments means that Aquinas is rather less occupied with the cross'.[78] These two pillars form the basis of the sacramental theology of the Council of Trent.

In the *Summa* it is taught that three effects were produced by original sin: the first is that the gift of original justice was lost, while the third is that the constitutive principles of nature were neither destroyed nor diminished. Up to this point, Thomas is placed in the wake of the biblical teaching from the Augustinian and Anselmian points of view. It is on the second effect, that is, on the inclination of nature towards virtue, that Aquinas takes an optimistic position. For him the natural inclination to virtue is only 'diminished':

---

76 Reeves, *Introducing Major Theologians*, pp. 151–52.

77 Although Thomas himself had relatively little to say about purgatory, his students gathered his opinions in the *Supplements*. See J. Le Goff, *The Birth of Purgatory* (Chicago, IL: University of Chicago Press, 1986), pp. 266–78.

78 R. Letham, *Gamechangers: Key Figures of the Christian Church* (Fearn, Tain, Scotland: Christian Focus Publications, 2015), pp. 94–95. For a present-day Thomistic account of Thomas's sacramentology, see R. Cessario, *The Seven Sacraments of the Catholic Church* (Grand Rapids, MI: Baker Academic, 2023). Cessario shows how Thomas shaped the Roman Catholic sacramental theology that emerged out of the Council of Trent and is embedded in the 1992 *Catechism of the Catholic Church*.

'Wherefore as sin is opposed to virtue, from the very fact that a man sins, there results in a diminution of that good of nature, which is the inclination to virtue' (*ST* I–II, q. 85, a. 1). Sin 'diminishes' the natural inclination to do good, dampens its energy, clouds its vision, but does not radically distort its direction. It slows down and confuses its progress without questioning its existence. There is a sense in which nature touched by sin is still inclined towards good and can be helped by grace to achieve it. Again, Thomas maintains that 'in so far as the reason is deprived of its order to the true, there is the wound of ignorance; in so far as the will is deprived of its order of good, there is the wound of malice; in so far as the irascible is deprived of its order to the arduous, there is the wound of weakness; and in so far as the concupiscible is deprived of its order to the delectable, moderated by reason, there is the wound of concupiscence' (*ST* I–II, q. 85, a. 3). 'Wound' is the key word here. In his understanding, the effects of sin are thought of in terms of weakening and narrowing, making thinking, willing and acting more difficult, but not in terms of the total corruption that follows the breaking of the covenant between God and humanity.

Further on in the *Summa*, Thomas addresses the theme of the need for grace and argues that human nature has not been 'completely corrupted by sin': a human being finds himself in the condition of a 'sick person' who, unlike a healthy human, is limited in function unless healed with the help of medicine. Furthermore, for Thomas, 'human nature is more corrupt by sin regarding the desire for good, than regarding the knowledge of truth' (*ST* I–II, q. 109, a. 2): the noetic effects of sin are more limited and attenuated than those on the will. Even in this differentiation between reason and will, Thomas does not have a theology of total corruption caused by sin. As Reeves clearly puts it, in the *Summa* 'grace can simply take nature as it is, extend and perfect it' as if our greatest problem is 'not so much sin as lack of grace'.[79]

For these reasons, the core of Thomas's vision and the Thomistic traditions that originated from him could be summarised with

---

79 Reeves, *Introducing Major Theologians*, p. 145.

the adage: 'grace does not annul nature, but perfects it'; for this reason, Thomism does not have a tragic understanding of sin; for this reason, the nature–grace relationship of Thomistic Roman Catholicism underestimates the effects of sin and has an optimistic view of human capabilities in cooperating with salvation. The grace of *reditus* corresponds to the nature of the *exitus*, but what about sin? The 'light' view of sin in Thomas touches on a crucial point in his understanding of the history of redemption, even in the presence of biblical language and themes in the *Summa*. In its micro-units of single questions, single articles and single topics, the *Summa* contains profound and ingenious elements, many of which are shaped by biblical wisdom, even if always imbued with Aristotelian motifs. It is the underlying movement lacking a biblical awareness of sin that is at stake and which appears to be an important part of the architecture of his theology.

3

Roman Catholic appropriations: from veneration to magisterial affirmation

In the Roman Catholic tradition, no other theologian has received the same recognition and praise as Thomas Aquinas. In the words of Leo XIII in the encyclical *Aeterni Patris* (1879), 'he is rightly considered the special defender and the glory of the Catholic church'. The reception of Thomas's thought has not always been linear, and its appropriation has taken different nuances, sometimes resulting in different schools of interpretation. From Thomas's work, various forms of Thomism within Roman Catholicism have extended his legacy over the centuries. This chapter will survey the main schools of thought that originated from Thomas, making his work mainstream in Western theology.

The beginning of the veneration and the early disputes

After the death of Thomas in 1274, two parallel phenomena took place. As Torrell puts it, 'A cult of the saint began quickly at the place of his death, and an opposition arose in Paris and Oxford that was not disarmed by his theological thought.'[1] It is interesting to notice that Thomas's legacy from day one took a devotional trajectory and a theological/philosophical one: neither one without the other, nor one at the expense of the other. Thomas's memory spoke both to the popular piety of the day and to the theological minds

---

1   Torrell, *Saint Thomas Aquinas, vol. 1*, p. 296.

of the academy. Moreover, while the Roman Catholic spirituality of the time began to appropriate him as fitting the category of a 'saint', the initial academic reception of his thought was subject to criticism.

Even before the burial of the body, a miracle was already attributed to Thomas: the first of a long series of supernatural interventions that were eventually used to support his canonisation as a saint within Roman Catholicism. After the funeral, the Dominican Order tried to get hold of the body, which belonged to the Cistercian Abbey of Fossanova, and they managed to behead it to keep at least the head with them. The issue became a political plot whereby several groups claimed the right to possess the body. Eventually, the Dominicans stole it by subterfuge, and the Cistercians appealed to Pope Urban V in Avignon to have it back. Finally, Thomas's body was taken to Toulouse (France) in 1369 along with his head, while his right arm ended up in Paris and his left arm in Naples to appease the Dominicans there.[2]

As the popular devotion to Thomas grew, some doctrinal agitation erupted in Paris. In 1270 the bishop of Paris, Étienne Tempier, had condemned thirteen philosophical propositions attributed to Aristotle and his Arab commentators, including panpsychism (one intellect for every human being), astrology (the correlation between earthly events and the movements of celestial bodies) and eternity of the world (and thus the denial of creation). Another list of condemnations followed in 1277 concerning 219 theses taken from Aristotelian philosophy that stipulated the superiority of reason.[3] In a sense, the 'compatibilist' and 'harmonising' reading of Thomas concerning Aristotle was being shattered. Aristotelianism was condemned in no uncertain terms. Given the close association between Aristotelianism and Thomas's theologised version of the relationship between philosophy and reason, a negative judgment was passed on these two and Thomas. Never had Thomas been

---

2   The whole macabre story is told by T. S. Centi, *Tommaso d'Aquino: nel segno del sole* (Milan: Ares, 2023), pp. 103–21.

3   Cf. L. Bianchi, *Il vescovo e i filosofi: la condanna parigina del 1277 e l'evoluzione dell'aristotelismo* (Bergamo: Ed. Pierluigi Lubrina, 1990).

explicitly critical of the Philosopher. Instead, Thomas sought to integrate him as much as possible within the categories of medieval Christianity.

True, Bonaventure had expressed reservations about the absorption strategy of Aristotelianism, but his critique was still within a developing theological debate. However, the condemnations of 1277 broke the synthesis attempted by Thomism. They fostered a divide between faith and reason, theology and philosophy, creating a climate of suspicion and opposition among proponents of one or the other. After the condemnations, 'theologians would rely on revelation and faith more than upon philosophical reasoning to ascertain the truth of theological conclusions'.[4] It can be said that 'concordist' theology accommodating to the instances of Aristotle's thought received a severe blow. The Parisian condemnations were followed by the University of Oxford in 1284, reinforcing the distance between those who practised philosophy and those who practised theology, also causing sparks between Franciscans (now lacking the diplomacy of Bonaventure) and Dominicans (defending the legacy of Thomas). At Oxford in 1278, the Franciscan friar William de la Mare drafted the *Correctorium fratris Thomae*, identifying 118 theses to censure from the works of Thomas. In response, the Dominicans wrote the *Correctoria corruptorii* arguing that William did not 'correct' Thomas but, if anything, 'corrupted' him by reading him maliciously. Trailing from these discussions were debates over the scientific status of theology, its speculative or practical nature, and the foundation of knowledge. Thomas was at the centre of them.

The canonisation by Pope John XXII (1323)

At the beginning of the fourteenth century, almost fifty years after his death, Thomas's reputation significantly improved. Within the

---

4   R. Van Nieuwenhove, *An Introduction to Medieval Theology* (Cambridge: Cambridge University Press, 2012), p. 227. The whole section on the 1277 condemnations (pp. 225–28) is useful.

Dominican Order, the reigning pope, John XXII, was asked to proclaim him as a 'saint'. The Church's official recognition of sanctity implies that the person may be publicly invoked as an intercessor. At this time, William of Tocco's biography was written as part of the documentation used to promote ecclesiastical recognition. In 1323 the process was finalised in Avignon, and the official decision was solemnly proclaimed on 18 July. Apart from highlighting the sanctity of Thomas's life, the text of the papal bull *Redemptionem misit* recalls ten miracles (mainly stories of healing but also of sweet odours) attributed to the intercession of Thomas in favour of different people who had visited his tomb or encountered his relics.[5] His theological achievements are hardly mentioned. The devotional dimension intertwined with medieval practices of veneration of relics and visitation of burial places appears to be one in which Thomas himself would be at ease. The canonisation process and final pronouncement shows that the Roman Catholic spiritual world of venerations and expectations has always been associated with Thomas and his theology. As Torrell acknowledges, 'the spontaneous spread of the saint's cult in the earliest days was very quickly relayed into the mustering of the Dominican Order around Thomas's doctrine'.[6] From the outset, there was no significant distinction perceived by his disciples and admirers between the lofty spheres of Thomas's theology and the accrued venerations of medieval spirituality.

John XXII also referred to what Thomas is reported to have said before dying and receiving the Eucharist. Here are his words: 'I have written and taught much about this very holy Body, and about the other sacraments in the faith of Christ, and about the Holy Roman Church, to whose correction I expose and submit everything I have written.'[7]

Thomas is depicted as totally immersed in the eucharistic theology of his day and considers himself submitted to the Roman

---

5   The text of the papal bull can be found here: https://florida.sspx.org/en/news-events/news/seventh-centenary-canonization-st-thomas-aquinas-4-81135 (accessed 5 July 2023).

6   Torrell, *Saint Thomas Aquinas*, vol. 1, p. 320. The story of the canonisation is told at pp. 317–26.

7   https://www.1517.org/articles/thomas-aquinas-the-doctor-of-the-church (accessed 24 January 2024).

Church and in the obedient service of it. There is total identification. The bull presents Thomas as a model of fidelity to the Roman
Church. Moreover, John XXII provides for those who 'go piously
to the tomb of the Saint to ask forgiveness . . . one year and forty
days of pardon' and to those who visit it seven days after his feast
'a hundred days of indulgence which they would still have to pay
for their sins'. Thomas's devotional legacy became embedded in the
practice of indulgences that his theology did not take issue with.

After the canonisation, in 1325, the bishop of Paris removed the
condemnations issued in 1277 regarding those propositions which
could be referred to as expressing Thomas's thought. This measure
was meant to clear any suspicion of heresy and stop further
polemical appraisals of Thomas's theology, especially from the
Franciscans. The Roman Church recognised Thomas as an example
of purity of life and adherence to its doctrine.

The transition from Thomas to Thomism

The canonisation was only a step in the process of identification of
early modern Roman Catholicism with Thomism.[8] At the beginning of the fifteenth century, the *Summa Theologiae* replaced Peter
Lombard's *Sentences* as the theological textbook in universities that
students had to study from and comment on as an essential part of
their academic journey, even outside of Dominican schools where
Thomism had become the official doctrine of the Order. Thomas's
thought was accepted as the standard representation of orthodox
Catholicism by Jesuits, Augustinians and others, and in places as
diverse as France, Germany, Poland, Italy and Portugal. In the
Jesuit Order, for example, the 1556 Constitutions of the Society
of Jesus provided for 'the scholastic doctrine of Saint Thomas' to
be taught to members. Because of his quasi-universal acceptance
across the board by the religious orders, it was at this point that

---

8   On these sections surveying the trajectory between Thomas and Thomism, useful sources are
    R. Cessario and C. Cuddy, *Thomas and the Thomists: The Achievement of Thomas Aquinas and
    His Interpreters* (Minneapolis, MN: Fortress Press, 2017) and R. Cessario, *Le thomisme et les
    thomistes* (Paris: Cerf, 1999).

Thomas was also named *Doctor Communis* (1567). Facing the theological challenges of the Reformation, Thomas also began to be considered the Roman Catholic bulwark against the rising tide of Protestantism in continental Europe.

After the early controversies over Thomas's orthodoxy, the Dominican John Capreolus (1380–1444) sparked a revival in Thomism in Paris, a century after his death. Capreolus's *Four Books of Defences of the Theology of St Thomas Aquinas* contributed to changing the perception of Thomas from being an individual Dominican theologian into the initiator of a school of thought that soon became mainstream in Roman Catholic theology. Commenting on Thomas's work was considered the main task of students and future theologians. Besides the circulation of Thomas's works, especially the *Summa Theologiae*, a Thomist commentatorial tradition was established.[9] Although not a monolith, this impressive body of writings functioned as introductions, interpretations and vulgarisations of Thomas. Since these early appropriations of Thomas, the tendency was to reinforce the systemic nature of his thought, perhaps beginning to harden certain features that Aquinas himself had left looser and more nuanced, especially in the fields of ecclesiology, moral theology, social doctrine and the relationship between faith and reason.

From the fifteenth century onwards, the School of Salamanca in Spain was a theological centre where Thomas's work was studied, taught and developed. In some way, Salamanca became what Paris had been in the thirteenth century: an international and influential university city where Thomism gained intellectual primacy. There were theologians of the calibre of Francisco de Vitoria (1492–1546), Domingo de Soto (1494–1560) and Melchor Cano (1509–60) who in their ways consolidated and expanded Thomas's system. Vitoria refined the nature of theology in the interplay between reason and

---

9 L. Lanza and M. Toste (eds), *Summistae: The Commentary Tradition on Thomas Aquinas's Summa Theologiae from the 15th to the 17th Centuries* (Leuven, Belgium: Leuven University Press, 2021).

faith and concentrated on the moral dimensions of Thomism.[10] Soto elaborated on Thomas's account of the relationship between nature and grace in an anti-Protestant way, giving theological ammunition to the Council of Trent. Against Luther, Soto also reinforced that Scripture is insufficient to establish doctrine: the light of reason and the Church Fathers' traditions are also necessary. Cano is the Salamanca theologian who participated in the Council of Trent. He had an important role in the discussions on the sacraments, especially the Eucharist, and always in an anti-Protestant tone. According to Cano, theology had two sources: one (Scripture and the Church's traditions) to be accepted *ab auctoritate*; the other (reason) to be accepted *a ratione*. Did he separate what Thomas had only distinguished or was it the 'natural' outcome of the still-shadowed relationship envisioned by Thomas?

In another university city, Padua, Tommaso de Vio (1468–1534), a professor of metaphysics, would become one of the most influential commentators on Thomas throughout the centuries. He was also known as Cajetan because he was born in Gaeta, north of Naples, and would eventually be appointed bishop there. This is the name he is normatively known by. After writing on Thomas's *De ente et essentia* and *De anima*, Cajetan wrote a monumental commentary on the *Summa Theologiae*. He was an Aristotelian because he was a Thomist. This work became the standard text-book for generations of theologians reading Thomas through the interpretative grid Cajetan provided. Suffice it to say that when Leo XIII came to write *Aeterni Patris* (1879) commending Thomas as the bulwark of Roman Catholic thought, Cajetan was the only commentator quoted in the papal encyclical.

Apart from Cajetan's commentaries on Thomas, Aristotle, Peter Lombard and numerous biblical books, his debate with Martin Luther in 1518 gave him a place in the history of theology. Pope Leo X entrusted him to meet with the German monk through whom the Reformation was sparked in Germany and beyond.

---

10 D. M. Lantigua, 'Aquinas and the Emergence of Moral Theology during the Spanish Renaissance' in Levering and Plested (eds), *The Oxford Handbook of the Reception of Aquinas*, pp. 173–90.

We will return to Luther's encounter with Thomism through his dealings with Cajetan. What matters here is the kind of proximity to Thomas. Cuddy has spoken of 'intensive reception':[11] Cajetan *defended* Thomas and his thought from alternative accounts such as Averroism, Scotism and incipient Lutheranism, and also *extended* its principles to questions and controversies of the day by applying them to contingent issues that Thomas had not dealt with directly. As argued by Cuddy, Cajetan 'consistently encourages his readers to approach the Thomistic corpus as a consistent whole'.[12] For him Thomas's thought was to be received as a system because it was framed according to universal principles and possessed an intrinsic cohesion. What is important to notice at this point is that '[t]hrough Cajetan the Thomist system was shaped and developed into a notable factor in the intellectual system of modern Catholicism'.[13] From Cajetan onwards, through the Council of Trent up to the First Vatican Council (1870), Thomas's legacy was considered a whole and became indistinguishable from mainstream Roman Catholicism. More than that, it was consecrated to the service of the Roman Church.

The anti-Protestant use of Thomas

After the first outbreak of enthusiasm culminated in Thomas being proclaimed a 'saint' in the fourteenth century, the second phase in the development of the movement of thought named after Aquinas was characterised by an increased apologetic thrust. In the fifteenth- and sixteenth-century expressions of Thomism, the Spanish commentators (e.g. Soto and Cano) and Cajetan had an anti-Protestant strand. The appeal to Thomas was seen as a protection against the perceived doctrinal errors of the Reformation and as the supreme theological guide to launch the renewal of

---

11 C. Cuddy, 'Sixteenth-Century Reception of Aquinas by Cajetan' in Levering and Plested (eds), *The Oxford Handbook of the Reception of Aquinas*, pp. 144–58.

12 Cuddy, 'Sixteenth-Century Reception of Aquinas by Cajetan', p. 150.

13 J. Wicks, 'Thomism Between Renaissance and Reformation: The Case of Cajetan', *Archiv für Reformationsgeschichte* 68 (1977), p. 11.

the Church that was increasingly sought. Of course, Thomas lived three centuries before the Reformation and did not anticipate the debates of the sixteenth century. On the Roman Catholic side, however, the principles of thought that Thomas had advocated for – from both reason and faith as interpreted by Rome – were considered the best ammunition to fight against the issues that the Reformation had brought to the fore.

This is evident in the discussions at the Council of Trent (1545–63) and the important documents that ensued, especially on doctrinal topics such as justification and the sacraments. Together with the measures aimed at giving new vigour to the structures and practices of the Roman Catholic Church, justification and the sacraments were the chief issues at stake. The Council Fathers found in Thomas an authority to appeal to in their deliberations.

Providing an overview of the influence exercised by Thomas on Trent, Cessario argues that 'a great deal of what was accomplished at Trent bore the stamp of St Thomas Aquinas'.[14] First of all, the Dominicans played a central role at the Council, although not being the largest number among the participants of different orders. Still, they had all been trained on Thomas's works and carried a distinct Thomist way of theologising.[15] Sure, Thomism was not the only school represented at the Council – there were also Franciscans and Augustinians – but it was perhaps the most influential one, especially thanks to the Spanish Dominicans such as Peter de Soto (1500–63) and the already mentioned Melchor Cano. While the story that the copy of the *Summa* was placed next to the Bible to indicate its eminency is more of a legend than a fact,[16] it is indisputable that Thomas stands behind what Trent decreed on justification (Sixth Session) and the sacraments (Seventh, Thirteenth, Fourteenth, Twenty-Second and Twenty-Third Sessions).

---

14 R. Cessario, 'Sixteenth-Century Reception of Aquinas by the Council of Trent and Its Main Authors' in Levering and Plested (eds), *The Oxford Handbook of the Reception of Aquinas*, p. 163.

15 Cf. A. Walz, *I Domenicani al Concilio di Trento* (Rome: Herder, 1961).

16 This is the view of Walz, followed by Cessario.

As already seen in chapter 2, Thomas's view on justification adhered to the transformative account whereby the sinner is made righteous through a reversible movement of different steps. Trent espoused the essence of it, and the Reformers departed from it. On this divisive issue, Trent sided with Thomas against the Reformation.

On the sacraments, the Council found in Thomas an advocate of the sacramental mediatorial role of the Church against the Reformers' view whereby grace is received by faith alone. Especially as far as the doctrine of the Eucharist is concerned, Trent used the *Summa Theologiae* as a theological framework for its deliberations on the doctrine of transubstantiation (III, q. 75), its sacrificial character (III, q. 73) and how Christ offers himself in it. Thomas's blueprint is also evident in the Council's views on penance, the extreme unction and the theology of the ecclesiastical hierarchy.

The earlier appeals to Thomas in the emerging theological fight against Protestantism became solidified in magisterial pronouncements and were internalised in Roman Catholic teaching, thus becoming theologically and symbolically associated with it. After the Council of Trent, it is no surprise that a Dominican pope like Pius V declared Thomas a Doctor of the Church in 1567,[17] in recognition of the theological support that Rome had found in him in countering the challenge of the Reformation. In post-Trent Roman Catholicism, not without nuances and shades of opinion, Thomas's doctrine was commonly held as the most solid, reliable and approved theological system in opposition to Protestantism.

This anti-Protestant version of Thomism is well epitomised by Roberto Bellarmino (1542–1621), the Jesuit defender of Roman Catholic orthodoxy as it had been reaffirmed at the Council of Trent over against the critical claims made by the various strands of the Protestant Reformation. As a controversialist theologian fully

---

17 A. Walz, 'San Tommaso d'Aquino dichiarato dottore della Chiesa', *Angelicum* 44 (1967), pp. 145–73.

immersed in Thomism, he was called *propugnaculum fortissimum* (the strong bulwark), and *haereticorum malleum* (the hammer of the heretics).[18] The most read work of his theological career is entitled *Controversies* (*Disputationes de controversiis Christianae Fidei adversus huius temporis haereticos*, published in Ingolstadt in three tomes from 1586 and 1593)[19] and became the standard Roman Catholic theological rebuttal of the Reformation up to the First Vatican Council (1870). The term 'controversy' indicates a cultural and theological milieu marked by the 'wars of truth', as John Milton put it in the *Areopagitica* (1644).[20] The 'oppositional' Roman Catholicism which had come out of the Council of Trent found in Bellarmine a thoughtful systematiser and an efficient apologist in the ongoing doctrinal and spiritual 'war' against the Protestant heresies. The Tridentine Conciliar Decrees and Canons – containing the rejection of Reformation doctrines and the affirmation of the Roman theological and sacramental system – were so well assimilated by Bellarmine that he successfully articulated them more comprehensively in response to the Protestant claims. All this was done by having Thomas as the chief reference point.[21] One important use of Thomism was to prove the incompatibility between Rome and the Reformation.

---

18 As reported by G. Domenici, 'La genesi, le vicende ed i giudizi delle controversie bellarminiane', *Gregorianum* 2:2 (1921), pp. 513–42. On Bellarmine, see my 'Robert Bellarmine and His Controversies with the Reformers'.

19 Partial English edition: R. Bellarmine, *Controversies of the Christian Faith* (Saddle River, NJ: Keep the Faith, 2016). This is the translation of the three controversies of Tome I: 1. On the Word of God; 2. On Christ; 3. On the Sovereign Pontiff. Tome I also includes On the Church. Tome II deals with the sacraments in general and with the seven sacraments. A partial English translation of the section on the Mass is R. Bellarmine, *On the Most Holy Sacrifice of the Mass* [1583–96] (Columbia, SC: Mediatrix Press, 2020).

20 On the importance of 'truth' for Counter-Reformation Roman Catholic thought, see S. Tutino, *Shadows of Doubt: Language and Truth in Post-Reformation Catholic Culture* (Oxford: Oxford University Press, 2014).

21 S. H. De Franceschi, 'Uniformité de doctrine et orthodoxie au temps de la synthèse bellarminienne: le statut doctrinal de Thomas d'Aquin dans la Compagnie de Jésus à la veille des Congrégations de auxiliis' in *Ripensare Bellarmino tra teologia, filosofia e storia* (Rome: Gregorian & Biblical Press, 2023), pp. 131–58.

From seventeenth-century internal debates to neo-Thomism

After the elevation of Thomas to the status of a venerated and prayed-to 'saint', and the appeal to his thought and legacy as a pro-Roman Catholic and anti-Protestant theology, there is a third important step in the appropriation process by the Roman Catholic tradition that needs to be briefly mentioned. Thomas was again at the centre of attention in the late sixteenth-century and seventeenth-century intra-mural Roman Catholic controversies over how human beings respond to God's grace or aid (*auxilium*; therefore, the *de auxiliis* controversy) and over moral theological issues (e.g. probabilism).

This time the debate was not between the Dominicans and the Franciscans but between the Dominicans and the Jesuits. The former, championed by Domingo Báñez (1528–1604), accused the Jesuits of semi-Pelagianism because they put too much stress on human beings' volitional handling of divine grace and ascribed only 'middle knowledge' to God. God's providence and action were moved by something preceding it. In turn, the Jesuits, represented by Luis de Molina (1535–1600), denounced the Dominicans as Calvinists because they insisted on the primacy of God's grace. Both parties appealed to Thomas to argue their case and to highlight the other's errors.[22]

The other major intra-mural Roman Catholic debate involving matters of interpretation of Thomas had to do with the role of probable opinions in moral discernment. Charting a middle way between extreme rigorism (i.e. ascribing little if no role to the moral weighting of situations) and laxism (i.e. coming close to moral indifferentism), Thomas's nuanced moral theology was taken as a point of equilibrium, thus reinforcing the conviction that his thought was the always relevant and needed stabiliser for theological controversies.

---

22 On the whole *de auxiliis* controversy, see S. H. De Franceschi, *Thomisme et théologie moderne: l'école de saint Thomas à l'épreuve de la querelle de la grâce (XVIIe–XVIIIe siècles)* (Paris: Artège Lethielleux, (2018). For a comparison between debates over salvation in Protestant and Roman Catholic theologies of the time, see J. J. Ballor, M. T. Gaetano and D. S. Sytsma (eds), *Beyond Dordt and De Auxiliis: The Dynamics of Protestant and Catholic Soteriology in the Sixteenth and Seventeenth Centuries* (Leiden, the Netherlands: Brill, 2019).

In the seventeenth century, the Thomist tradition was aptly represented by John of St Thomas (1589–1644), a Portuguese Dominican.
His commentary on the *Summa*, the eight-volume *Cursus Theologicus*,
was another monumental addition to the immensely vast body of
literature dealing with the thought of Thomas. What is particularly
interesting in John of St Thomas is his view of what it means to be a
Thomist, i.e. a disciple of Thomas Aquinas. As Robertson summarised it: 'A true disciple of St Thomas would (i) hold to the teaching
of the continuous succession of his disciples such as Hervaeus,
Capreolus, Cajetan, Ferrara, Vitoria, Soto, Flandria, and the like; (ii)
make efforts to defend and develop St Thomas's teaching; (iii) seek
the glory of St Thomas and not his own opinions; (iv) apply himself
to reconciling apparent contradictions in his writings; and (v) strive
for unity and agreement in following the teaching of St Thomas'.[23]
John of St Thomas testifies to the much-consolidated awareness
of belonging to a Thomist tradition that desires to remain faithful
to Thomas, honour his legacy and develop his thought within the
already provided theological framework.

After the French Revolution and the downfall of the French
emperor Napoleon Bonaparte, the Congress of Vienna of 1814–15
tried to redesign a layout of the European political and constitu-
tional order. The Roman Catholic Church wanted to overcome
the threats of the Revolution and reconnect to the Tridentine and
scholastic tradition as if nothing had happened. Rome presumed
that the challenges of the modern world could be easily removed.
All the deviations of modernity, e.g. the Enlightenment, deism and
fideism, were considered as nothing but outcomes of Protestantism's
subsidence to subjectivism. As Thomas was used to defend the
Roman Catholic identity against the Reformation, even now – three
centuries later – Thomas's thought was evoked as the best and most
efficacious representation of traditional Roman Catholicism seeking
to reaffirm itself against the derailing effects of modernity. The
'objectivity' of the Aristotelian–Thomist account of reality was used

---

23 C. Robertson, 'Seventeenth-Century Catholic Reception Outside the *De auxiliis* Controversy'
in Levering and Plested (eds), *The Oxford Handbook of the Reception of Aquinas*, p. 281.

as a shield to be protected from and as a weapon to fight against all 'modern' attempts at reconstructing the Christian world view, be they 'romantic' or 'rationalistic' ones. According to the Roman Catholic theology of the time, as exemplified by a German Thomist, Christian Wolff (1679–1754), Thomas, as interpreted by the Council of Trent and further received by subsequent Thomistic trends, provided the best apologetics for the Roman *status quo*, both intellectually and symbolically. In the ideological and political turbulence brought about by the Enlightenment and the French Revolution, the patronage of Thomas gave the Roman Catholic system a sense of doctrinal stability, rational defensibility and epistemological certainty over against philosophies of appearance (phenomenalism), of becoming (evolutionism) and of the ego (psychologism).

In confronting modernity, Thomas, the philosopher more than the theologian, came to be appreciated. His thought was elevated to being the *philosophia perennis* (everlasting philosophy) that the teaching authority of the Church would cling to in confronting the claims of autonomy made by modern reason. The primary importance given to the Aristotelian–Thomist philosophical framework and the association of this tradition with the teaching authority of the Roman Catholic Church made Thomism go through a further step in its historical development. It was more than a new form of Roman Catholic rationalism: it had become neo-Thomism. In Thomism, the ideal of Christian philosophy and theology had come to a full and unsurpassable accomplishment. The whole Church needed to think *ad mentem Sancti Thomae* (according to the mind of Saint Thomas).

Leo XIII, *Aeterni Patris* (1879) and the magisterial affirmation of Thomism

When Pope Leo XIII signed the encyclical *Aeterni Patris* (*AP*) on 4 August 1879, nobody was surprised.[24] Before becoming

---

24 *Aeterni Patris*, encyclical letter of Pope Leo XIII on the restoration of Christian philosophy. See: https://www.vatican.va/content/leo-xiii/en/encyclicals/documents/hf_l-xiii_enc_04081879_aeterni-patris.html (accessed 27 July 2023).

pope, Gioacchino Pecci as bishop of Perugia had been a staunch promoter of the Thomist reorientation of seminary studies and a representative of the growing neo-Thomistic movement. In the second year of his pontificate, Leo issued *AP* as a programmatic manifesto for the whole Church.[25] Against the background of the challenges put forward by modern thought, the encyclical sketches the history of Christian philosophy from the early Apologists to the Western Fathers (e.g. Augustine) and the medieval Doctors. In this context, the supreme recognition given to Thomas flowed from the perceived need to counter the pressures of modernity with the reaffirmation of a giant of Roman Catholic thought:

> Among the Scholastic Doctors, the chief and master of all towers Thomas Aquinas, who, as Cajetan observes, because he most venerated the ancient doctors of the Church, in a certain way seems to have inherited the intellect of all. The doctrines of those illustrious men, like the scattered members of a body, Thomas collected together and cemented, distributed in wonderful order, and so increased with important additions that he is rightly and deservedly esteemed the special bulwark and glory of the Catholic faith (*AP*, n. 17).

According to Leo XIII, Thomas and Thomism, taken together as an indistinguishable whole, provide the scientific account of Christian wisdom and thought, and the most reliable reference point to be pitted against modern, anti-religious trends.

Especially as far as the relationship between reason and faith is concerned, 'Reason, borne on the wings of Thomas to its human height, can scarcely rise higher, while faith could scarcely expect more or stronger aids from reason than those which she has already obtained through Thomas' (*AP*, n. 18). The encyclical claims that reason as interpreted by Thomas has its own methodological autonomy that faith supplements to elevate it. Faith is *ultra* (beyond) but not *contra rationem* (against reason). Little

---

25 See G. Morra, 'La "Aeterni Patris" cent'anni dopo', *Sacra Doctrina* 92 (1980), pp. 5–19.

if no awareness here is given to the noetic effects of sin, i.e. the disruptive impact of human sin on the trustworthiness of reason. Moreover, claiming Thomas on his side, Leo acknowledges reason's autonomy and considers faith a supplement capable of elevating it to its supernatural end.

Besides recognising Thomas's epistemological commitments regarding the relationship between reason and faith, the encyclical also underlines the centrality of his thought in the decisions made by Church Councils: 'In the Councils of Lyons, Vienna, Florence, and the Vatican I might almost say that Thomas took part and presided over the deliberations and decrees of the Fathers, contending against the errors of the Greeks, of heretics and rationalists, with invincible force and with the happiest results. But the chief and special glory of Thomas, one which he has shared with none of the Catholic Doctors, is that the Fathers of Trent made it part of the order of conclave to lay upon the altar, together with sacred Scripture and the decrees of the supreme Pontiffs, the *Summa* of Thomas Aquinas, whence to seek counsel, reason, and inspiration' (*AP*, n. 22).

For Leo XIII, the Roman Catholic Church has always followed Thomas's legacy and should continue to be the North Star in confronting the day's issues. There is such a strong connection between Thomas and Rome, almost an identification, to the point where to be Roman Catholic means to think and live 'in conformity with the teaching of the Church, such as is contained in the works of Thomas Aquinas' (*AP*, n. 28).

As already mentioned, one of the outcomes of *AP* was the republication of the complete works of Thomas Aquinas, called the Leonine Edition, the reprinting of the commentaries on the *Summa* by Cajetan, the establishment of a Thomistic academy in Rome and the founding of the Roman Dominican university, the Angelicum, to promote academic studies and to train future scholars. The full support given by Leo XIII to Thomistic studies also encouraged the founding of several dedicated academic journals: *Divus Thomas* (Piacenza, Italy, 1880), *Revue Thomiste* (Fribourg, Switzerland, 1889), *Revue néoscolastique* (Leuven, Belgium, 1894), *Rivista di filosofia neoscolastica* (Milan, Italy, 1909), *New Blackfriars Journal* (Oxford,

1920), *The Thomist* ((Washington, DC, 1939), *Sacra Doctrina* (Bologna, Italy, 1956). This form of Thomism became the standard philosophical and theological grid for the generations of scholars and priests between the nineteenth and the twentieth centuries.

According to Leo XIII and neo-Thomism, the restoration of the traditional social order that the French Revolution had challenged and the reaffirmation of the traditional world view that the Enlightenment had put into question needed the recovery of a fully orbed Thomism as its dorsal spine. The Christian society (*societas christiana*) under attack urged the Roman Church to uphold Thomas's framework of thought to be defended and relaunched. Since Thomas was the safe and approved philosophy and theology teacher for Roman Catholics, his ideas were the safe and approved norms for navigating the challenges of modern times.

The rather intellectualist and reactionary interpretation of Thomism continued and even intensified after Leo XIII. Everything that would not formally resemble and resound Thomistic (i.e. the way neo-Thomism interpreted Thomas) was accused of 'modernism' and fought against.[26] Any attempts to reconcile the Roman Catholic Church and modern culture away from Thomistic thought patterns were accused of betrayal. The confrontation became so intense that in 1907 Pius X issued the encyclical *Pascendi Dominici gregis* on the errors of the modernists.[27] Among other measures to stop the spreading of modernist ideas, the pope made sure to ordain that 'scholastic philosophy be made the basis of the sacred sciences' (n. 45) and admonished teachers to stay as close as possible to Thomas: 'Let Professors remember that they cannot set St. Thomas aside, especially in metaphysical questions, without grave detriment' (n. 45).

The further official declaration came in 1914 when the Congregation of Studies published what has come to be known

---

26 G. Daly, *Transcendence and Immanence: A Study in Catholic Modernism and Integralism* (Oxford: Oxford University Press, 1980).

27 https://www.vatican.va/content/pius-x/en/encyclicals/documents/hf_p-x_enc_19070908_pascendi-dominici-gregis.html (accessed 31 July 2023).

as 'The Twenty-Four Thomistic Theses'.[28] Several professors from different institutions drew up a set of philosophical theses – particularly metaphysics – which they had been teaching and defending as Thomas's principles. These twenty-four theses all concern metaphysics (i.e. ontology, cosmology, psychology, theodicy), since it was chiefly upon the metaphysical teaching of Thomas that the popes, particularly Pius X, insisted. Appealing to experience, tradition and historical studies was the wrong way to pursue the truth. The point of the 24 Theses was to secure a relative autonomy of the natural order with its intrinsic teleology within the context of the demonstrability of God through the cosmological argument. Grace was a super-added gift. The physical world had to be shown to work on its own principles.

Thomas's theological system was also refuelled in a neo-Thomistic way by Dominican theologian Réginald Garrigou-Lagrange (1877–1964).[29] This is to say that neo-Thomism, while having a prevalent interest in Thomism as a philosophical framework, also insisted on the perennial viability of Thomas's theology. In 1917, publishing the Canon Law, Pope Benedict XV ordered the method, doctrines and principles of St Thomas to be followed (can. 1366, § 2) and gave as reference the decree of the Sacred Congregation that had approved the 24 Theses. Furthermore, on the 600th anniversary of Thomas's canonisation in 1923, Pope Pius XI declared Thomas the *studiorum ducem*, the supreme guide in the study of higher disciplines.[30] He went on to say that 'it behooves the whole of Christendom worthily to celebrate this centenary [the 600th anniversary of his canonisation] because in honouring St. Thomas something greater is involved than the reputation of St. Thomas and that is the authority of the teaching Church' (n. 31). Thomas and the teaching authority of the Church are totally

---

28 http://www.catholicapologetics.info/catholicteaching/philosophy/thomast.htm (accessed 31 July 2023).

29 Garrigou-Lagrange, *La sintesi tomistica* [1950]. For a survey of neo-scholastic theology, see R. W. Nutt, 'The Reception of Aquinas in Early Twentieth-Century Catholic Neo-Scholastic and Historical Theologians' in Levering and Plested (eds), *The Oxford Handbook of the Reception of Aquinas*, pp. 392–407.

30 https://www.papalencyclicals.net/pius11/p11studi.htm (accessed 31 July 2023).

identified. As Thomas had been used as the pre-eminent anti-Protestant Roman Catholic source of inspiration, he was now indicated as Rome's chief defender in its anti-modernist battle. The ideological and apologetic use of Thomas had come full circle.

The twentieth-century *ressourcement* and the emergence of a 'living Thomism'

The flip side of neo-Thomism was that, while it sought to solidify an objective and principle-based system for the preservation and implementation of Roman Catholic influence in modern society, it also generated opposition within the Church and was not entirely successful in eradicating modernism from within. The irony was that neo-Thomism had built a theological–philosophical system that, to fight against the Enlightenment, ended up assimilating the rationalistic outlook of its plausibility structures. The neo-Thomism that was carved into the encyclical *Aeterni Patris* of Leo XIII and beyond was perceived to be a closed, sophisticated and intellectualist apparatus that lost sight of the 'mystery' of faith expressed in the liturgy and the sacraments. Regarding its alleged Thomism, its anti-modernist edge looked like a fundamentalist use of Thomas, which had lost his thought's historical context and inner dynamism. These concerns were given voice by the *nouvelle théologie* (new theology), a stream of Roman Catholic thought (mainly French) that developed in the first half of the twentieth century and that sought to renew the theological vision of Roman Catholicism by re-engaging its biblical, patristic and liturgical sources in conversation with philosophical, cultural and scientific discourses of the time. This strain of theology was initially looked upon with suspicion by Rome's ecclesiastical authorities and even fought against, although it became highly influential at the Second Vatican Council and afterwards.

The *nouvelle théologie* was a reaction to this stiffening of Thomism through the rediscovery of a 'living Thomism' that opened the eyes of faith to the world (M. Blondel, J. Maréchal, P. Rousselot), promoted the historical appropriation of Thomas away

from the 'eternal' principles distilled by the scores of commentators (M.-D. Chenu), made fluid the distinction between the natural
and the supernatural (H. de Lubac and H. Bouillard), insisted
on the category of incarnation and human 'participation' in the
Incarnation (H. U. von Balthasar and M.-D. Chenu), rediscovered
the 'spiritual' interpretation of Scripture and tradition (J. Daniélou
and H. de Lubac), and invested a great deal in ecclesiology in sacramental terms (H. de Lubac and Y. Congar). In short, under the
leadership of Dominicans like Chenu and Congar and then Jesuits
like Bouillard and de Lubac, it proposed re-appropriating the
pre-modern heritage of the Christian faith (Thomas included) to
appreciate its Roman Catholicity afresh and to deal with the quests
of modern culture.[31] Everything revolved around the category of
ressourcement: return, re-appropriation, re-assimilation of the biblical, patristic and liturgical tradition and, in our case, of Thomas.

The New Theology expressed one direction of what McCool has
termed 'the internal evolution of Thomism'.[32] After centuries of reliance on the Thomist commentators as providing a rather dry, static
and one-sided presentation of Thomas, the change brought about
in the twentieth century was a renewed interest in Thomas's works
in their historical context and in Thomas's person as 'the Christian
believer seeking understanding, the poet and preacher, mystic
and doctor captivated by the wonderful order of created reality
made simultaneously more perspicacious and mysterious through
divine revelation'.[33] Beyond theological circles and even besides
the contribution of the New Theology, the works of philosophers
and historians like Jacques Maritain (1882–1973)[34] and Étienne

---

31 I am following the interpretation of *nouvelle théologie* found in H. Boersma, *Nouvelle Théologie
and Sacramental Ontology: A Return to Mystery* (Oxford: Oxford University Press, 2009). On
this whole section F. Kerr, *Twentieth-Century Catholic Theologians* (Oxford: Blackwell, 2007),
is extremely helpful.

32 G. A. McCool, *From Unity to Pluralism: The Internal Evolution of Thomism* (New York, NY:
Fordham University Press, 1989).

33 A. G. Cooper, 'The Reception of Aquinas in *Nouvelle Théologie*' in Levering and Plested (eds),
The Oxford Handbook of the Reception of Aquinas, p. 427.

34 As part of his prolific production, see his *The Angelic Doctor: The Life and Thought of St.
Thomas Aquinas* [1930] (New York, NY: Lincoln MacVeagh; Toronto: Longmans, 1931).

Gilson (1884–1978)[35] pictured Thomas as the symbol of an open-minded attitude and as the nuanced genius theologian–philosopher grounded in biblical revelation, the tradition of the Fathers and the Church, and also steeped in Aristotelian and Platonic philosophies. An exclusively Aristotelian – and by extension – philosophical reading of Thomas was too one-sided to reflect his legacy's complexity and depth. According to Maritain, Thomas's thought could not be equated with an anti-modernist, anti-scientific, anti-secular perspective, but positively with a form of 'integral humanism', i.e. a generous account of Christian thought capable of embracing whatever good can be found in other religious and philosophical traditions and of informing political discourse and policy in a pluralistic age.[36]

No longer was it the abrasive and 'dead' Thomas; rather, the welcoming and 'living' Thomas was the Roman Catholic saint and patron who emerged out of the *ressourcement* of the twentieth century and broke away from the rigidity of neo-Thomistic accounts that had prevailed before. Unsurprisingly, retrieving Thomas's thought as it was reinterpreted by the New Theology would play a significant role at the Second Vatican Council (1962–65). According to Congar, 'it could be shown . . . that St. Thomas, the *Doctor communis*, furnished the writers of the dogmatic texts of Vatican II with the bases and structure (*les assises et la structure*) of their thought'.[37] It is not so much the direct quotations or interactions with Thomas's texts that count as the deep structures of his thought that helped the Council Fathers to shape the overall orientation of conciliar processes and texts.

More specifically, direct references to Thomas are found in two places. One deals with priestly training and the indication that it should be implemented 'under the guidance' of Thomas. Here is

---

35 Indicative of his interpretation of Thomas as it can be found in many books is *Thomism: The Philosophy of Thomas Aquinas* [1922] (Toronto: Pontifical Institute of Medieval Studies, 2002).

36 J. Maritain, *Integral Humanism* [1936] (New York, NY: Scribner's, 1968).

37 Quoted by Guarino, *The Disputed Teachings of Vatican II*, p. 25. We will need to come back to this quote in ch. 5 as attention will be given to the influences of Thomas's doctrine of analogy and participation in post-Vatican II Roman Catholicism.

the text: 'in order that they may illumine the mysteries of salvation as completely as possible, the students should learn to penetrate them more deeply with the help of speculation, under the guidance of St. Thomas, and to perceive their interconnections' (Decree on Priestly Training *Optatam Totius*, 1965, n. 16).[38] Following an uninterrupted tradition, Thomas is considered the theological guide for Roman Catholic priests and leaders. The indication given by Vatican II was then codified in the 1983 *Codex of Canon Law* where one reads, 'Students are to learn to penetrate more intimately the mysteries of salvation, especially with St. Thomas as a teacher' (can. 252, par. 3).[39] In post-Vatican II Roman Catholicism, Thomas is the guide and the teacher for the priesthood, a role the Roman Church gives no one else. This was the first time an Ecumenical Council had recommended an individual theologian, and Thomas was deemed worthy of the honour.

The other place where Thomas is mentioned in Vatican II texts is always in the context of training, but this time in general education. The new issues and challenges that the conversation with modern times brings to the fore must be dealt with 'according to the example of the doctors of the Church and especially of St. Thomas Aquinas' (Declaration on Christian Education *Gravissimum educationis*, 1965, n. 10).[40] Here again, as in 1923 with Pius XI referring to Thomas as *studiorum ducem* (supreme guide for higher studies), Thomas is seen as an exemplary and special guide for navigating the rough waters of cultural engagement. Whether dealing with the neo-Thomistic Thomas or the post-*nouvelle théologie* portrait of Thomas, the Roman Catholic Church has consistently uplifted him as her theological leader and supreme teacher. The interpretation of Thomas may have changed, but the overall identification with him has certainly not.

---

38 https://www.vatican.va/archive/hist_councils/ii_vatican_council/documents/vat-ii_decree_19651028_optatam-totius_en.html (accessed 2 August 2023).

39 https://www.vatican.va/archive/cod-iuris-canonici/eng/documents/cic_lib2-cann208-329_en.html#TITLE_III. (accessed 2 August 2023).

40 https://www.vatican.va/archive/hist_councils/ii_vatican_council/documents/vat-ii_decl_19651028_gravissimum-educationis_en.html (accessed 2 August 2023).

The retrieval of Thomas in recent popes

The long wave of the present-day Roman Catholic appropriation of Thomas has seen recent popes being part of the process,
indeed strong supporters and promoters.[41] After Vatican II, Paul
VI issued an apostolic letter, *Lumen Ecclesiae* (Light of the Church,
1974), to celebrate the 700th anniversary of Thomas's death and to
underline the permanent value of the doctrine and the method of
Thomas.[42] Thomas is rightly called 'a light for the Church and the
whole world' because the Church acknowledges 'the teaching of
St Thomas to be a complete, faithful and sublime expression both
of her own doctrine and of "the sense of the faith" that is inherent
in the people of God as a whole' (n. 22). The inherent relationship
between the Roman Church and Thomas is further reiterated when
Paul VI writes that 'the Church officially approves the teaching of
the Angelic Doctor and uses it as an instrument superbly adapted
to her purposes, thus casting the mantle of her own magisterial
authority over Aquinas' (n. 22). In summarising his legacy, the
pope argues that Thomas 'united faith and reason while preserving
the rights of each . . . The Church has shown a preference for the
teaching of St Thomas by declaring it to be her own . . . and pre-
ferring it on the basis of centuries-old experience. Even today, the
Church makes the teaching of the Angelic Doctor the basis of the
theological training given to those whose role it will be to confirm
and strengthen their brothers in the faith' (n. 23). Looking to
the future, Paul VI is convinced that 'There can be no authentic,
fruitful fidelity unless we receive from St Thomas himself the principles which act as beacons, shedding light on the more important
philosophical questions and rendering the faith more intelligible to
our age. Thomas's main positions and dynamic ideas must likewise
be accepted' (n. 29).

Along similar lines, John Paul II reinforced the identification of
Roman Catholic theology with that of Thomas. The publication of

---

41 We have already touched on Pope Francis's reverence for Thomas in the Introduction.
42 https://www.superflumina.org/paulvi_on_stthomas.html (accessed 3 August 2023).

the encyclical letter *Fides et Ratio* (*FR*) on 14 September 1998 by the pope brought to the attention of the religious world and public opinion a theme of fundamental importance for Christianity, i.e. the relationship between faith and reason.[43] This document is considered one of the most important contributions of the Roman Catholic Church to the interplay between theology and philosophy, Christianity and culture, and the Church and the world. *FR* shows the vastness and depth of Roman Catholic wisdom in a condensed and meditated form. In the classic style of the encyclicals, *FR* is a document that brings together a series of ideas woven into a discourse that tends towards a synthesis. To address the question of the relationship between faith and reason, *FR* lays the foundations, starting by reading some biblical data, taken above all from the Wisdom literature and from Pauline writings. These biblical references are put in a theological framework that uses some patristic sources summarised in the expressions *credo ut intelligam* (i.e. I believe in order to understand) and *intelligo ut credam* (i.e. I understand in order to believe).

FR is interesting in what it says and what it omits to say. Its silences are just as revealing as its explicit citations. The catholicity of Rome is not all-encompassing but responds to the selective logic of Roman catholicity. Above all, the lack of any reference to evangelical Protestant authors or sources is worth noting. There is no citation of the Protestant Reformers, and the same negligence can be extended to Protestant orthodoxy (seventeenth century), to philosophers such as Jonathan Edwards, and to neo-Calvinism (e.g. Abraham Kuyper and Herman Bavinck). On the one hand, *FR* tries to include the tradition of Eastern Orthodoxy (n. 74); on the other, it excludes Protestantism. Evidently, the Roman Catholic centre of gravity of Thomism, on which the encyclical rests, may lean in one direction but not another.

From its beginning, *FR* has had an unmistakable Thomistic inspiration. The encyclical can be considered an authoritative

43 https://www.vatican.va/content/john-paul-ii/en/encyclicals/documents/hf_jp-ii_enc_14091998_fides-et-ratio.html (accessed 2 August 2023). We shall return to this important encyclical in ch. 5.

affirmation of the importance of Thomism for the Roman Catholic world view. Without the scaffolding provided by Thomism, *FR* would be unthinkable. *FR* explicitly supports the 'enduring originality' of Thomas's thought (nn. 43–44). It endorses the philosophical framework of the 1870 dogmatic constitution *Dei Filius* of Vatican I (nn. 52–53), the 1879 encyclical *Aeterni Patris* (n. 57), and the neo-Thomistic renewal of the twentieth century (nn. 58–59). Thomism is the trajectory that joins medieval Roman Catholicism to the post-conciliar faith. It represents 'the most elevated synthesis ever attained by human thought' (n. 78).

Another confirmation of a full papal endorsement of the whole of Thomas and Thomism comes from Benedict XVI. At a general audience in 2010 centred on Thomas and his teaching for today's Church, Benedict said, 'The content of the Doctor Angelicus' preaching corresponds with virtually the whole structure of the *Catechism of the Catholic Church.*'[44] It is important to notice that the pope says what Thomas taught provides the theological framework of what the 1992 *Catechism* teaches. The point is made again that Thomas's theology needs to be received as a whole and that the present-day Roman Catholic Church adheres to it.

In the audience, Benedict made a further comment not often found in previous papal statements. Whereas other aspects of Thomas's work were highly praised and commended, the pope drew attention to Thomas's Mariology: 'Like all the Saints, St Thomas had a great devotion to Our Lady. He described her with a wonderful title: *Triclinium totius Trinitatis; triclinium,* that is, a place where the Trinity finds rest since, because of the Incarnation, in no creature as in her do the three divine Persons dwell and feel delight and joy at dwelling in her soul full of Grace. Through her intercession we may obtain every help . . . With a prayer that is traditionally attributed to St Thomas and that in any case reflects the elements of his profound Marian devotion we too say: "O most Blessed and sweet Virgin Mary, Mother of God . . . I entrust to your

---

44 https://www.vatican.va/content/benedict-xvi/en/audiences/2010/documents/hf_ben-xvi_aud_20100623.html (accessed 24 January 2024).

merciful heart . . . my entire life . . . Obtain for me as well, O most sweet Lady, true charity with which from the depths of my heart I may love your most Holy Son, our Lord Jesus Christ" '. According to Benedict XVI, Thomas's theology cannot be separated from his Marian theology and spirituality. This is another important feature of the Roman Catholic appropriation of Thomas.

4
Protestant readings of Thomas: circling around evangelical eclecticism

Thomas Aquinas is the Roman Catholic theologian *par excellence*. He has embodied the letter and the spirit of the theology of the Church of Rome over the centuries. Combining rationality and contemplation, rigour and passion, study and devotion, his thought has touched on the different traits of Catholic life, inspiring intellectual sophistication and popular beliefs, academic pursuits and devotional imaginations. The reception of his legacy has not been without conflicts of interpretation and different seasons of greater or lesser influence. Yet, the *Wirkungsgeschichte* (history of effects) indicates that there would not have been the anti-Protestant Roman Catholicism of the Council of Trent (1545–63), the anti-modernist Roman Catholicism of Vatican I (1869–70), and then the ecumenical Roman Catholicism of Vatican II (1962–65) without Thomas Aquinas inspiring them all in different ways. Difficult to dispute is church historian David Schaff's claim that 'the theology of the Angelic Doctor and the theology of the Roman Catholic Church are identical in all particulars except the immaculate conception. Anyone who understands Thomas understands medieval theology at its peak and has access to the doctrinal system of the Roman Church.'[1] At least symbolically, if not theologically, Thomas is to Roman Catholicism in all its internal versions what Luther and Calvin are to the Reformation in all its variants: father-like figures.

---

1   Quoted by his father P. Schaff, *History of the Christian Church, vol. 5: The Middle Ages. A.D. 1049–1294* [1907] (repr. Grand Rapids, MI: Eerdmans, 1960), p. 662.

By contrast, until a few years ago, few would have dreamed of seeing Thomas associated with a 'Protestant' sensibility because of his close identification with Roman Catholicism. It is true that, in Thomistic studies, there is a vein that interpreted Thomas from the point of view of his being associated with evangelical traits. For example, Chenu refers to this when he claims that 'the evangelical vocation of Brother Thomas Aquinas is the source of the development of his theology'.[2] Certainly, the reference to 'evangelical' must be interpreted here in a very broad sense that the gospel vaguely inspires in a form compatible with traditional Roman Catholic doctrine and experience.

In this chapter, we turn to concentrate on Protestant readings of Thomas and Thomism, understanding Protestant or evangelical in a confessional and historical way, beginning from Martin Luther up to the twentieth century in four steps, which can be thought of as being different evangelical patterns of dealing with Thomas. The sketched survey will present a very different story from that of the Roman Catholic appropriations of Thomas. It will also underline that the reception, interpretation and engagement with Thomas is an open-ended issue for Protestant theologians across the centuries.

Martin Luther's negative yet principled approach to Thomas

Even a beginner in theological studies knows that when dealing with Martin Luther, she should be aware of the hyperbolic nature of Luther's theological language and the controversialist tone of doctrinal discussions. Of course, he was not alone in doing theology this way. The point is that when examining Luther's assessment of Aquinas and scholastic theology, one is confronted with a 'crass polemical style'.[3] In perhaps the abrupt judgment that speaks for all, Luther labels Thomas as 'the source and foundation of all heresy,

---

2   Chenu, *Aquinas and His Role in Theology*, p. 11.

3   D. Luy, 'Sixteenth-Century Reception of Aquinas by Luther and Lutheran Reformers' in Levering and Plested (eds), *The Oxford Handbook of the Reception of Aquinas*, p. 106.

error and obliteration of the Gospel'.[4] Some background information can explain why Luther could conceive such a harsh comment.
In the early years of the Reformation, Luther's Roman Catholic
opponents on the topic of indulgences were Thomist theologians
belonging to the Dominican Order: this is the case with Johann
Tetzel (1465–1519), Ambrosius Catharinus (1484–1553) and the
already mentioned Cajetan. Even other theological opponents, while
not Dominicans, would appeal to Thomas as the theological authority
to argue against Luther. Since the issue of authority was at stake in
those early debates, and since Thomas was used as representing
the authority of the Roman Church, Luther identified Thomas as
the authority of Rome he was fighting against. While Luther could
accept Thomas as a Doctor of the Church, he would treat his writings as 'opinions' among others to be evaluated according to biblical
teaching and the consensus of the Church Fathers. In distancing
himself from Thomas, Luther first questioned the supreme authority
attributed to him as representative of Roman Catholic teaching.
Luther's Thomas was more than the medieval theologian he could
agree or disagree with on points of theology: symbolically, he
embodied the established theological authority he was challenging
on key points. Institutionally the face of the Church of Rome was the
pope, but theologically it was Thomas who was the principal voice.

Besides the theological identification with the papal Church,
Luther took issue with Thomas because of his distaste for scholastic
theology. Even before penning his 1517 *Disputation Against
Scholastic Theology*, Luther had developed acrimony against
scholastic theology, which, according to him, had rather uncritically appropriated the premises of Aristotle's thought, especially
in critical areas such as works-righteousness.[5] In Luther's understanding, Aristotle had taught that righteousness is a quality that
can be fostered by habitual action, thus not having any sense of
the doctrine of original sin whereby original righteousness is lost

4   Weimarer Ausgabe 15:184; *Predigten und Schriften* (1524): http://www.lutherdansk.dk/
    WA%2015/WA%2015%20-%20web.htm (accessed 7 August 2023).
5   See A. M. Johnson, *Beyond Indulgences: Luther's Reform of Late Medieval Piety, 1518–1520*
    (University Park, PA: Penn State University Press, 2017).

and in need of being received as a gift of divine grace. According to Luther, scholastic theology had built on this positive view of human righteousness, a low view of original sin, arriving at its synergistic outlook. Luther fiercely opposed this view with his account of the gospel according to which justification is received by faith *alone*. In thesis 50, Luther states in his typical blunt fashion: 'the whole Aristotle is to theology as darkness is to light.' As scholastic theology had surrendered to Aristotelian philosophy (and especially his *Ethics*) and compromised the gospel at crucial points, so 'Aquinas had become more or less synonymous in Luther's mind with scholasticism's fateful embrace of Aristotle.'[6] Luther charged Thomas with having built his theological system over the Aristotelian thought structure, thus blurring Christian theology with pagan philosophy. His attack on scholasticism was a way for Luther to call the Church back to biblical authority rather than being embedded in a spurious system. Because of this fatal mistake, Thomas read and interpreted Scripture through Aristotelian lenses, distorting its meaning. As argued by Luy, 'Luther regarded Aquinas' theology as marred by errors and confusions so fundamental that the very Gospel had been obfuscated as a result.'[7] This was particularly true regarding the sharp difference between Luther's view of justification (imputed and forensic) and what he perceived was Thomas's view (infused and brought about by habituation). For Luther, when Aquinas was mentioned or referred to, he saw the abusive Church and the wrong theology of Rome.

Scholars have questioned the feasibility of Luther's portrait of Thomas and the sources from which he painted it. Rather than having an immediate and direct acquaintance with Thomas's works, Luther had read Thomas through secondary sources, namely the *via moderna* and nominalist thinker Gabriel Biel (1415–95)[8]

---

6 Luy, 'Sixteenth-Century Reception of Aquinas by Luther and Lutheran Reformers', p. 109.

7 Luy, 'Sixteenth-Century Reception of Aquinas by Luther and Lutheran Reformers', p. 108.

8 J. L. Farthing, *Thomas Aquinas and Gabriel Biel: Interpretations of St. Thomas in German Nominalism on the Eve of the Reformation* (Durham, NC: Duke University Press, 1988) and H. A. Oberman, *The Harvest of Medieval Theology: Gabriel Biel and Late Medieval Nominalism* (Cambridge, MA: Harvard University Press, 1963; repr. 2001).

and Andreas Karlstadt (1486–1541), a former Thomist who had become a colleague of Luther in Wittenberg. Whether it was Biel's and Karlstadt's interpretation of Thomas as purporting an anthropologically optimistic and soteriologically synergistic theology or Thomas himself who had such a position, Luther understood it as a Pelagian-influenced type of view that opposed his Augustinian doctrines of sin and grace. One way or the other, Luther suspected that Thomas's theology was marred with a semi-Pelagian error that needed to be fought against.

With all his hyperbolic tone and polemical force, Luther's distaste for Thomas and scholasticism was not an absolute denial of the value of his work nor a lack of recognition of good in the schoolmen. Despite his controversialist attitude, Luther was a discerning theologian who could parse theological arguments and evaluate sources and authors. In a 1518 letter to his art professor at Erfurt, Jodocus Trutfetter, he could write: "'Permit me to treat the schoolmen as you yourself have treated them" (that is, accepting their authority only where it is consonant with Scripture and the Fathers)'.[9] Luther introduces a theological criterion in his approach to the schoolmen, among whom Thomas would be surely enlisted. It is not a visceral opposition nor an emotional antipathy that drives his theological acumen. It is not an anti-Thomas attitude or an anti-scholastic posture that governs his theology. The primary concern is accepting and submitting to the authority of Scripture and the Fathers. As an embodiment of the Roman Catholic authority that had undermined biblical teaching and as a champion of a theological compromise with pagan anthropology and soteriology, Thomas's system was considered inimical to gospel fidelity and, therefore, to be rebutted. However, if and where Thomas's theology

---

9   Quoted by D. V. N. Bagchi, 'Sic et Non: Luther and Scholasticism' in C. R. Trueman and R. S. Clark (eds), *Protestant Scholasticism: Essays in Reassessment* (Carlisle: Paternoster Press, 1999), p. 8. Similar views can be found elsewhere in Luther's writings: 'I simply believe that it is impossible to reform the church if the canons, the decretals, scholastic theology, philosophy, logic as they are now practiced will not be pulled out radically and other studies established; and in this opinion I proceed so that I ask the Lord daily that it will happen soon that the very pure studies of the Bible and the Holy Fathers will be resuscitated', quoted by T. Dieter, 'Martin Luther and Scholasticism' in D. Marmion, S. Ryan and G. E. Thiessen (eds), *Remembering the Reformation: Martin Luther and Catholic Theology* (Minneapolis, MN: Fortress, 2017), p. 55.

was 'consonant with Scripture and the Fathers', Luther would readily acknowledge its soundness and goodness. It is a theologically principled approach to Thomas: neither entire dismissal nor uncritical submission. According to Luther, Thomas's theological system was seriously flawed and needed a biblical re-orientation. Having said that, since his works are many, nuanced and complex, the theologian should weigh them in terms of their biblical consistency. If they are in line with Scripture, Luther is willing and ready to receive them, thus showing that his critical stance is not a negative prejudice against Thomas but a principled and cautious approach. Christoph Schwöbel sums it up well: 'Where he engages with Thomas and the ST on specific theological issues . . . he treats him like another important theologian whose opinions are to be taken seriously, indeed so seriously that they have to be criticised. Where Luther suspects that appeal to Thomas in dealing with doctrinal matters is a symptom of misplaced authority leading to displaced foundations, his criticism can be savage, as in the case of the accusation of doing theology on the basis of Aristotle and not on the basis of God's self-disclosure as testified in Scripture.'[10]

Regarding scholasticism, Luther was not opposed to it as a theological method. Indeed, he used it, and his theology is imbued with it to a large extent, as was already evident in the 1517 *Disputation Against Scholastic Theology*.[11] His concern was ultimate consonance with Scripture. Provided that scholastic ways of arguing (e.g. distinctions, questions and disputations) were used following biblical teaching and to express it, he approved them. Thomas's theological architecture was rejected in some fundamental pillars in that, in Luther's eyes, it resembled a semi-Pelagian account of the gospel. However, some of Thomas's materials, arguments and points were affirmed if they matched biblical standards. Luther's

---

10 C. Schwöbel, 'Reformed Traditions' in P. McCosker and D. Turner (eds), *The Cambridge Companion to the Summa Theologiae* (Cambridge: Cambridge University Press, 2016), p. 322.

11 Dieter, 'Martin Luther and Scholasticism', and M. Allen, 'Disputation for Scholastic Theology: Engaging Luther's 97 Theses', *Themelios* 44:1 (2019), pp. 105–19. Examples of scholastic distinctions in Luther's theology, including the most famous *simul iustus et peccator* (both righteous and sinner) of his doctrine of justification by faith, are given by Bagchi, 'Sic et Non: Luther and Scholasticism', pp. 11–14.

engagement with his understanding of Thomas's teaching was largely negative and critical but, as far as he was concerned, biblically principled.

Early Protestant Thomists?

Protestant theology is not confined to Martin Luther, so his dealings with Thomas do not amount to the only approach found in Protestantism since the sixteenth century. Opening the view to contemporary and subsequent protagonists of Protestant theology is also an exercise that helps grasp the range of receptions and interpretations of Thomas. As a general and introductory comment, one can relate to Protestant theologians what a Renaissance scholar such as Paul Oskar Kristeller wrote when thinking of how humanist culture dealt with Thomas. Kristeller distinguished three types of appropriation of Thomas: 1. Those who drew on the authority of Thomas and endorsed his system; 2. Those who connected some of his ideas with others, thus trying to expand and elaborate his intuitions and ideas; 3. Those who borrowed some insights and issues from Thomas without espousing his system.[12] While the first type aptly applies to various forms of Roman Catholic Thomism surveyed in the last chapter, the second and especially the third type indicate the range of Protestant interactions with Thomas.

In touching on Protestant engagements with Thomas, the larger issue concerns the relationship between Protestantism and scholasticism. Everything related to Thomas was part of and filtered through the issue of how Protestant theologians were influenced by and part of scholastic culture and practices. As already seen in chapter 1, scholasticism was primarily a scientific method based on philosophical distinctions and argumentative techniques from the Middle Ages and, at the time of the Reformation, coexisted with

---

12 P. O. Kristeller, *La tradizione aristotelica nel Rinascimento* (Padua: Antenore, 1962). On the Protestant reception of Thomism and more generally scholasticism, see R. A. Muller, 'The Problem of Protestant Scholasticism: A Review and Definition' in W. J. van Asselt and E. Dekker (eds), *Reformation and Scholasticism: An Ecumenical Enterprise* (Grand Rapids, MI: Baker Academic, 2001), pp. 45–64, and P. Bolognesi, *Tra credere e sapere: dalla Riforma protestante all'Ortodossia riformata* (Caltanissetta: Alfa & Omega, 2011), pp. 43–61.

humanist expertise in rhetoric and philology. Epistemologically, the Reformation emerged from a blending of scholastic and humanist strands of thought, using both the former's insistence on the scientific methods of the day (e.g. using the technical language and categories of posing questions) and the latter's concern for literary studies (e.g. studying the Bible in the original languages). This attitude was a mark of the age. As Schmitt argues, 'The sixteenth century . . . though it saw a certain purifying tendency, was in large measure an age of differing blends of eclecticism.'[13]

In turn, medieval scholasticism was appropriated by different schools such as Thomism, Occamism and Scotism. The scholastic method was the same for all three theological schools, while the philosophical and theological outcomes differed. In some way, all Protestant theologians from the sixteenth to the eighteenth century were influenced by scholastic methods while navigating through the debates of their time in their attempt to be faithful to Scripture and the Church Fathers.[14] This phenomenon intensified as the centuries passed, thus making the alleged opposition between Protestantism and scholasticism a false historical issue. The point at stake is to what extent Protestant theologians were impacted by scholasticism in their ways of doing theology and what portrait of Thomas and his thought they had in mind while doing so.

Scholars have argued that while John Calvin was more of a humanist than a scholastic who had little awareness of Thomas's writings, although not entirely foreign to scholastic tendencies and not at all ignorant of Aquinas,[15] other first- and second-generation Reformed theologians like Martin Bucer (1491–1551) and Peter Martyr Vermigli (1499–1562) showed a much deeper scholastic frame of mind and a much better acquaintance with

---

13 C. B. Schmitt, *Aristotle and the Renaissance* (Cambridge, MA: Harvard University Press, 1983), p. 102.

14 J. J. Ballor, 'Deformation and Reformation: Thomas Aquinas and the Rise of Protestant Scholasticism' in M. Svensson and D. VanDrunen (eds), *Aquinas Among the Protestants* (Oxford: Wiley Blackwell, 2018), pp. 27–48.

15 D. C. Steinmetz, 'The Scholastic Calvin' in Trueman and Clark (eds), *Protestant Scholasticism*, pp. 16–30. On the relationship between Calvin and medieval theologians see also A. N. S. Lane, *John Calvin: Student of the Church Fathers* (Grand Rapids, MI: Baker, 1999), pp. 15–66.

the work of Thomas. Both men studied his theology in their academic training and before becoming Protestants. From the earliest years of the Reformation and beside Luther's idiosyncratic yet principled approach, these giants of Reformed theology can be located on a spectrum when considering their relationship with Aquinas. Some were closer, others were farther. David Luy speaks of 'maximalist' and 'minimalist' interpretations of the proximity or distance between Luther and Thomas.[16] David Sytsma talks about 'strict' and 'wide' connections between Reformed theologians and Aquinas.[17] In other words, from the early stages of the development of Protestant theology, there was no single and definitive approach to Thomas. Rather, there was a web of closer or more distant links against the background of a pendulum that could occasionally swing from one extreme to another (sympathetic to antagonistic) while maintaining an 'eclectic' orientation on the whole. None of the Protestant theologians ever wrote a commentary on the *Summa Theologiae* or other major works, so there is nothing comparable with the Roman Catholic appropriation of Thomas, where an entire commentarial tradition developed.

Beginning with the theologians who had a 'stricter' consideration of Thomas and a 'maximalist' exposure to him, two names must be considered: Jerome Zanchi (1516–90) of the Reformed camp[18] and Johann Georg Dorsche (1597–1669) of the Lutheran camp.[19] Zanchi was the Reformed theologian and theology professor at Strasbourg and Heidelberg whose systematic work, the eight-volume *Operum theologicorum*,[20] draws on the *Summa* as a model. Zanchi plans the structure and the disposition of his topics against the background of the *Summa*.

16 Luy, 'Sixteenth-Century Reception of Aquinas by Luther and Lutheran Reformers', pp. 114–17.

17 D. S. Sytsma, 'Sixteenth-Century Reformed Reception of Aquinas' in Levering and Plested (eds), *The Oxford Handbook of the Reception of Aquinas*, pp. 121–43.

18 P. Bolognesi, 'Un cristiano riformato: Girolamo Zanchi (1516–1590)', *Studi di Teologia* 55 (2016), pp. 3–24.

19 W. Zeller, 'Lutherische Orthodoxie und mittelalterliche Scholastik: das Thomas-Verständnis des Johann Georg Dorsch', *Theologie und Philosophie* 50 (1975), pp. 527–46.

20 The Latin text can be found here: http://www.juniusinstitute.org/sources/Zanchi_Opera_v01.

There are parallels and overlaps in treating divine attributes and other aspects of the doctrine of God and natural philosophy.[21] However, as Systma acknowledges, 'Zanchi displays independence of thought, both in content and method.'[22] As a Reformed theologian, his primary commitment was to Scripture, and he had no sense that Thomas was a guide to be followed regardless of the adherence to biblical teaching as Zanchi understood it. He was not a Thomist in the sense that his contemporary Roman Catholic theologians Domingo de Soto or Melchor Cano were, not even a self-defined disciple of Thomas. He was indebted to Thomas for his methodology but much less regarding his overall theology. This is why the 'eclectic nature' of his use of Thomas has been rightly remarked.[23] We must return to the eclecticism of Protestant theologians in dealing with Thomas.

As for Dorsche, professor of theology in Strasbourg, in 1656 he published the book *Thomas Aquinas, Called the Angelic Doctor, Shown to be a Confessor of the Evangelical Truth that was Repeated in the Augsburg Confession.*[24] The work is polemical against Roman Catholic theology but claims Thomas's support for all distinct evangelical doctrines as they are enshrined in the 1530 Lutheran confession. Dorsche tries to subvert the standard Roman Catholic appeal to Thomas against Reformation doctrine as championed, for example, by Robert Bellarmine by attempting to show that Thomas is on the Reformation side regarding the interpretation of the Bible and the doctrines of creation, sin, predestination, the mysteries of Christ and salvation. The main train of the argument is that Thomas supports the Lutheran position better than that of the Council of Trent. In his counter-apologetic, Dorsche displays a positive view of Thomas and a sincere interest in his writings, not only the *Summa*. He viewed Thomas as a 'confessor' of evangelical

---

21 S. Lindholm, 'Jerome Zanchi's Use of Thomas Aquinas' in Svensson and VanDrunen (eds), *Aquinas Among the Protestants*, pp. 75–91.

22 Sytsma, 'Sixteenth-Century Reformed Reception of Aquinas', p. 127.

23 Lindholm, 'Jerome Zanchi's Use of Thomas Aquinas', pp. 86–87.

24 The Latin title is *Thomas Aquinas, dictus doctor angelicus, exhibitus confessor veritatis evangelicae Augustana confessione repetitae* and the text can be found here: https://www. digitale-sammlungen.de/en/view/bsb11230518?page=2,3 (accessed 10 August 2023).

doctrine rather than an opposer, and because Thomas had much authority among his opponents, he wanted to prove that the Angelic Doctor is on the Protestant side of the debates. Was his subversive interpretation of Thomas feasible? Soon after the book's publication, Roman Catholic theologians like the Dominican Thomas Leonardi remarked that Dorsche's reading of Thomas was marred with out-of-context references, wrong summaries and cherry-picked quotations.[25] He tried dismantling Bellarmine's Thomistic artillery against the Reformation by reversing it, but perhaps at the expense of a fair reading of Aquinas and resulting in a methodological flaw. The impossibility of bringing Thomas to the position of being a proto-Protestant, let alone a 'confessor', rather than a proto-Tridentine Catholic is why Dorsche's attempt, despite his genuine apologetic motivations, has been an isolated exercise in Reformation theology.

Protestant eclectic yet always controversialist engagements with Thomas

Both Zanchi and Dorsche, in their own ways, are the closest Protestant theologians could get to a 'strict' form of connection with Thomas: the former with a more methodological than theological thrust, the latter running the risk of constructing his own view of Thomas which was drastically different from the real one or from the one that all others understood. Ultimately, Zanchi and Dorsche sit at one extreme of the spectrum of Protestant interaction with Thomas. Various forms of eclecticism are features of more mainstream and centrist approaches.

In general, Protestant theologians feel free to gather ideas and borrow insights from Thomas in the awareness of his being on the other side (the Roman Catholic one) concerning the Protestant commitment to the 'Scripture alone' formal principle and to the

---

25 B. T. G. Mayes, 'Seventeenth-Century Lutheran Reception of Aquinas' in Levering and Plested (eds), *The Oxford Handbook of the Reception of Aquinas*, especially pp. 229–34.

'Faith alone' material principle, the foundations of Protestant theology. Within a theology firmly anchored in Scripture and the lesson of the Protestant Reformation that provides its structure, Protestant intellectuals read Thomas with intelligence and spiritual acumen, using various elements without embracing his system, which, in their eyes, sided with the Tridentine Roman Catholicism they were theologically fighting against. The eclecticism allowed even the friendlier theologians to oppose and correct Thomas when they thought he had departed from Scripture and had taken positions contrary to it. They merely borrowed some of his ideas when they felt they had been derived from the Bible and affirmed by the Church Fathers (Augustine above all) on the general contours of the doctrines of God, creation, and salvation, without embracing the specific architectural structure that Thomas had brilliantly devised, and that Roman Catholic Thomism had further solidified. They were eclectic in the service of their controversialist theology with regard to Roman Catholicism.

Examples of Protestant eclecticism abound, and here we can only sample a few. The already mentioned Bucer and Vermigli exemplify what it meant for first- and second-generation Reformers embodying an eclectic posture. Bucer came from the Dominican Order and received his training in Thomistic theology. He owned a copy of many of Aquinas's works and Cajetan's commentary on the *Summa*. In his writings, Thomas's quotations are sprinkled everywhere, especially in his treatments of free will and predestination, and his tone is generally more irenic than other Reformers. However, while acknowledging the Thomistic upbringing of Bucer, one needs to come to terms with what Stephens argues when he says that 'it is not clear how far the influence of Thomism is more than superficial, affecting Bucer's language rather than his fundamental understanding of the Christian faith.'[26] Bucer held Thomas in high esteem, considering him as one of the *saniores scholastici*

---

26 W. P. Stephens, *The Holy Spirit of the Theology of Martin Bucer* (Cambridge: Cambridge University Press, 1970), p. 18, n. 3.

(sounder scholastics),[27] but he was not the only medieval theologian to reckon with (one can think of the importance of Anselm, the Victorines and Bernard of Clairvaux for Reformation theology), nor was this recognition a wholesale theological submission to Thomas. The soundness of Thomas's theology was measured by its fidelity to Scripture (on all topics) and Augustine (on the doctrine of grace). Moreover, it was a case-by-case endorsement of what was under discussion and not a general approval.

Following similar patterns, one can evaluate the Thomist strand that can be traced in Peter Martyr Vermigli. Trained in Aristotelian philosophy at the University of Padua, Vermigli maintained an interest in Aristotle to the point of giving a series of lectures in his Strasbourg sojourn (1554–56), posthumously printed as *Commentary on the Nicomachean Ethics*.[28] In cleverly reviewing it, Baschera notices that 'his approach to both Aristotelianism and scholasticism, as that of his contemporaries, remained critical and selective, and it was characterized by a fundamental eclecticism'.[29] While using the fourfold Aristotelian concept of causality and the Philosopher's categories of substance, accidents and habits, Vermigli was not bound to Aristotelianism as a philosophical normative grid. The final arbiter and comprehensive framework of his theology was the Bible. As far as his relationship with Thomas and Thomism was concerned, while paying attention to Aquinas and often borrowing from his insights throughout his extensive writings, Vermigli felt free to agree with Thomas on predestination because of the

27 The same or similar expressions can be found in Zanchi, Vermigli and William Whitaker (1548–95). See Sytsma, 'Sixteenth-Century Reformed Reception of Aquinas', pp. 129–33. On Whitaker and Aquinas, see F. G. M. Broeyer, 'Traces of the Rise of Reformed Scholasticism in the Polemical Theologian William Whitaker (1548–1595)' in van Asselt and Dekker (eds), *Reformation and Scholasticism*, pp. 155–80, and D. S. Sytsma, 'Thomas Aquinas and Reformed Biblical Interpretation: The Contribution of William Whitaker' in Svensson and VanDrunen (eds), *Aquinas Among the Protestants*, pp. 49–74.

28 Modern English translation: E. Campi and J. C. McLelland (eds), *Commentary on Aristotle's Nicomachean Ethics*, The Peter Martyr Library, vol. 9 (Kirksville, MO: Truman State University Press, 2006).

29 L. Baschera, 'Aristotle and Scholasticism' in T. Kirby, E. Campi and F. A. James III (eds), *A Companion to Peter Martyr Vermigli* (Leiden, the Netherlands: Brill, 2009), p. 159.

biblical foundation of his arguments.[30] He also, however, felt free to depart from Thomas whenever the superior authority of Scripture demanded that he do so and Thomas failed to follow biblical teaching, as was the case with his treatment of virtues.[31] Even Patrick Donnelly, the Jesuit scholar who introduced the portrait of Vermigli as the representative of 'Calvinist Thomism', has moderated the argument by acknowledging that Vermigli's theology was an eclectic synthesis of scholasticism and humanism whose primary commitment was biblical fidelity.[32] More precisely, the Florentine Reformer combined 'such polarities as humanist aims and scholastic logic, Platonic-Augustinian and Aristotelian-Thomistic method, Reformed hermeneutics and medieval rabbinic commentary'.[33] His alleged Thomism is not a dominant feature of his thought but a presence among others, and all fall under the scrutiny of Scripture. According to Vermigli, Thomas is a 'sound' scholastic only as far as he is in line with Scripture, neither because of an inherent property of his thought nor assuming that the whole of this thought is equally sound.

While Thomas and Thomism are certainly part of the theological substratum of these Protestant theologians, their approach is a world apart from their contemporary Roman Catholic counterparts who were reading the same Thomas but getting a very different theology out of him and positioning themselves differently. As a supporter and medieval interpreter of Augustine in his anti-Pelagian writings, Thomas was considered part of the Augustinian tradition traceable to Scripture. This explains why Reformation theologians did not take issue with the basic metaphysics (creation,

30 D. S. Sytsma, 'Vermigli Replicating Aquinas: An Overlooked Continuity in the Doctrine of Predestination', *Reformation & Renaissance Review* 20:2 (2018), pp. 155–67.

31 E. M. Parker, 'Fides Mater Virtutum Est: Peter Martyr Vermigli's Disagreement with Thomas Aquinas on the "Form" of the Virtues', *Reformation & Renaissance Review* 15:1 (2014), pp. 49–62.

32 See his 'Calvinist Thomism', *Viator* 7 (1976), pp. 441–55, and *Calvinism and Scholasticism in Vermigli's Doctrine of Man and Grace* (Leiden, the Netherlands: Brill, 1976).

33 J. C. McLelland, 'Vermigli's "Stromatic" Theology' in Kirby, Campi and James (eds), *A Companion to Peter Martyr Vermigli*, p. 497.

providence, law) and the trinitarian doctrine of God derived from medieval sources.[34] They assumed and elaborated on them not because Thomas had taught them but because they were biblically defendable, and Thomas was among the many who had endorsed them before. On trinitarian grounds, they contested Thomas's doctrine of 'created grace' whereby God gives *something* that enables the Christian to love (*ST* I–II, q. 110, a. 1). The Reformers offered a biblically better alternative that resulted in a trinitarian view of salvation whereby grace is nothing less than God giving himself to us in Christ by the Spirit.[35] The point is that they were not about retrieving Thomas as their theological project. They were about reforming the Church according to God's Word. As for Thomas's reliance on scholastic methods and categories, he was seen as a generally sound reference point, given that these Protestant theologians also used scholastic practices, as was the custom in the early modern period. If they resembled Thomas in his methodology and language, it was not because they were strictly speaking Thomists, but because they were influenced by scholastic practices broadly understood and widely used. In biblical interpretation, Thomas was generally approved if and when he insisted on the literal sense of the biblical text and before constructing his sacramental and devotional attachments. On all other theological matters, they did not consider themselves committed to Thomas or Thomism, but rather to Scripture and the Augustinian doctrine of grace. Whereas the Roman Catholic commentators admired Thomas as a venerated master and took him as a sure and solid guide, 'their Reformational contemporaries did not. They could not accept Thomas's system as it stood. They read Thomas Aquinas, or his followers, only to find arguments and views that they could use for their purposes.'[36]

---

34 See the 'monumental' work of R. A. Muller, *Post-Reformation Reformed Dogmatics: The Rise and Development of Reformed Orthodoxy*, 4 vols (Grand Rapids, MI: Baker Academic, 1987–2003), especially vol. 1, p. 34.

35 M. Reeves, 'The Holy Trinity' in M. Barrett (ed.), *Reformation Theology: A Systematic Summary* (Wheaton, IL: Crossway, 2017), especially pp. 192–94. Reeves comments: 'Because Aquinas gave prominence to an Aristotelian, unrelational doctrine of God, his soteriology inevitably defaulted away from the idea of God giving us *himself* by his Spirit', p. 194 (italics in the text).

36 Broeyer, 'Traces of the Rise of Reformed Scholasticism in the Polemical Theologian William Whitaker', p. 161.

This flexible, selective, apologetic-oriented yet principled approach allowed them to be eclectic in their partial reception and rejection of Thomas. Siding with Thomas on a single issue, whatever it was, did not mean they were Thomists in any comprehensive sense of the word. Their governing and programmatic principle was to be faithful to Scripture.

Similar engagement patterns can also be seen in the following decades to confirm that Protestantism was continually facing the issue of relating to the medieval heritage of Christian thought. In surveying seventeenth-century Lutheran theologians who dealt with Thomas, Mayes speaks of their 'eclectic freedom' towards the Thomistic heritage to the point where Lutheran and Thomist would not be overlapping categories.[37] Again, the eclecticism of Protestant readings of Thomas is underlined as a general observation. When observable, the proximity can be understood as stemming from the influence of the Bible and the Augustinian tradition, but without a specific and direct dependence on Thomas. Schwöbel is again helpful here where he argues that 'If one surveys the whole field of Protestant school theology in the seventeenth century one finds that the *Summa* could be referred to constructively as part of the received tradition in all philosophical matters and critically in those theological questions where the teaching of the Reformation differed from the theology of the *Summa*.'[38]

In the early years of the Reformation, Protestantism faced the challenge of appropriating the conceptual pedagogical tools to transmit the newly recovered doctrines of the biblical gospel to present-day and future generations and to train students within a university context. Philip Melanchthon (1497–1560), Luther's co-Reformer in Wittenberg, was the first Protestant theologian to present biblical doctrines under the heading of *loci communes theologici* (theological commonplaces), thus following a scholastic methodological pattern, through gathering passages on given topics to interpret them harmoniously. The first edition of *Loci*

---

37 Mayes, 'Seventeenth-Century Lutheran Reception of Aquinas', p. 222.
38 Schwöbel, 'Reformed Traditions', pp. 329–30.

Communes dates to as early as 1521 and is mainly concerned with soteriological issues arranged according to the model of Paul's epistle to the Romans.[39] Subsequent editions would add more doctrinal topics, such as the doctrines of God, creation and ethics. In doing so, Melanchton expanded the *Loci* thematically and integrated quotations and arguments from the Church Fathers and the medieval theologians. His reasons were apologetic, i.e. to demonstrate that what the Reformation was upholding was nothing less than the 'catholic' doctrine that the Roman Church had gradually abandoned and to subvert Roman claims to the contrary. Following the tradition set by Melanchthon, a century later, Johann Gerhard (1582–1637) wrote a work with the same title: *Loci Communes Theologici* (1610–22)[40] with similar pedagogical and apologetic motivations. Here, as expected, he eclectically appropriated the pre-Reformation traditions, including Thomas, on the proofs of God's existence and the analogy of being, at times incorporating his insights, at times rejecting them. After investigating his treatment of the analogy of being, Kilcrease argues that Gerhard 'neither demonizes nor completely accepts Thomas's formulations. His reception is one of embrace and critique, dialogue and debate.'[41]

A similar tendency is observable in Reformed orthodoxy. Driven by pedagogical and apologetic concerns, the Reformed theologians would also confront Roman Catholic, Socinian (anti-trinitarian) and Arminian writers to defend Reformed doctrine and to foster academic training in their schools. In their endeavours marked by scholastic language and methodology, they dealt with metaphysical issues as they are related to the doctrine of God, e.g. divine simplicity, the proofs of God's existence, and the role of natural law. Thomas is chief among the medieval authors they engage with in proving their points and promoting their programme. On these points, they find areas of agreement and acknowledge

39 *Commonplaces: Loci Communes* [1521], tr. C. Preus (St Louis, MO: Concordia, 2014).
40 English translation by Ralph Winterton (1632): https://quod.lib.umich.edu/cgi/t/text/text-idx?c=eebo;idno=A01638.0001.001 (accessed 11 August 2023).
41 J. Kilcrease, 'Johann Gerhard's Reception of Thomas Aquinas's *Analogia Entis*' in Svensson and VanDrunen (eds), *Aquinas Among the Protestants*, p. 123.

them, although neither the category of simplicity nor of causality is unique to Thomas and therefore their treatment of these issues is part of a larger discourse than just commenting on Aquinas or referring to him.

In surveying the contributions of Francis Turretin (1623–87) and John Owen (1616–83) in particular, Carl Trueman rightly underlines their 'nuanced and eclectic approach' to Thomas's works, which results in their 'judicious use of metaphysics in the move from biblical exegesis to doctrinal synthesis'.[42] Faithfulness to Scripture is what moves them to use metaphysical categories and language that are not exclusive to Thomas. This is just one part of the picture, though, and should make neither Turretin nor Owen a Thomist in any comparable way to their Roman Catholic counterparts. For example, for all his inclination towards scholasticism, Owen can derogatorily talk of Aquinas as a 'vassal of the Papacy'[43] and point out that he belongs to the opposite camp than his. As for Turretin, in his *Institutio theologiae elencticae* (1679–85),[44] he respectfully discusses and quotes Thomas on aspects of the doctrine of providence (e.g. VI, q. 4 and q. 8), the state of humankind before the Fall (VIII, q. 5, ii), the ninth commandment (XI, q. 20, v), the interpretation of 1 Peter 3:19 on Jesus having preached to the spirits in prison (XIII, q. 15, xii), Christ's sitting at the right hand of the Father (XIII, q. 19, x), the perfection of the satisfaction of Christ (XIV, q. 12, xx), and ceremonial works (XVI, q. 2, xi). Turretin disapproves of Aquinas on the veneration of images (XI, q. 9, xviii), sworn faith and oaths (XI, q. 11, viii), aureolas in heaven (XVII, q. 5, xxxix), conditions for membership in the Church (XVIII, q. 3, viii), the marriage of the clergy (XVIII, q. 26, iii), various sacramental issues, and the mode of the beatific vision

---

42 C. R. Trueman, 'The Reception of Thomas Aquinas in Seventeenth-Century Reformed Orthodoxy and Anglicanism' in Levering and Plested (eds), *The Oxford Handbook of the Reception of Aquinas*, pp. 207–21. The quotation is from p. 211.

43 *Of Schism* (1657), p. 196: https://ota.bodleian.ox.ac.uk/repository/xmlui/bitstream/handle/20.500.12024/A90276/A90276.html?sequence=5&isAllowed=y (accessed 11 August 2023).

44 F. Turretin, *Institutes of Elenctic Theology*, 3 vols, ed. J. T. Dennison Jr (Phillipsburg, NJ: P & R Publishing, 1992–96).

(XX, q. 8, v). He clearly distances himself from Aquinas's account of justification as motion from sin to righteousness (XVI, q. 2, xxiv) and ascribes also to Aquinas the 'blind superstition' of the veneration of images (XVIII, q. 14, xiii), the 'falsity' (XIX, q. 28, xix) and 'the crime of idolatry' of transubstantiation (XIX, q. 30, xi). In all his respect for the 'sounder scholastics' to whom Aquinas belongs, Turretin is free to point out that 'Thomas, Cajetan and others are deceived' (IX, q. 9, viii) on the consequences of Adam's sin and includes Aquinas in the list of 'distinguished papists' (XI, q. 7, xiv) that he continually opposes. While dialoguing with Thomas, both Owen and Turretin are eclectic in their approach to him.

Between eclectic and elenctic Reformed approaches to Thomas

The reference to Francis Turretin widens the spectrum of Reformed engagements with Thomas and introduces another nuance of evangelical eclecticism, i.e. the elenctic dimension. Biblically speaking, the verb *elenchō* and its derivative nouns are used in the New Testament to convey the idea of convicting someone of his/her error, rebuking a mistake, denouncing a flaw, and judging a case. The forensic framework is evident as if the actions associated with elenctics happened in the context of a court. On the positive side, elenctics speaks about the need to demonstrate faith and to defend its reliability and truthfulness against its critics and competitors. In the biblical passage that has been considered as the 'foundation of elenctics', John 16:8–11,[45] we are told that the Holy Spirit, through the gospel, convicts people of sin, righteousness and judgment. In so doing, he is the one who does the elenctics. The inspired Word of God has also a distinct elenctic role in that it is profitable 'for teaching, for reproof, for correction, and for training in righteousness' (2 Timothy 3:16 ESV). The Holy Spirit working with and

---

45 C. J. Haak, 'The Missional Approach: Reconsidering Elenctics (part 1)', *Calvin Theological Journal* 44:1 (2009), p. 42.

through the written Word has both a deconstructive and a reconstructive role in building the Christian character.

In the Reformed tradition, the reference to elenctic theology was relaunched by Francis Turretin in his already mentioned *Institutio theologiae elencticae* (1679–85). In this magnum opus, Turretin expounds God's truth and refutes its adversaries, e.g. the Socinians, the Papists, the Remonstrants, in his day's thought-forms and theological constructions. In Bolognesi's words, for Turretin 'the didactic perspective needs to be associated with the polemical one'.[46] Although not explicitly referring to elenctics, the link between didactic and polemical theology was also found in the name given to the chair at Princeton Seminary, where B. B. Warfield (1851–1921) taught.[47] In the twentieth century, but in a different regional context and another theological discipline, the elenctic emphasis was given importance in the missiological reflection of Johann Herman Bavinck (1895–1964),[48] whereby mission was understood as an exercise of deconstructing other religions when presenting the gospel. In a nutshell, 'Elenctics can be seen as the activity through which the Holy Spirit works to refute the idols.'[49]

Traces of an elenctic approach can be discerned in important Reformed readings of Thomas in the twentieth century, with different degrees of intensity and especially coming from the neo-Calvinist or Reformational tradition. Scholars like John Bolt have recently termed and questioned this critical attitude as 'Reformational Anti-Thomism'.[50] While I see a pronounced critical edge in some accents of their interpretation of Thomas and Thomism, especially in the more recent exponents, locating their

46 P. Bolognesi, 'La teologia come disciplina elenctica', *Studi di Teologia* 46 (2011), p. 137.

47 See his 1888 inaugural address to the chair 'The Idea of Systematic Theology Considered as a Science', reprinted in *The Works of Benjamin B. Warfield*, vol. 9 (New York, NY: Oxford University Press, 1932), pp. 49–87.

48 J. H. Bavinck, *An Introduction to the Science of Mission* (Phillipsburg, NJ: P & R Publishing, 1960). For a fresh presentation of Bavinck's missiologial elenctics, see D. Strange, *Make Faith Magnetic* (Epsom: The Good Book Company, 2021).

49 Bolognesi, 'La teologia come disciplina elenctica', p. 142.

50 J. Bolt, 'Doubting Reformational Anti-Thomism' in Svensson and VanDrunen (eds), *Aquinas Among the Protestants*, pp. 129–48.

contribution in the context of the elenctic tradition of modern Reformed theology seems more appropriate. In the end, what they did is generally in line with the previous controversialist and polemical tradition of Reformation theology, which was neither anti-Thomist nor embracing Thomism as a theological system. On the other hand, while stressing the theme of antithesis with other world views, neo-Calvinism nonetheless wants to honour its desire to be both 'catholic and modern' without being assimilated into the Roman kind of Catholicity and the liberal kind of modernity.[51]

Abraham Kuyper (1837–1920), the Calvinist theologian-statesman, provides an example of such an elenctic approach.[52] In his 1898 *Lectures on Calvinism*, he argues that Calvinism has three main competitors: 1. Paganism in the contemporary form of modernism imbued with Enlightenment and revolutionary ideology, 2. Islam which, although a minority in Europe, faces the Western world with 'missionary' ambitions, and 3. Roman Catholicism (which he calls 'Romanism'), a traditional competitor of the Protestant faith since the time of the Reformation.[53] These four movements are visions of life representing 'four different worlds in the one world of life' (17). The focus of his elenctic exercise is concerned with the understanding of Roman Catholicism as a 'life-system' in comparison and competition to Calvinism.[54] According to Kuyper, Rome as a 'life-system' has shaped entire societies and, unlike the multiformity of Protestantism, has maintained a certain uniformity thanks to the 'papal system', which had recently been strengthened with the dogma of papal infallibility (1870). Concerning Rome, Calvinism is a 'fundamental antithesis' (183) because the 'mother principle' coming out of the relationship

---

51 C. Brock and N. Gray Sutanto, *Neo-Calvinism: A Theological Introduction* (Bellingham, WA: Lexham Press, 2022), pp. 44–70.

52 More on this in my 'Retrieving Elenctics: Kuyper, Machen, and Van Til on Roman Catholicism' in B. B. Green (ed.), *Thinking God's Thoughts After Him: Essays in the Van Til Tradition* (Eugene, OR: Wipf and Stock, forthcoming).

53 *Lectures on Calvinism* (Grand Rapids, MI: Eerdmans, 1931; 10th reprint 1978). Page numbers will be referred to in the main text.

54 I have analysed in greater detail the reference to 'life-system' by Kuyper and his critique of Rome in my book *Evangelical Theological Perspectives on Post-Vatican II Roman Catholicism* (Oxford: Peter Lang, 2003), pp. 166–85.

with God, neighbour and the world of the two systems is different. Concerning the relationship with God, Roman Catholicism establishes this relationship 'by means of a mystic middle-link, which is the Church'. It does so in such a way that the Church, as a visible and palpable institution, 'stands between God and the world'. The relationship is, therefore, 'mediated' by the Church (21). As for relationships in society, Roman Catholicism configures them 'hierarchically', therefore in an aristocratic sense (26–27). The need for mediation by the Church means that a hierarchical scale is established in society. Rome always needs to establish a hierarchical mediation in spiritual and social relations. The third axis has to do with the relationship with the world. Roman Catholicism, forced by its principle of hierarchical mediation, sees the Church as an institution under whose 'protection' the world must submit (29–30). The Catholic attitude translates into either an ecclesiastical dominion over the world or a monastic flight from the world. For this unresolved tension between domination and flight, Kuyper defines Roman Catholicism as a 'dualistic system' (52).

The whole hierarchical and pyramidal structure of Roman Catholicism serves as the unifying principle of its cultural and institutional system. Thomas is not mentioned, but his theology stands behind it as an architectural structure. Making implicit reference to the encyclical *Aeterni Patris* by Leo XIII (1879), and to the flourishing of neo-Thomism, Kuyper expresses appreciation for the Catholic incentive given to philosophical studies. While he notes the declining character of Roman Catholicism in countries where it is the majority (in southern Europe and Latin America), he records its cultural vitality in regions where it is a minority (Holland, United States, England), stimulated by live competition with different majorities and committed to ensuring survival. The point to be recognised is that the analysis is not only doctrinal (as if Roman Catholicism were only a theological system) and not even monolithic (as if Roman Catholicism was the same everywhere and has always been the same). Roman Catholicism is considered a 'life-system', resembling Thomas's theological work's holistic and all-encompassing nature.

Where Thomas gets more frequently mentioned by Kuyper is in his 1894, three-volume *Encyclopaedie der Heilige Godgeleerdheid* (Encyclopedia of Sacred Theology)[55] where Aquinas's historical significance is acknowledged.[56] In surveying the history of theology and philosophy, Kuyper calls Augustine *pater ecclesiae* (Church Father) and Thomas *doctor* (I, 98). The former is a foundational figure, the latter is a teacher and 'whoever refuses to go back to Thomas weakens himself as a theologian' (II, 613). In his view, Thomas tried to combine Aristotelian and Christian legacies and the outcome was mixed, brilliant on the one hand, perplexing on the other. In Eglinton's words, 'In Kuyper's reading, Thomas's greatest strengths and weaknesses are interlinked. The former is found in his perception of the need to relate theology to the other sciences, whereas the latter lies in the precise manner by which their relationship was posited.'[57] While Kuyper appreciates the effort, he questions a certain rationalistic and ethical optimism based upon a view of human beings, human reason and natural capacities. According to Kuyper, Thomas's epistemological optimism has little or no sense of the antithesis of believing and unbelieving and the fallenness of unregenerate human knowing brought about by sin. It is not that Thomas does not teach sin's corruption, but that he does not consider it as total corruption. He is a *doctor* insofar as he courageously and brilliantly engages his intellectual milieu (i.e. Aristotelianism) with Christian thought, but the specific way he deals with it concedes too much to an overly optimistic view of humanity and cannot be taken as a reliable guide.

Herman Bavinck (1854–1921) is another great Reformed theologian who adopts an approach to Thomas that has been defined as eclectic, not only as far as his dealings with Aquinas but also

---

55 https://archive.org/details/encyclopdieder01kuyp/page/n7/mode/2up?ref=ol&view=theater (accessed 12 August 2023).

56 J. Eglinton, 'The Reception of Aquinas in Kuyper's *Encyclopaedie der heilige Godgeleerdheid*' in Levering and Plested (eds), *The Oxford Handbook of the Reception of Aquinas*, pp. 452–67.

57 Eglinton, 'The Reception of Aquinas in Kuyper's *Encyclopaedie der heilige Godgeleerdheid*', p. 458.

with modern and liberal theology.[58] His magnum opus, the four-volume *Reformed Dogmatics*, deals extensively with Aquinas.[59] In his summary of the history of dogma, Bavinck links Thomas with Albert the Great and Bonaventure and openly admits that they 'secured for theology a place of honour among the sciences, and treated the most profound problems with extraordinary intelligence' (I, 147). The eclectic reading of Thomas is evidenced in the fact that while Bavinck can side with Thomas on useful distinctions between the natural and the supernatural and various other theological points, he can also criticise him for having contributed to the Roman Catholic ontological framework in which the relationship between nature and grace is viewed (for example in II, 542–48). For Bavinck, Thomas and subsequent Thomists began to think of grace as a 'superadded gift' that elevates nature, rather than grace counteracting sin. They figured out the relationship in terms of an ontological move rather than soteriological significance. Bavinck retains the language of nature and grace derived from the Augustinian and then Thomist traditions.[60] In so doing, he seems to fit the conversation that was going on in the neo-Thomism of his day while just adding new nuances. However, for Bavinck the issue was not that grace elevates nature to its supernatural end. As divinely created nature, nature is already supernaturally oriented. The doctrine of 'common grace' better fits the operations of grace in nature (I, 319). The problem of nature is not its need to be complemented but rather lies in the entrance of sin that corrupted and disrupted it. The issue at stake is, therefore, ethical, not ontological. It follows that the Christian solution (grace) is soteriological (redemptive), which Thomism underestimates. So, as Bavinck summarises his view, grace restores nature rather than perfects it.

---

58 C. Brock and N. Gray Sutanto, 'Herman Bavinck's Reformed Eclecticism: On Catholicity, Consciousness and Theological Epistemology', *Scottish Journal of Theology* 70:3 (2017), pp. 310–32. See also C. Brock, *Orthodox Yet Modern: Herman Bavinck's Use of Friedrich Schleiermacher* (Bellingham, WA: Lexham, 2020).

59 *Reformed Dogmatics*, 4 vols [1895–1901], ed. J. Bolt (Grand Rapids, MI: Baker, 2003–08). Page numbers will be referred to directly in the main text.

60 See J. Veenhof, *Nature and Grace in Herman Bavinck* (Sioux Center, IA: Dordt College Press, 2006).

Grace is not a substance to be added to the natural in order to raise it to a higher supernatural order (a quantitative transformation). No dualism is implied. Instead, grace liberates people from sin (a qualitative transformation). Grace is not opposed to the natural, but only to sin. In short, Bavinck believed that the Reformers replaced the physical opposition of the natural and supernatural in Thomistic Roman Catholicism with an ethical opposition of sin and grace.[61]

Just because Bavinck uses the language of nature and grace in critical dialogue with the neo-Thomism of his day does not make him a 'Thomist' or a 'neo-Thomist'.[62] His acquaintance with the German neo-Thomist Jesuit theologian Joseph Kleutgen (1811–83) is well documented (Bavinck quotes him fifty-four times). Kleutgen was the Thomist theologian behind the drafting of both the 1870 constitution *Dei Filius* at Vatican I and Pope Leo XIII's encyclical *Aeterni Patris*, which are the two main magisterial affirmations of Thomism in the last part of the nineteenth century. While sharing with Kleutgen areas of agreement on points regarding faith and reason and theology and philosophy, Bavinck, as Brock argues, was 'adamantly opposed to the centre of Kleutgen's neo-Thomistic program: a dualism, as he understood it, between the natural and supernatural orders'.[63] To reinforce the point, 'While Bavinck and Kleutgen share aspects of agreement along the lines of Thomistic epistemology, theology as science, and use much of Thomas's philosophical framework, they are opposed at the center'.[64] For neo-Thomism, the problem is metaphysical; for Bavinck it is entirely ethical. It is not a matter of emphasis but a foundational difference central to the opposition between Reformed theology as Bavinck understands it and Thomistic Roman Catholicism. Bavinck's

---

61 The epistemological issues stemming out of this contrast are elucidated by N. Gray Sutanto, *God and Knowledge: Herman Bavinck's Theological Epistemology* (London: T&T Clark, 2020). The chapter 'Between Aquinas and Kuyper' is of particular significance, pp. 75–93.

62 I depend here on C. Brock, 'Herman Bavinck the Neo-Thomist? A Reevaluation of Influence' in J. Eglinton and G. Harinck (eds), *Neo-Calvinism and Roman Catholicism* (Leiden, the Netherlands: Brill, 2023), pp. 114–33.

63 Brock, 'Herman Bavinck the Neo-Thomist?', p. 124.

64 Brock, 'Herman Bavinck the Neo-Thomist?', p. 127.

eclecticism combines his scholarly and 'catholic' recognition of medieval doctors like Thomas and church traditions like Thomism, and his sharp awareness that their theological centre differs from that of the Reformation: ontology vs ethics; limits vs sin; elevation vs salvation. This is a vibrant showcase of Reformed elenctics retaining high degrees of eclecticism and catholicity.

In chapter 2, the critique of Cornelius Van Til (1895–1987) of Thomas was already introduced in the context of his analysis of Thomas's programme to integrate Aristotelian philosophy into the doctrinal body of Christianity. Van Til's elenctic approach to Thomas takes over the eclectic interest already seen in Kuyper and Bavinck. Van Til calls the outcome of Thomism the 'Aristotle-Christ' of traditional Roman Catholicism with its well-established Thomistic legacy built over centuries of Roman Catholic history.[65] In arithmetical terms, Roman Catholicism is 'a synthesis of Aristotle plus Christ',[66] i.e. the 'Aristotle-Christ'.[67] Historically, the key figure of Aristotelianism's penetration into Christianity is Thomas, whereas the larger movement that eventually promoted and consolidated the compromise between Christian theism and Greek philosophy is Roman Catholic scholasticism.[68]

Van Til thought that the traditional Roman Catholic nature-grace scheme is an attempt to mesh the god of Aristotle's framework, in its relationship to the world of space and time, with the God of Christianity and the creation that he has made. In this respect, according to Van Til, Thomas has imposed 'the Christian world-view on top of Aristotle's scheme of abstract form and chaotic matter'.[69] Nature is thought of in an Aristotelian way, whereas grace is thought of in Christian terms. At most, grace brings an elevation

---

65 C. Van Til, *The Reformed Pastor and Modern Thought* (Phillipsburg, NJ: P & R Publishing, 1971), pp. 73–105. See also my '"The Clay of Paganism with the Iron of Christianity": Cornelius Van Til's Critique of Roman Catholicism'.

66 Van Til, *A Christian Theory of Knowledge*, p. 175.

67 Van Til, *A Christian Theory of Knowledge*, p. 185.

68 Van Til, *The Reformed Pastor and Modern Thought*, pp. 83–104. John Frame devotes two useful chapters on Van Til's treatment of both Aquinas and scholasticism: Frame, *Cornelius Van Til: An Analysis of His Thought*, pp. 257–68 and 339–52.

69 Frame, *Cornelius Van Til*, p. 267.

supra naturam (above nature) but does not shape it. Nature maintains a status of independent life. For Van Til, the fact that the sphere of nature, even if to a limited extent, enjoys a certain degree of autonomy from the Creator God is wholly unacceptable because it would compromise the doctrine of the absolute sovereignty of God who, instead, as Van Til repeatedly affirms, controls whatsoever comes to pass. According to Van Til, the Roman Catholic world view rests on the grand synthesis systematically framed by Thomas Aquinas and updated by the modern post-Kantian trajectory.

Apart from Van Til but along similar critical lines, Thomas's other Protestant twentieth-century critical voice is the Reformed apologist Francis Schaeffer (1912–84). Here again, Thomas's thought is primarily analysed in terms of the nature–grace relationship with a particular interest in the account of the Fall and the mild consequences of sin.[70] According to Schaeffer, 'Aquinas's view of nature and grace did not involve a complete discontinuity between the two' (10). Moreover, 'In Aquinas's view the will of man was fallen, but the intellect was not. From this incomplete view of the biblical Fall flowed subsequent difficulties' (11). Out of this, as time passed, the human intellect was seen as autonomous and 'a really autonomous area was set up' (11). The fundamental difference between Thomas and the Bible is between an incomplete fall and a total fall (19). In Schaeffer's interpretation of Thomas, 'the whole man had been made in the image of God, but now the whole man is fallen, including his intellect and will' (19). Contrary to previous Protestant readers of Thomas who grappled with his work, parsing arguments and evaluating individual points, both Van Til's and Schaeffer's approach rests on a 'big picture' interpretation of Thomas which emphasises the nature–grace relationship and mainly applies it to epistemological issues.

---

70 *Escape from Reason* (Downers Grove, IL: IVP, 1970). Page numbers will be referred to in the main text.

The recent 'Aquinas-ation' tendency in evangelical thought

In recent decades and with increasing intensification, Thomas has been brought closer to a Protestant theological sensibility. In the German and Lutheran context, in 1964, Ulrich Kühn wondered whether Thomas belonged only to the Roman Church. Was Thomas only the apex of the medieval synthesis or is there an 'evangelical Thomas or at least a Thomas who has important things to say to evangelical theology'? Was there a need to rediscover Thomas as one of 'our own fathers in faith'?[71] In Anglo-Saxon circles, in 1985, a book by Arvin Vos critically scrutinised the perceived distrust of contemporary evangelical thought towards Thomas, considering it more of a reaction against nineteenth-century neo-Thomist images of Thomas rather than against Aquinas himself.[72] Vos contends that Thomas 'does not hold the position [his critics] have attributed to him', namely, that Aquinas had compromised Christianity with Aristotelianism and taught the autonomy of human reason.[73] Their views of Thomas were more the reflection of 'textbook Thomism' stemming from neo-Thomist readings which had departed from Thomas's more nuanced and complex thought.[74] In this line of assessment, Van Til is one of the many scholars who have mistakenly exchanged the rigid and dualistic essentialism of modern Thomism (i.e. neo-Thomism) with the nuanced fluidity of Thomas himself, attributing to the latter what is instead a feature of the former.

The issue of an evangelical interpretation of Thomism in general, and Aquinas in particular, remains open. Van Til's interpretation of Thomas is part of what needs further investigation. This is a debate

---

71 U. Kühn, *Via Caritatis: Theologie des Gesetzes bei Thomas von Aquin* (Berlin: Ev. Verlagsanstalt, 1964), p. 14.

72 A. Vos, *Aquinas, Calvin, and Contemporary Protestant Thought: A Critique of Protestant Views on the Thought of Thomas Aquinas* (Washington, DC: Christian University Press, 1985). Vos has particularly in mind the writings of Herman Dooyeweerd, Cornelius Van Til, Nicholas Wolterstorff, Alvin Plantinga, Carl Henry and Francis Schaeffer.

73 Vos, *Aquinas, Calvin, and Contemporary Protestant Thought*, p. 148.

74 Vos, *Aquinas, Calvin, and Contemporary Protestant Thought*, pp. 152–58.

that also involves Roman Catholic thinkers. The colossal legacy of Thomas, his scholastic schools of interpretation, his magisterial re-appropriation in the nineteenth century, and his reappraisal in the twentieth-century *ressourcement* movement indicate that Van Til and Schaeffer are not the only ones to blame for an overly narrow and rigid reading of Thomas. These Reformed authors were not historians, certainly not Thomas scholars. Their summary of Thomas lacks precision and nuances, and their intent was not to provide academic monographs on him, but to give an overall theological interpretation for apologetic purposes.

Then, in a milder way and with less provocative intentions, some evangelical theologians like Norman Geisler worked hard to provide a very positive 'evangelical' evaluation of Thomas, rehabilitating above all his metaphysics and epistemology for apologetics.[75] Geisler has also suggested that the 'traditional Evangelical criticism' of Thomas (including Van Til, but also Os Guinness, Gordon Clark, Carl Henry, E. J. Carnell, Arthur Holmes, Roland Nash) is too rigid, negative, and unfair to Thomas Aquinas himself. Distancing himself from fellow evangelical readers of Thomas and trying to overcome 'Evangelical antipathy', Geisler finds Thomas's philosophy to be perfectly compatible with classic Protestant thought. He only quibbles with some excessive sacramental features that already mark Thomas's theology to the point of not being acceptable to mainstream Protestant theology.

In the mid-1990s, an unassuming little article opened a crack that later became a gash when a respected North American evangelical theologian peremptorily entitled his essay: 'Aquinas Was a Protestant'.[76] According to the article's daring thesis, Thomas's theology was close to, if not to say overlapping with, the 'formal principle' of the Protestant Reformation (*Scripture alone*) and its

---

75 N. L. Geisler, *Thomas Aquinas: An Evangelical Appraisal* (Grand Rapids, MI: Baker, 1991). See also R. A. Purdy, 'Norman Geisler's Neo-Thomistic Apologetics', *Journal of the Evangelical Theological Society* 25 (1982), pp. 351–58.

76 J. Gerstner, "Aquinas Was a Protestant", *Tabletalk* 18:5 (May 1994), pp. 13–15, 52. The push-back by R. L. Reymond is worth referring to: 'Dr. John H. Gerstner on Thomas Aquinas as Protestant', *Westminster Theological Journal* 59 (1997), pp. 113–21.

'material principle' (*faith alone*), making him a forerunner of the Reformation, also with regard to the doctrine of justification. In more recent years, academic circles influenced by the theology of Karl Barth have also begun an operation of re-appropriating Thomas in the form of theological ecumenism referred to as 'Protestant Thomism' or 'Thomistic Protestantism'.[77] Similar phenomena can be found in the works stemming from 'radical orthodoxy'.[78]

In fact, there seems to be a widespread perception today that Thomas is no longer a heritage for Roman Catholics alone[79] and that evangelicals can and should learn a great deal from Thomas.[80] On the Roman Catholic side, there are even those who have gone so far as to argue that the Roman Catholic Thomas Aquinas is both Protestant and evangelical:[81] the real *Doctor Communis*! Would Thomas have joined the Reformation had he lived 250 years later? If even a theologian critical of Thomas like Oliphint can reply: 'perhaps',[82] then it is not far-fetched theologically to ask if Thomas could indeed be an evangelical.

The long history of Protestant interactions with Thomas Aquinas can be summarised with a series of theological exercises in evangelical eclecticism. Thomas was never regarded as belonging to the Protestant camp as if he were a proto-Reformer. However, he did belong to the medieval tradition, with which the Reformation has always been in critical dialogue, at times retrieving and expanding it, other times radically departing from it to recover biblical

77 Cf. J. Bowlin, 'Contemporary Protestant Thomism' in P. Van Geest, H. Goris and C. Leget (eds), *Aquinas as Authority* (Leuven, Belgium: Peeters, 2002), pp. 235–51, and B. L. McCormack and T. J. White (eds), *Thomas Aquinas and Karl Barth: An Unofficial Catholic-Protestant Dialogue* (Grand Rapids, MI: Eerdmans, 2013). See also K. Oakes, 'Karl Barth's Reception of Thomas Aquinas' in Levering and Plested (eds), *The Oxford Handbook of the Reception of Aquinas*, pp. 468–82.

78 For example: J. Milbank and C. Pickstock, *Truth in Aquinas* (London: Routledge, 2001).

79 C. Trueman, 'Thomas Aquinas: Not Just for Catholics Any More', *Public Discourse* (19 August 2018): https://www.thepublicdiscourse.com/2018/08/39373 (accessed 2 January 2023).

80 'What Can Protestants Learn from Thomas Aquinas?', *Credo Magazine* 12:2 (2022): https://credomag.com/magazine_issue/what-can-protestants-learn-from-thomas-aquinas (accessed 2 January 2023).

81 Beckwith, *Never Doubt Thomas*.

82 Oliphint, *Thomas Aquinas*, p. 123.

doctrine in the Augustinian interpretation of it. This is especially true as far as the doctrine of grace is concerned. While it is possible to make Thomas and Thomism overlap with Roman Catholicism, it is impossible to do the same with Protestantism. The best link that can be established is eclectic, on a case-by-case, issue-by-issue basis, with strong resistance, if not opposition, to embracing Thomas and Thomism as shapers of the theological architecture of Protestant thought.

5

Legacy and critical issues: the contours and the trajectories of Thomas's architectural thought

As explored in chapter 2, Thomas's theology is often compared to a 'cathedral' of medieval thought, i.e. an impressive, solid and comprehensive construction where theology and philosophy, church and academy, ecclesiastical items and moral issues, high sophistication and popular devotion all intersect in a coherent and well-grounded system of thought. To better grasp some of the components of Thomas's structure of thought and their long-term impact on pivotal Roman Catholic theological doctrines and attitudes, we now deal with the nature–grace interdependence, the axis of analogy and participation, and the integrative theological method that Thomas championed. These pillars can all be traced to Thomas but have also been elaborated in Thomism and are constitutive parts of the present-day Roman Catholic framework. Thomas's work is not a self-contained unit but a seminal thought that has inspired further and, at times, different advancements. A case study for each pillar will try to demonstrate the vitality and centrality of Thomas not only in medieval Christian thought but also in current Roman Catholic theology.

Thomas's nature–grace interdependence and the core of 'ontological' optimism

The 1992 *Catechism of the Catholic Church* begins with a section interestingly entitled *Homo est Dei capax* ('Man's Capacity for God') and deals with whether men and women are naturally open to God and recipients of his grace. The answer of the *Catechism* is 'yes,' and this affirmative answer is the backdrop of the Roman Catholic way of relating nature and grace. Indeed, one of the axes of the Roman Catholic system is the 'nature–grace interdependence'.[1] Briefly put, here is a way to introduce it:

[T]he spheres of nature and grace are in irreversible theological continuity, as 'nature' in Roman Catholicism incorporates both creation and sin, in contrast to the Reformed distinction between creation, sin, and redemption. This differing understanding of sin's impact means grace finds in nature a receptive attitude (enabling Roman Catholicism's humanistic optimism), as against a biblical doctrine whereby entrenched sin leaves us unaware of our reprobate state. Nature is seen as 'open' to grace. Although sin has touched nature, it is still programmatically open to be infused, elevated, and supplemented by grace. The Roman Catholic 'mild' view of the Fall and sin makes it possible for Rome to hold a view of nature that is tainted by sin but not depraved, obscured but not blinded, wounded but not alienated, morally disordered but not spiritually dead, inclined to evil but still holding on to what is true, good and beautiful. There is always a residual good in nature that grace can and must work with. After Vatican II, more recent interpretations of the nature–grace interdependence argue that nature is always graced from within. If traditional Roman Catholicism maintained that grace was *added* to nature, present-day Rome prefers to talk about grace as an *infrastructure* of nature. Despite the differences between the two versions, the interdependence is nonetheless underlined.[2]

This brief description highlights that the Roman Catholic Church has historically built its theological system along the lines provided

---

1   For a brief presentation and pointed critique, see G. R. Allison, *Roman Catholic Theology and Practice* (Wheaton, IL: Crossway, 2014), pp. 46–55.

2   L. De Chirico, *Same Words, Different Worlds: Do Roman Catholics and Evangelicals Believe the Same Gospel?* (London: Apollos, 2021), p. 105.

by the nature–grace interdependence. In the history of theology, the lasting combination of the motif has been solidified by Thomas. It is, therefore, useful to better grasp the historical trajectory of the Roman Catholic appropriation and elaboration of that relationship. An old but still significant article by Johannes Beumer (1901–89), a Jesuit theologian at the Gregorian University of Rome, covers much ground in sketching such a history up to the first half of the twentieth century[3] and can be the starting point for some further comments and evaluations.

Gratia supponit naturam (grace supposes nature) is the traditional expression, used also by Thomas, that encapsulates the nature–grace interdependence envisioned by Roman Catholic theology. It conveys that human beings can receive grace as a natural desire and disposition. As nature is open to grace, so grace is in continuity with nature. The two are distinct but intertwined.

Where does this understanding come from? From the patristic age, there are several interwoven threads, but the contours of the motif are still loose and undefined. Both in the West (e.g. Irenaeus and Athanasius) and in the East (e.g. Gregory of Nazianzus and Basil the Great), there was language of grace 'perfecting' nature as well as the recognition of the pervasive consequences of sin which have marred that disposition of nature to be elevated by grace. These two elements somehow coexist. While the Fathers contained some ambiguities in this respect, their main focus was to underline the power of grace to perfect the *Christian* life, i.e. the life of someone who has already received God's grace, not *natural* life per se. Theirs was not an abstract reference to nature as such but to the kind of nature that has already been touched by grace and continues to be impacted by it.

In the East, however, the stress was increasingly put on the participation of nature with grace as an inherent capacity maintained

---

3   J. Beumer, 'Gratia supponit naturam: zur Geschichte eines theologischen Prinzips', *Gregorianum* 20 (1939), pp. 381–406, 535–52. I had access also to the Italian translation provided by Simone Billeci, *Gratia supponit naturam: storia di un principio teologico* (Venice: Marcianum Press, 2020). For another Roman Catholic historical interpretation of the motif, see A. Vanneste, *Nature et grâce dans la théologie occidentale* (Leuven, Belgium: Leuven University Press, 1996).

by nature regardless of sin's effect. In Maximus the Confessor, John of Damascus and Pseudo-Dionysius, there is a growing insistence that grace cannot work apart from the assumption that nature is disposed to receive grace, welcome it, and be perfected by it. In their view, there is a harmony between nature and grace. Obviously, in this theological understanding, the impact of sin recedes from the foreground and becomes less relevant than in a Church Father like Augustine. What is prominent is the continuity between nature and grace and their interdependence.

In the medieval period, it was Albert the Great (1200–80) who taught that we are by nature disposed to receive grace and that grace presupposes what is natural in us. He is famous for saying, 'what is in nature is also in grace' (*sicut est in naturis, sic et in gratia*). In his view, grace does not distance itself from or modify nature; rather, grace perfects nature. Along this line, Bonaventure of Bagnoregio (1221–74) coined the phrase 'grace presupposes nature' (*gratia praesupponit naturam*). At this point, sin had largely disappeared from the forefront of the discussion, and its impact was no longer seen as having involved a radical breach or a tragic disruption.

According to Beumer, Thomas Aquinas is the one who has articulated the theological aspect of the relationship more forcefully, providing its mainstream Roman Catholic outlook in the second millennium. In a famous passage of the *Summa*, Thomas writes that 'Since grace does not scrap nature but brings it to perfection, so also natural reason should assist faith as the natural bent of the will yields to charity' (*ST* I, q. 1, a. 8). Building on what had already been envisaged by the preceding medieval theologians, Aquinas believed that grace needs nature as its substrate, logical presupposition, and the substance that could receive it. There is concordance between nature and grace. Grace fits nature and vice versa. In Chenu's words, 'Divine life is not laid over the surface of our understanding like an external additive; rather it is infused at the root of our being. Divine life is built up in us according to the framework of our nature, even it surpasses our nature ontologically. We can say that grace is within us after the fashion of a (*super*)nature; that is to say, after the fashion of a principle most interior to ourselves, most our own, at the same time that it is divine.'[4] Sin, though formally acknowledged, is swallowed up in nature, and considered a weakness or a sickness of nature, which maintains its original openness to and capacity for it. Aquinas can speak of sin as a 'stain', 'infection', 'corruption', 'defect' and 'disorder' (*ST* I–II, q. 81, a. 2), and can acknowledge that sin impacted both the mind and the will, although the latter more than the former, but has no sense of the total corruption of sin and retains a positive view of nature's inherent capabilities to interface with grace.[5] The fact that sin has had no radically corruptive effects and that the discontinuity brought about by sin is relative makes it possible for *gratia creans* ('creating grace'), *gratia elevans* ('elevating grace') and *gratia sanans* ('healing grace') to be in fundamental unity.[6]

In the subsequent development of the Thomistic tradition (e.g. Bellarmine), one finds an account of the relationship that stresses the distinction between nature and grace while maintaining their organic link. In scholastic Thomism grace is seen as the added gift to nature (*donum superadditum*), which can function even without grace. Grace is *super*-natural, placed on top of nature, as if it were an added layer. In this scholastic view, nature can exist without grace, but grace cannot exist without or apart from nature. One consequence of this Thomistic account is that the difference between *natura pura* ('pure nature') and *natura lapsa* ('fallen nature') is even more blurred than in previous versions of the relationship. Sin is always formally acknowledged, but its

---

4   Chenu, *Aquinas and His Role in Theology*, p. 47.

5   D. Haines, 'Thomas Aquinas on Total Depravity and the Noetic Effects of Sin', *Themelios* 48:2 (2023), pp. 366–80, rightly corrects some misconceptions about Thomas not having a pervasive doctrine of sin. However, Schaeffer, Oliphint and other Protestant authors he criticises don't argue that Thomas lacked a high view of sin. They do contend that his account of sin is not totally corruptive and therefore leaves room for a too positive and 'neutral' view of reason and the will. More than exegeting Thomas's fine points, they see the 'big picture' of the consequences of his lighter view. Haines also wants to demonstrate that Thomas and Calvin said similar things about sin. Again, though this is true at a superficial level, Calvin and the subsequent Reformed tradition stress the total corruption brought about by sin in ways that Thomas does not.

6   As argued by Farrow, 'Thinking with Aquinas about Nature and Grace', p. 37. Here Farrow quotes Thomas's *Quaestiones disputatae de veritate* (*On Truth*), q. 10, a. 11: https://isidore.co/aquinas/english/QDdeVer10.htm#11 (accessed 17 August 2023).

effects are considered as not having entailed breaking a covenant and, therefore, having brought about spiritual death. Nature is still intact as it has always been since its beginning. Grace is supernaturally added to a nature that has never lost its openness to it. The addition aims to elevate nature to a supernatural end, i.e. a higher and superior status. Only secondarily and incidentally does grace deal with the problem of sin. The latter is a kind of road accident that has not stopped the elevation journey; it has only made the journey more difficult. Ultimately, there is no tension between nature and grace, but rather harmony and coordination.

Beumer's historical sketch ends here, but the Roman Catholic development of the 'nature–grace interdependence' does not. The twentieth century witnessed a significant theological debate over the exact interpretation of the Thomistic understanding of the relationship. Before entering the contemporary Roman Catholic discussions on nature and grace, some provisional conclusions can be drawn from this bird's-eye view. In all its variations up to the twentieth century, the 'nature–grace interdependence' had shown how impactful it was on the Roman Catholic view of sin's gravity (or lack thereof). Without a tragic view of sin, Roman Catholic anthropology tends to be optimistic about people's natural ability to cooperate with salvation, and salvation itself looks like an addition wrought by grace rather than a regenerating miracle of God who brings about life where death reigns. As the opening section of the 1992 *Catechism of the Catholic Church* indicates with its reference to 'man's capacity for God', the whole theological system of Roman Catholicism owes its architectural outlook to Thomas.

If one wants to come to terms with Roman Catholic theology, sooner or later one needs to address the 'nature–grace interdependence'. Roman Catholicism is pervaded by an attitude that is confident in the capacity of nature and matter to objectify grace (the bread that becomes Christ's body, the wine that becomes Christ's blood, the water of baptism that regenerates, the oil of anointing that conveys grace, and the institutional Church that is in some significant sense the prolongation of the Incarnation), in the person's ability to cooperate and contribute to salvation with his/her own works, in the capacity of the conscience to be the point of reference for truth. In theological terms, according to this view, grace intervenes to 'elevate' nature to its supernatural end, relying on it and presupposing its untainted capacity to be elevated. Even if weakened or wounded by sin (as argued in Roman Catholic teaching), nature can interface with grace because grace is indelibly inscribed in nature. Roman Catholicism does not distinguish between 'common grace' (with which God protects the world from sin) and 'special grace' (with which God saves the world) and, therefore, is pervaded by optimism that whatever is natural is graced.

As already seen in chapter 3, in the nineteenth century, two important Roman pronouncements gave the nature–grace interdependence an authoritative status from a magisterial viewpoint. First, the First Vatican Council dogmatic constitution *Dei Filius* (1870) affirmed the nature/super-nature distinction as the normative framework for the Roman Catholic faith in epistemology and in the relationship between reason and faith. Second, the encyclical *Aeterni Patris* (1879) by Leo XIII elevated Thomas Aquinas's thought (of which the 'nature–grace interdependence' is a pillar) as the supreme reference point for Roman Catholic thought. So, when we talk about the nature–grace scheme, we deal with a fundamental axis of traditional Roman Catholicism with the magisterium's *imprimatur* (i.e. stamp of approval).

Though well established in magisterial teaching, the 'nature–grace interdependence' went through a significant intra-mural discussion in the twentieth century.[7] The debate was sparked by the 'New Theology' (*nouvelle théologie*) and saw the involvement of the best theological minds of Rome, such as Henri de Lubac, Yves Congar, Karl Rahner and Hans Urs von Balthasar. According to Duffy, 'this "new theology" marked the end of the static theology of nature and grace that had been in vogue since the era of the

---

7 I am following the account given by S. J. Duffy, *The Graced Horizon: Nature and Grace in Modern Catholic Thought* (Collegeville, MN: Liturgical Press, 1992).

Counter-Reformation.[8] In a certain sense, Thomist theology began to be 'rewritten' by this new interpretation of Thomas.[9]

The perception of these new theologians was that, after the Council of Trent, Thomas Aquinas's account of nature and grace had been hardened to the point of making nature and grace 'extrinsic', i.e. separate, sealed off, apart from one another, resulting in a static outlook of a super-imposition of grace on top of nature. In his seminal work *Surnaturel* (1946)[10] and in subsequent books, de Lubac in particular argued that this rigid interpretation of Thomas Aquinas had brought about a dichotomy between nature and grace, thereby losing the continuity between the two. Nature and grace had become juxtaposed rather than integrated: grace was associated with a superior degree of nature rather than its original and pervasive matrix. Grace needed to be rethought of as being immanent to nature, as nature was to be re-appreciated as organically open and disposed to grace. According to this view, grace is not *added* to nature as though nature is void of it; rather, grace is *always* part of nature as a constitutive element. In Henri Bouillard's terms, grace is the 'infrastructure of nature',[11] not an external addition. Grace makes nature what it is. For the New Theology, grace constitutes nature, even before receiving salvation. There is a natural desire for God that is already a manifestation of grace. Rather than being totally corrupted by sin, that desire for God is only blurred or attenuated. Nature is already affected by grace as part of what nature is (i.e. already graced). Grace is primary and inherent, not secondary and superimposed on nature. In de Lubac's poignant expression: grace is the 'heart's desire' of the natural human being and continues to be there even in the presence of sin.[12] Interpreting Thomas in this way, White

8 Duffy, *The Graced Horizon*, p. 49.

9 M. Jordan, *Rewritten Theology: Aquinas After His Readers* (Oxford: Blackwell, 2006).

10 English edition: *The Mystery of the Supernatural* [1965] (Chestnut Ridge, NY: Herder & Herder, 1998).

11 H. Bouillard, *Conversion et grâce chez saint Thomas d'Aquin* (Paris: Aubier, 1944).

12 J. Milbank, *The Suspended Middle: Henri de Lubac and the Debate Concerning the Supernatural* (Grand Rapids, MI: Eerdmans, 2005).

can argue that 'what grace promises is a yet higher beatitude of seeing God face to face, it does not act extrinsically to our natural end . . . there exists a natural point of contact in us such that grace is not alien to human nature and can lead human nature without violence through the ascent upward into the supernatural life of God.'[13]

The Roman Catholic magisterial authorities were initially suspicious about this line of interpreting the Thomistic tradition. Without naming it, Pope Pius XII's encyclical *Humani Generis* in 1950 expressed concerns over any possible reinterpretation of the Thomistic legacy away from the patterns established by *Aeterni Patris*. Years of 'internecine warfare among Thomists' over the exact interpretation of Thomas followed.[14] It is true to say that only fifteen years later, at the Second Vatican Council (1962–65), the Roman Catholic Church embraced the main thrust of the New Theology's account of the 'nature–grace interdependence' with its positive view of the modern world, its nuanced yet redemptive understanding of world religions, and its reiteration of people's openness to God because of their natural disposition. By updating the traditional teaching on nature and grace, Vatican II 'developed' it to overcome the rigid framework inherited from the nineteenth century and adopted a more 'catholic' (embracing and inclusive) understanding of it.

One of the consequences of this recent move is that sin, already overlooked in the traditional version, has become even less impactful on the overall Roman Catholic theological mindset. If grace is inherent in nature and by definition present in it, sin cannot be thought of as having brought about a radical breach between God and humanity. Rather, that relationship is only wounded. Grace was in nature before sin and continues to shape nature after sin. If sin is only a serious wound and not a state of spiritual death, then nature and grace intermingle from beginning

---

13 T. J. White, 'Imperfect Happiness and the Final End of Man: Thomas Aquinas and the Paradigm of Nature-Grace Orthodoxy', *The Thomist* 78 (2014), p. 288.

14 The expression is by Farrow, 'Thinking with Aquinas about Nature and Grace', pp. 36–40.

to end at various intensity levels. The issue is no longer exclusively epistemological, but also soteriological.

This present-day reinterpretation of the 'nature–grace inter-dependence' that emerged from the New Theology and that was subsequently endorsed by Vatican II is the theological background out of which Pope Francis can talk of atheists going to heaven,[15] argue that humanity is made of 'all brothers',[16] regardless of their faith in Christ, pray with Muslims and people of other religions assuming that we pray to the same God,[17] and insist, as he did in the 2013 apostolic exhortation, *The Joy of the Gospel*, that mission is the joyful willingness to extend the fullness of grace to the world that is already under grace. Because of this view, the gospel appears not to be a message of salvation from God's judgment, but instead access to a fuller measure of salvation already given to all human-kind and that all already experience in a defective, yet real way.[18]

All these expressions of the Roman Catholicism of our time find their historical origin and theological legitimacy in the 'nature–grace interdependence' whereby grace is pervasively and soteriologically present and active in all aspects of human life, inside and outside of explicitly Christian influences, and in the presence or absence of professed faith in Jesus Christ. This is some-thing that Thomas himself never envisaged in these exact terms, but his work contained the seeds of them, and the development of his thought led the Roman Catholic Church to endorse them in following Thomas's lead. In his thought, an inherent disposition

15 See my 'Do Atheists Go to Heaven? Pope Francis Says Yes', *Vatican Files* N. 149 (1 May 2018): https://vaticanfiles.org/en/2018/05/149-atheists-go-heaven-pope-francis-says-yes (accessed 17 August 2023).

16 Pope Francis, encyclical letter *Fratelli tutti* (3 October 2020): https://www.vatican.va/content/francesco/en/encyclicals/documents/papa-francesco_20201003_enciclica-fratelli-tutti.html (accessed 17 August 2023).

17 See my 'Would You Ever Ask a Muslim to Pray for You? Pope Francis Did', *Vatican Files* N. 139 (1 July 2017): https://vaticanfiles.org/en/2017/07/139-would-you-ever-ask-muslims-to-pray-for-you-pope-francis-did (accessed 17 August 2023).

18 Pope Francis, apostolic exhortation *Evangelii gaudium* (24 November 2013): https://www.vatican.va/content/francesco/en/apost_exhortations/documents/papa-francesco_esortazione-ap_20131124_evangelii-gaudium.html. See my 'The Joy of the Gospel: A Window into Francis's Vision', *Vatican Files* N. 69 (2 December 2013): https://vaticanfiles.org/en/2013/12/69-the-joy-of-the-gospel-a-window-into-francis-vision (accessed 17 August 2023).

of even unredeemed humanity renders it suitable and 'open' for receiving salvation. What the new interpretation of Thomas appreciated in him is not the precise language he used nor the scholastic procedures he employed, but the 'openness', the open-mindedness, the positive approach to reality that was used to further stretch the catholicity of Roman Catholicism.

According to this Roman Catholic view, grace is infused in nature from the beginning and will ever be so. The sacraments of the Church infuse more grace in the faithful, but even those who do not receive the seven particular sacraments live in a state of grace because of who they are, i.e. natural creatures of God inherently oriented towards him. Remember that according to Thomas and subsequent Roman Catholic teaching, there is no distinction between 'common grace' (providence) and 'special grace' (salvation). This explains the universalist tendency of Rome's view of salvation, its optimistic outlook on the human capacity to cooperate with God to merit salvation, and the positive view of human religions as vessels of grace. The Polish scholar Swiezawski summarises Thomas's thought as being driven by an 'ontological optimism'.[19] This ontological optimism entails epistemological, moral and soteriological layers. One may see similarities in language between Thomas and the Reformed tradition on aspects of natural law or natural reason, but the distinction between 'common' grace and 'special' grace, whether acknowledged explicitly or not, is at work in Protestant writers, not in Thomas and the Thomistic tradition.[20] Even informed readings of the nature–grace debate can fall short of taking notice of this and instead overstress the continuity between Thomism and Reformation theology.[21]

In Roman Catholicism, both accounts of the 'nature–grace interdependence', the *gratia supponit naturam* of the medieval and

---

19 S. Swiezawski, *Redécouvrir Thomas d'Aquin* (Paris: Nouvelle Cité, 1989), pp. 135–39.

20 The distance is sampled in studying the nature–grace relationship in H. de Lubac and H. Bavinck. See G. W. Parker Jr, 'Reformation or Revolution? Herman Bavinck and Henri de Lubac on Nature and Grace', *Perichoresis* 15:3 (2017), pp. 81–95. The language is similar, but they are theologically two worlds apart.

21 As is the case with P. Helm, 'Nature and Grace' in Svensson and VanDrunen (eds), *Aquinas Among the Protestants*, pp. 229–48.

modern ages, and the idea of 'grace as the heart's desire' in our time, coexist. They differ in accents rather than basic theological assumptions. The Council of Trent (sixteenth century, endorsing the former) and Vatican II (twentieth century, affirming the latter) are both pillars of Roman Catholic theology stemming from Thomas. As acknowledged by Farrow, 'Both/and is the only solution'.[22] Rome has no static or rigid doctrinal system, as Thomas's thought leans towards one and the other. It moves without losing its fundamental commitment concerning 'man's capacity for God', despite sin. According to Chenu, 'Thomas Aquinas is the spiritual master of a conception of grace and nature in which their mutual involvement immediately illuminates their meaning, while still safeguarding their real distinction'.[23]

The nature–grace motif strongly impacts the understanding, confession and living of the gospel in that it imagines the relationship on a spectrum characterised by imperfection–perfection, limited–complete, natural–supernatural, ordinary–elevated, but not radically impacted by sin. The theology of Thomas assumes that there is 'naturally an inclination to good in all creatures'.[24] In addition to knowing God, all can love him, albeit to a limited extent. Again, grace elevates the natural capacity for love and alleviates the effects of sin. Whichever way one looks at it, Thomas's theology does not have a conception of the radical effects of sin; thus, it rests on a nature-grace schema that does not take due account of the Fall and the change of direction of sinful human beings in all their faculties, none excluded. In Thomas, a person's *inclinatio naturalis* (natural inclination) towards God is still maintained, even if obscured and disordered by sin, but not broken. The sense of the tragedy of the covenant break brought about by sin is completely missing. One can debate whether Thomas positioned grace externally (the neo-Thomist interpretation) or internally to nature (the New Theology interpretation). Roman Catholic

---

22 Farrow, 'Thinking with Aquinas about Nature and Grace', p. 39.

23 Chenu, *Aquinas and His Role in Theology*, p. 85.

24 Sarmenghi, *Rimuovere l'oscurità: conoscenza e amore nella Somma di Teologia di Tommaso d'Aquino*, p. 185.

theologians still argue about this, and they do so animatedly:[25] Thomas lends himself to both readings. However, this is not the point. As Vanhoozer rightly argues, 'The problem is not that God (or the supernatural) is "external" to creation but rather that the whole realm of creation has become alienated from God through sin. Stated differently: the gospel is the good news that men and women can be adopted as children of God, not because human nature has by grace been "elevated", but because human sinners (persons) have by grace been forgiven.'[26] In Oliver Crisp's words, 'it is not merely that grace must perfect that which is imperfect, but functional. It is more that grace must repair what is severely damaged'.[27] This biblically tragic sense of sin (and all that follows for the Christian world view) is lacking in Thomas, and it has ripple effects in Roman Catholicism.

Case study: nature and grace in the theology of Joseph Ratzinger

The relationship between nature and grace is the framework that explains how humankind and God cooperate in bringing about salvation. In Roman Catholicism, the interdependence between the two is such that grace intervenes to elevate nature to its supernatural end, fully relying on its untainted capacity to be elevated and even to contribute to the process. Even if wounded by sin, Roman Catholic theology argues that nature maintains the ability to be graced because nature is always open to grace (the traditional view) and because grace is indelibly embedded in nature (the contemporary view).

To further expand the analysis of the nature–grace interdependence in Roman Catholicism and the influence of Thomas, it might be of some interest to look at how an outstanding Roman Catholic theologian like Joseph Ratzinger (1927–2022) has accounted for

---

25 Fergus Kerr comments that current interpretations of Thomas are incommensurably conflicting: Kerr, *After Aquinas*, pp. 15–16.

26 K. J. Vanhoozer, *Biblical Authority After Babel: Retrieving the Solas in the Spirit of Mere Protestant Christianity* (Grand Rapids, MI: Brazos, 2016), p. 49.

27 O. Crisp, 'On Being a Reformed Theologian', *Theology* 115:1 (2012), p. 21.

and developed the theme in his work. Ratzinger's importance does not need to be argued: a theological expert at the Second Vatican Council (1962–65), an eminent professor in Munich, Bonn, Münster and Regensburg (1957–77), archbishop of Munich (1977–81) and cardinal, then prefect, of the Congregation for the Doctrine of the Faith (1981–2005), Pope Benedict XVI (2005–13), and, since 2013, pope emeritus after his somewhat tragic resignation, Ratzinger remains one of the most authoritative voices of Roman Catholic theology today. One cannot deal seriously with present-day Roman Catholicism without coming to terms with his person and work.

Specifically, Ratzinger has worked on the interdependence in a twofold way:[28]

1 In his early books on Augustine's view of the people of God (1954) and on Bonaventure's understanding of revelation and history (1955).[29]
2 In Ratzinger's mature works where he revisits the relationship in the light of a new appreciation of the legacy of Thomas Aquinas[30] and the heated Roman Catholic debates on the issue around and after Vatican II.[31]

In a sense, the vocabulary of the entire discussion was framed by Augustine, whose famous *On Nature and Grace* (AD 415) contains reference to both nature and grace individually and to their relationship. In writing against the Pelagians, who had an optimistic view of nature and a correspondingly lower appreciation of grace, Augustine wanted to highlight the supremacy of grace over nature.

---

28 S. Billeci, *Gratia Supponit Naturam nella teologia di Joseph Ratzinger* (Trapani: Il Pozzo di Giacobbe, 2020).

29 *Volk und Haus Gottes in Augustins Lehre von der Kirchen* (Munich: Karl Zink, 1954) and *Offenbarungsverständnis und Geschichtstheologie Bonaventuras* (1955). The English edition of both books can be found in his *Opera Omnia* (Freiburg, Basel, Vienna: Herder Verlag, 2011), vol. 1 and 2 respectively.

30 E.g. *Der Gott des Glaubens und der Gott der Philosophen* (Munich-Zurich: Schnell & Steiner, 1960), now in *Opera Omnia*, vol. 3.

31 E.g. *Einführung in das Christentum* (Munich: Kösel-Verlag, 1968); English edition: *Introduction to Christianity*, 2nd edn (San Francisco, CA: Ignatius Press, 2004).

One limitation of the way the whole issue was framed was that it neglected to mention sin, leaving it out of the big picture. True, Augustine had a somewhat radical view of the Fall and the consequences of sin, but in comparing and contrasting 'nature' and 'grace' and not referring to sin in framing the relationship, he gave the impression that it all revolves around an ontological issue, i.e. the properties of nature as distinct from those of grace and vice versa, rather than presenting the discussion in the historical and moral trajectory of a good creation having fallen into sin and in need of redemption in Jesus Christ. Augustine has a proper view of *natura decaduta*, i.e. fallen nature, but his overall title *Nature and Grace* and the structure of his argument are still dependent on ontological categories.

It is no surprise that Ratzinger follows the Augustinian discussion on nature and grace by grappling with it in ontological terms rather than in historical and moral terms. For him 'neither pure nature, nor pure grace' is the crux of the matter. Nature is never purely nature detached from grace, and grace is never purely grace existing outside of nature. The biblical emphasis in its historical sequence, i.e. God's creation, the disruption of sin, and God's salvation, is swallowed up in the abstract and ontological distinctions and relationships between nature and grace, more defined by Christianised patterns of Greek thought than the biblical flow of salvation history.

In studying Bonaventure of Bagnoregio's theology of revelation and history, Ratzinger focuses on the insistence of the medieval Franciscan monk that is summarised in the sentence, *gratia non destruit sed perficit naturam*, i.e. grace does not destroy but perfects nature. The overall framework is still characterised by the Augustinian imprinting which underlies the ontological properties of nature and grace. Bonaventure understood grace as an upward movement, an upgrade of nature that elevates it to a perfected state. Nature is open to be graced and, in perfecting nature, grace does not destroy it, but relies on it. Put in this way, nature and grace appear to be two steps in the chain of being, one implying the other, rather than a story of creation–Fall–redemption culminating in the consummation of all things according to God's plan.

Ratzinger's interpretation of Bonaventure appreciates the dynamic movement of perfecting nature by grace. There is indeed a movement, a story, and not just the juxtaposition of two ontological realities. However, despite that, the underestimation of the impact of the Fall and sin shows that it is not yet the Bible's story that shapes the overall understanding of nature and grace. In Bonaventure, and Ratzinger's examination of him, it is not the *biblical* nature, i.e. creation, as it is permeated by common grace, that then falls in sin and whose only hope is in the special grace of redemption. Rather, it is still the kind of nature thought of in philosophical terms, and it is still an objectified kind of grace that is added to nature.

Ratzinger's interpretation of the nature–grace interdependence also depends on Thomas Aquinas. After surveying Aquinas's interpretation of the nature–grace motif, which does not significantly differ from the accounts above, Billeci offers a summary of what it means for Thomas to recognise the impact of the Fall on human nature and what it is that grace does in response: 'The kind of nature that subsists after sin is that of man who, from his first instant, had God as his ultimate end, was, therefore, able to know him and to love him at a supernatural level and who had been called to live in intimate fellowship with him in beatitude. The loss of his highest capacity to reach that end leaves him in a nasty state of dissatisfaction to which the renewed gift of grace will be able to bring remedy.'[32]

We are here confronted with the nuances of Aquinas in a nutshell. On the one hand, he reiterates the natural openness of nature to grace; on the other, he argues that after the Fall, grace still relies on nature's residual ability to be graced by way of healing it and elevating it to its supernatural end. The primary metaphor is that of 'healing' a wound rather than 'regenerating' the dead. Be it *integra*, i.e. integral and whole, or *corrupta*, i.e. corrupted and fallen, nature maintains the capacity for grace that opens up the possibility of human merit and the mediation of the sacraments through human agency, i.e. the Church. According to this

---

32 Billeci, *Gratia Supponit Naturam nella teologia di Joseph Ratzinger*, p. 245.

Thomistic view that Ratzinger made his own, the biblical teaching of salvation that comes by *faith alone* in *Christ alone* is rejected because human nature is still open to cooperate with grace, even in its corrupted state. Grace is necessary but not sufficient to attain salvation because nature is only weakened and not spiritually dead. Grace presupposes a weakened but still sufficiently reliable nature.

As indicated, Ratzinger endorsed that there is 'neither pure nature, nor pure grace'. His dense historical studies and theological reflections remain in the traditional categories of Roman Catholicism since they have been received in the Thomistic interpretation of Augustine's *Nature and Grace*, and they continue to be discussed in present-day Roman Catholic theology. Instead of applying biblical categories in approaching 'nature' and 'grace', the Roman Catholic tradition, in all its nuances and subtleties, is framed in ontological terms rather than historical and moral ones in the context of biblical revelation. Instead of considering the radical disruption of the Fall and sin, Rome has preferred to view it more mildly to safeguard nature's inherent ability to cooperate with grace and the Church's role of mediating agency through the sacraments. Instead of receiving God's grace as a divine gift that reaches us from the outside, Rome has built a theological system whereby grace will always be found within us. With all his theological acumen, Ratzinger's theology perfectly fits the Roman Catholic nature–grace interdependence along the lines envisioned by Thomas.

Thomas's doctrines of analogy and participation as the grammar of Roman Catholic inclusivity

The cathedral of Thomas's thought is also built on a distinct view of analogy and participation. The term 'analogy' comes from the Greek *ana-logon* (according to proportion) and envisages a relationship between items that do not belong to the same species. Thomas employs it in two areas: logic and metaphysics. Regarding logic, analogical is used in distinction and contraposition with univocal (i.e. identity between the two elements) and equivocal (i.e. difference between the two). Analogical combines identity and difference. According to McInerny, Thomas understands analogy according to attribution (i.e. the same predicament is present in both elements because one depends on the other) and proportion (i.e. the same predicament belongs to different elements in proportion to the degree of their beings).[33] In Thomas, the main use of analogy regards theological language.[34] God cannot be approached univocally or equivocally, but only analogically (*ST* I, q. 13, a. 5). In so doing, Thomas follows the line of the Fourth Lateran Council in 1215, which had reinforced the view that 'between Creator and creature no similitude can be expressed without implying an even greater dissimilitude'.[35] The Creator is not the same as the creature (univocal), nor is he unrelated (equivocal), but he stands in a relationship of similitude and dissimilitude that can only be expressed analogically, more specifically, an analogy of attribution.[36] In this way, God's transcendence is preserved while limited knowledge of him is made possible.

The theory of analogy is often associated with the natural theology of Thomas, according to which there is correspondence on the level of being between the created order and God, because of his being Creator (*analogia entis*). This analogy allows for the theoretical justification of God's inductive and natural knowledge through human faculties. Thomas's doctrine of analogy is part of the wider motif of the nature–grace interdependence, and therefore, as already argued in the preceding section, one of its problems is that it does not fully account for the noetic effects of sin, that is, the consequences of the Fall in the order

---

33 R. McInerny, *The Logic of Analogy: An Interpretation of St. Thomas* (The Hague: Martinus Nijhoff, 1961) and 'San Tommaso e l'analogia', ed. S.-T. Bonino, G. Mazzotta, L. F. Tuninetti, *Doctor Communis* 5 (2023).

34 W. J. Hoye, *Divine Being and Its Relevance According to Thomas Aquinas* (Leiden, the Netherlands: Brill, 2020), pp. 187–201, and B. Davies, 'The Limits of Language and the Notion of Analogy' in Davies and Stump (eds), *The Oxford Handbook of Aquinas*, pp. 390–400.

35 Fourth Lateran Council, Constitution 2 on the Error of Abbot Joachim: https://www.papalencyclicals.net/councils/ecum12-2.htm#2 (accessed 18 August 2023).

36 For a beginners' introduction to medieval discussion on univocity and analogy, see Leithart, 'Medieval Theology and the Roots of Modernity', especially pp. 167–75.

of knowledge. Thomas tends to posit too much optimism in the fallen human capacity to think, know, and even desire God based on this analogy. Karl Barth strongly and notoriously reacted against Thomas's analogy of being.[37] As a reaction to the biblically unjustified optimism, Protestant theology has developed an account of analogy with God's self-revelation as its pivot. It, not the natural human capacity, allows one to recognise correspondences between the created order and God based on divine revelation accepted with faith. Hence the definition of *analogia revelationis* (analogy of revelation) or *analogia fidei* (analogy of faith). Taking the classical Protestant position to an extreme, Karl Barth (1886–1968) made use of the expression *analogia fidei* to point to divine revelation as the sole source of knowledge of God, contrasting it with the *analogia entis* as the foundation of the path taken by natural reason to know God. In doing so, Barth risks failing to appreciate important biblical doctrines such as general revelation, common grace and the thought of eternity that God has implanted in the human heart.[38]

If the *analogia entis* runs the risks of making general revelation primary, the *analogia fidei* tends to disregard the value of general revelation and focus exclusively on special revelation. From an evangelical perspective, general and special revelation complement each other, while recognising the primacy of Scripture (*sola Scriptura*) as the norm of both.[39] Sin attempts to subvert the order of knowledge by denying the authority of revelation and seeking forms of autonomy. Yet, the task of human knowledge redeemed by Christ is to submit to divine revelation through which one has true access to reality.

37 See T. J. White, 'Thomas Aquinas and Karl Barth on the Analogy of Being', *Doctor Communis* 5 (2023), pp. 213–42.

38 On this debate see T. J. White (ed.), *The Analogy of Being: Invention of the Antichrist or the Wisdom of God?* (Grand Rapids, MI: Eerdmans, 2011); S. J. Duby, 'Reformed Catholicity and the Analogy of Being' in J. Minich (ed.), *Reforming the Catholic Tradition: The Whole Word for the Whole Church* (Leesburg, VA: The Davenant Institute, 2019), pp. 47–76; S. J. Duby, *God in Himself: Scripture, Metaphysics, and the Task of Christian Theology* (Downers Grove, IL: IVP, 2019), pp. 232–291.

39 I follow J. M. Frame, 'Theology' in G. North (ed.), *Foundations of Christian Scholarship: Essays in the Van Til Perspective* (Vallecito, CA: Ross House Books, 1976), pp. 295–330.

What matters here is not to dig into the depths of the debate around analogy, but to underline that in Thomas's view of analogy, what is implied is the proximity of things and their relatedness. Certainly, Thomas has a sense of God's 'greater dissimilitude', but at the same time, he places great trust in the ability of human nature to express and investigate the 'similitude'.[40] As we shall see, this has massive consequences on the posture of the Roman Catholic faith in its dealings in the world.

A corollary to the analogy of being is Thomas's doctrine of participation, which he particularly expounds in his *Exposition on the Hebdomads of Boethius*. He writes: 'Now everything seeks its own increase and completion, and on this account what is like, inasmuch as it is such, is for each reality that which is sought' (2,271).[41] Already used in Platonism to explain how the world of ideas intersects the sensible world (by way of participation), Thomas employs participation to account for the relationship between the finite and the infinite. Because of its importance in the structure of Thomas's thought, a scholar like Battista Mondin can convincingly say that the most appropriate definition of Thomas's philosophy is the 'metaphysics of participation'.[42] The context of participation is the link between cause and effect that is not mechanical or impersonal but involves a deeper nexus, one of likeness between what is caused and what causes it. As far as the God–world relationship is concerned, Thomas argues that we 'participate' in God (he being the cause) as creatures (we being the effects). Each reality participates in God according to the relationship that unites the two on a scale of weaker or stronger intimacy. This relationship can move according to the

---

40 In stressing the similitude, John Webster sees a danger of compromising the asymmetrical nature of the Creator–creature distinction. See J. Webster, 'Perfection and Participation' in White (ed.), *The Analogy of Being*, pp. 379–93.

41 Thomas Aquinas, 'An Exposition of the "On the Hebdomads" of Boethius', tr. E. A. Synan and J. L. Schultz: https://isidore.co/calibre#panel=book_details&book_id=8355 (accessed 21 August 2023). On this text, see Porro, *Tommaso d'Aquino*, pp. 408–17.

42 B. Mondin, *Dizionario enciclopedico del pensiero di San Tommaso d'Aquino* (Bologna: Edizioni Studio Domenicano, 2000), p. 488. See also J. W. Koterski, 'The Doctrine of Participation in Thomistic Metaphysics' in D. W. Hudson and D. W. Moran (eds), *The Future of Thomism* (Mishawaka, IN: American Maritain Association and University of Notre Dame Press, 1992), pp. 185–96.

criteria of proximity and distance. This immediately suggests an order of goods perfected in different ways, an ordering of the creature to the Creator that is in one sense simply given by the fact of the participation of composite creatures in existence, but in another sense an ordering that must be achieved and developed (participation as imitation) according to a pattern of goals and perfections.

Thomas combines God's causality of creation (understood in Aristotelian terms) with creation's participation in the divine (understood in Neoplatonic terms). Combining these two traditions allows him to justify true rational knowledge of God through analogy. Creation is, by analogy, like God since he created it. And in receiving its being from God, creation emanates from him and tends towards him who is the perfect Being by tending towards the perfection and continuation of its own being. The point here is that participation is a dynamic category derived from Thomas by which Roman Catholicism understands the relationship between God and humanity and between human beings. In all these vertical and horizontal connections, there is always something in common: an irreducible link and a mutual belonging. This participation accounts for Rome's inclusivity and catholicity as they were relaunched at Vatican II.

Case study: Thomas's doctrines of analogy and participation as foundational for Vatican II

As one might expect, Thomas's doctrines of analogy and participation have been commented on over the centuries. However, the present-day appropriation is of particular interest, especially in the way it influenced the Second Vatican Council. The re-reading of Thomas away from the rigid interpretations of neo-Thomism was part of the *ressourcement* movement that led to the preparation of the Council and the shaping of its texts and 'spirit'.[43] In a recent study on Vatican II,[44] Guarino contends

---

43 See D. Grumett, 'Movements of *Ressourcement* in Theology: Foundations for a Council of Renewal' in C. E. Clifford and M. Faggioli (eds), *The Oxford Handbook of Vatican II* (Oxford: Oxford University Press, 2023), especially pp. 45–49, 53–54.

44 Guarino, *The Disputed Teachings of Vatican II*. Page numbers will be referred to in the main text. Here I reuse some of the material already presented in my book *Same Words, Different Worlds*, pp. 89–97.

that 'analogical and participatory thinking is a crucial, though generally overlooked, theme at Vatican II' (25). In his view, analogical and participatory categories derived from Thomas form the backbone of the Council. Analogical thinking means that similarities are stressed (rather than differences); everything is analogous to something else and, therefore, close, similar, next to it. Participatory thinking means that everything participates in one way or another in everything else; therefore, mutual indwelling and inter-relationships are underlined (rather than distance and separation). If pre-Vatican II Roman Catholicism operated with a 'univocal' approach (i.e. defining reality in one way only) followed by dialectical thinking (i.e. distancing itself from what was not aligned with its univocal definition), Vatican II Rome learned to reframe its whole theological vision according to what is in common with everything else and what unites it with the rest of the world. 'Dialectical difference was not the style of the Council – analogical similarity was' (73). Antinomies were replaced by analogies (75).

Indeed, Vatican II does not use traditional terms of technical Thomistic language such as 'primary and secondary analogates and intrinsic and extrinsic attribution' (27), but analogical and participatory thinking undergirds whatever Vatican II says. The Church of Rome is never called the 'primary analogate' and the non-Catholic churches are never addressed as the 'secondary analogates'; yet Vatican II stresses what is common between the two because they are analogous. The same is true as far as participatory categories are concerned. When Vatican II speaks of the modern world in friendly terms, wanting to affirm and embrace it, it assumes that 'all human beings participate in the same created human nature, the ultimate ground of similarity among people' (26–27). The notion of a 'diversified participation in a perfection' (80) undergirds modern Roman Catholic thought.

This theological background allows Vatican II to talk about mutuality, friendship, partnership and cooperation with Protestants, Jews, Muslims, peoples of other religions, people of goodwill, and the whole world. The Council promotes a 'conciliatory approach

– emphasising unity with, rather than difference from, all others' (26). Again, in Guarino's words, 'the "others" formally participate in the unique attributes of Catholicism and are therefore intensively related to it' (28). This is not the fruit of a generic kindness, but the result of a particular theological project based on analogical and participatory categories. This does not mean that the traditional claims of Rome being the only church, the perfect society, etc., are obliterated. They are no longer seen in exclusive and oppositional forms but in analogous and participatory ways. It is no longer a matter of being 'in' or 'out', inside, or outside, but it is a matter of participating at various degrees in the same reality. 'Without losing Catholic exceptionalism . . . the conciliar accent was placed on Catholicism's similarity' (29) with other faiths. They are now considered 'partially similar to the Catholic faith and analogically related to it' (201). Guarino argues, 'Catholicism did not change its self-understanding – but it did stress its close proximity to others' (131). Vatican II presents the view whereby Rome has the fullness of grace, but those who do not belong to it still participate in it at various levels of intensity. Guarino says all this happened and is happening 'without betraying the material continuity of the faith' (44, i.e. the Roman Catholic faith).

Guarino concurs with Congar in stressing that 'it could be shown . . . that St. Thomas, the *Doctor Communis*, furnished the writers of the dogmatic texts of Vatican II with the bases and structure ('les assises et la structure') of their thought' (25).[45] Following Congar, Guarino further argues that the real theological mind behind Vatican II is not a modern theologian, but Thomas Aquinas himself. Thomas's doctrine of analogy and his reinterpretation of the Neoplatonic doctrine of participation form the foundational axes of the theology of Vatican II. While the Council avoided 'the *language* of scholasticism', it did make use of seminal 'scholastic *ideas*' (74); again, 'while Thomistic *language* was absent at Vatican II, Thomist *ideas* were in plain sight' (201). While Vatican II

---

45 Here Guarino quotes Y. Congar, 'La théologie au Concile: le "théologiser" du Concile' in *Situation et tâches présentes de la théologie* (Paris: Cerf, 1967), p. 53.

practised an eclectic *ressourcement*, Thomas Aquinas was its main source. A modernised form of Thomism in dialogue with the modern world was and is the framework that provides 'the bases and the structure' of present-day Roman Catholicism.

In pointing to the importance of this 'paradigm change' (31) that has occurred, Guarino stands on the shoulders of the giants of twentieth-century Catholic theology, such as Gérard Philips, Karl Rahner, Yves Congar and Joseph Ratzinger (30–31). His is not an isolated, fancy interpretation of Vatican II, but the mainstream reading of the theological principles at work in the Roman Catholic Church since the last Council. According to this view, Vatican II did not move away from Thomism, but went deeper into it.

One of the implications of such a 'paradigm change' brought about by the use of analogical and participatory categories is that, after Vatican II, Rome does not have an 'oppositional' posture in relating to non-Catholics but always tries to find commonalities, underline unity, stress fellowship and embrace evangelicals as much as possible. Even after Vatican II, Rome is dedicated to the all-embracing gospel of 'analogy' and 'participation' translated into Rome's ecumenism, Mariology, ecclesiology, inter-religious dialogue, mission, etc. Pope Francis may not even use the language of 'analogy' and 'participation', but his message of 'unity', 'mercy' and 'all brothers' (including therefore ecumenical, missiological and soteriological dimensions) is steeped in it.

For example, the pope speaks of mercy as 'the bridge that connects God and man, opening our hearts to the hope of being loved forever despite the limits of our sins'.[46] There are a couple of strategic theological points in this dense sentence. First, the nature–grace interdependence is implied concerning the 'bridge'

---

46 Bull of Indiction of the Extraordinary Jubilee of Mercy *Misericordiae Vultus* (2015), n. 2: https://www.vatican.va/content/francesco/en/bulls/documents/papa-francesco_bolla_20150411_misericordiae-vultus.html (accessed 22 August 2023). The English translation of the papal text on the Vatican website is blurred and incorrect. It says 'the bridge that connects God and man, opening our hearts to the hope of being loved forever *despite our sinfulness*' (italics added). However, the Latin official text says *praeter nostri peccati fines* which needs to be translated as 'despite the limits or bounds of our sins' as the Italian, French and Spanish versions rightly translate.

between the two. In the pope's theology, sin is at most a human limit but not the breaking of the covenant, the rebellion against God, disobedience to his commandments, or the subversion of divine authority that results in God's righteous and holy judgment. If sin is a 'human limit', then the cross of Christ did not atone for sin but only manifested God's mercy in an exemplary way. Second, as Cardinal Matteo Zuppi comments on the papal bull, the pope means that 'at the centre of the biblical message is not sin, but mercy'.[47] If that is the case, the consequences are massive. In Naro's words, Christian theology must be freed from 'hamartiocentrism', i.e. from the centrality of sin. Sin must be replaced by the pervasiveness of God's mercy which 'can help us to break free from hamartiocentrism and to rediscover the tenderness of God'.[48] In his view, Pope Francis has replaced sin with mercy at the centre of his message. Again, there is no direct reference to Thomas's doctrines of analogy and participation, nor the nature–grace interdependence. However, as it has been re-appropriated at Vatican II, the Thomistic framework forms 'the bases and the structure' of this theological vision. The words used may be the same as those found in the evangelical account of the gospel (e.g. mercy, sin, hope, love), but their meaning is different because Rome uses them within the theological framework that Rome itself traces back to Thomas.

The *pax Thomistica* between faith and reason and its bearings on theological method

Within the context of the nature–grace motif and related to his doctrines of analogy and participation, Thomas's theological method is another foundational aspect of his thought that has had seminal importance. Paraphrasing the medieval language found in discussions on nature–grace and building on the Thomist train

---

47 M. Zuppi, 'Foreword' to M. Naro, *Protagonista è l'abbraccio: temi teologici nel magistero di Francesco* (Venice: Marcianum Press, 2021), p. 16.

48 Naro, *Protagonista è l'abbraccio*, respectively p. 93 and 114.

of thought, Pinckaers notes that 'theology does not destroy but perfects philosophy,'[49] or in Duby's words, '*sacra doctrina* perfects the true insights of philosophy.'[50] This harmonious and developmental connection has led Douglas Farrow to speak of the *pax Thomistica*:[51] according to Thomas, between nature and grace, reason and faith, humanity and God there is peace, concordance, cooperation and agreement. Between theology (read: the Bible) and philosophy (read: Aristotelian thought), Thomas envisions 'a cooperative and peaceful cohabitation along a respected border.'[52]

We have already explored and discussed in chapter 2 how Thomas develops the 'peaceful' interaction in the *Summa against the Gentiles* and the *Summa Theologiae*. In that context, we have also referred to various forms of criticism generated by his conciliatory approach. They can be summarised in a too high view of whatever is 'natural' and a too low view of the impact of sin: perhaps a case of epistemological and hamartiological semi-Pelagianism,[53] with huge implications in all areas of Christian doctrine. To further explore the significance of the *pax Thomistica* in present-day Roman Catholicism, here are two case studies on the integration between Christianity and Hellenism and the relationship between faith and reason. In both cases, what is at stake is Rome's rejection of the ultimate authority of Scripture based on Thomas's theological method.

Case study 1: 'Faith, Reason and the University' and the clash with the Reformation

The long-term influence of Thomas can be seen in a relatively recent incident that attracted much attention and stirred some

---

49 S. Pinckaers, 'The Place of Philosophy in Moral Theology', *L'Osservatore Romano* (15 June 1999), p. 15.

50 Duby, *God in Himself*, p. 87.

51 Farrow, 'Thinking with Aquinas about Nature and Grace', especially pp. 16–27.

52 Farrow, 'Thinking with Aquinas about Nature and Grace', p. 27.

53 I am aware that 'epistemological Pelagianism' was an expression used to raise uneasiness towards natural theology by a Barthian theologian: G. Husinger, *Evangelical, Catholic, and Reformed: Doctrinal Essays on Barth and Related Themes* (Grand Rapids, MI: Eerdmans, 2015), p. 92.

controversies. Although Thomas is not explicitly referred to, the shadow of his theological system is at stake as far as the theological method is concerned. The case has to do with the speech by Pope Benedict XVI which was delivered at the University of Regensburg (Germany) on 12 September 2006 on the topic 'Faith, Reason and the Universities: Memories and Reflections'.[54] This lecture caused widespread turmoil in some countries where Muslims felt offended by the reference made by the pope to the dialogue between Emperor Manuel II Paleologus and an educated Persian man in 1391 about Christianity and Islam. For some Muslims, the pope did not distance himself from Manuel's words concerning the coercive and violent nature of Islamic expansion at the expense of the use of reason. International media immediately mounted a case that turned this reference to an instance of Byzantine history into a political and diplomatic issue.

Unfortunately, much attention has been devoted to this rather secondary aspect of the lecture with the result of obscuring and downplaying its real content. What is really at stake in Ratzinger's speech is his view of the relationship between faith and reason as championed by biblical faith and Greek reason. For Ratzinger, Christianity stems from the 'inner rapprochement between Biblical faith and Greek philosophical enquiry'. This 'synthesis', a category that is often applied to Thomas's attempt to bring together Christianity and Aristotelian philosophy, is already envisaged in the 'I am' saying of Exodus 3 whereby God reveals himself in a way that overcomes mythology, and the Johannine prologue whereby the *logos* is both word and reason.[55] The instance of Paul's mission whereby the Macedonian man appears to the apostle to plead with him to go to Macedonia (Acts 16:6–10) is considered a vivid picture of the 'intrinsic necessity' of the rapprochement. In medieval Christianity, the 'synthesis between the Greek spirit and

---

54 The text is available at http://www.vatican.va/holy_father/benedict_xvi/speeches/2006/september/documents/hf_ben-xvi_spe_20060912_university-regensburg_en.html (accessed 21 August 2023).

55 The exegetical and canonical feasibility of these readings of the biblical material is beyond the scope of this book. However, this 'metaphysical' hermeneutics leaning towards Greek categories has been and must be seriously questioned.

the Christian spirit' finds its culmination, and it is 'an encounter between genuine enlightenment and religion'. What for Thomas was a historical contingent challenge for the theology of his time, i.e. the integration of Aristotle into Christian discourse, for Ratzinger has become a convergence that is quintessential for Christianity. This is true not only in terms of its historical past but also in its overall theological profile. Thomas is not mentioned, but the papal argument stands on the *pax Thomistica* that has become the model for Roman Catholicism. This is an instance of the profound impact that Thomas's theology has had on Roman Catholic thought.

In the lecture, Ratzinger singles out the main threats this synthesis has encountered since medieval times to modernity and beyond. There have been attempts to 'dehellenise' Christianity which the pope considered dangerous and fatal mistakes. First, Duns Scotus's voluntarism sunders the synthesis whereby God's transcendence is so exalted as to become unattainable and hidden to reason. The analogy of being of Thomistic derivation is therefore broken. Second, the sixteenth-century Reformation with the *sola Scriptura* principle is for the pope another blow to the virtuous synthesis. In Ratzinger's words, according to the Reformation 'faith no longer appeared as a living historical Word but as one element of an overarching philosophical system'. The pope thought that Christianity not only needs such an 'overarching philosophical system', namely Greek thought, to be Christianity, but that without it there would be no Christianity at all. *Sola Scriptura* is, therefore, a dangerous undercutting of the hellenised version of the Christian faith. The third threat comes from the liberal theology of the nineteenth and twentieth centuries. For Benedict XVI, the German liberal theologian Adolf von Harnack epitomises another facet of the 'programme of dehellenisation' whereby Christianity wishes to return simply to the man Jesus and his simple message underneath the accretions of hellenised theology. The final danger for the synthesis between faith and reason is 'cultural pluralism', which argues that the hellenisation of Christianity was an initial inculturation that is not binding on other cultures. It goes without saying that Ratzinger rejected all these threats to safeguard the peaceful, cooperative, Thomistic embrace between the Bible and Greek philosophy.

A critique of Ratzinger's views on faith and reason, as presented here, would require much work. Suffice it to mention his negative consideration of the *sola Scriptura* principle, which clashes with his profound convictions on the interplay between faith and reason. He was right that the Reformation wanted to re-discuss the relationship between biblical and philosophical presuppositions concerning the Christian faith. He was right to see the Reformation as a question mark on the Thomistic balance. What Ratzinger perceived as an essential and inherent part of the Christian faith (i.e. Greek reason combined with biblical faith), Reformation theology considered a point to be reconstructed, ensuring that the final authority of Scripture is recognised. The only 'intrinsic necessity' for the Christian faith is its submission to God's Word. Regarding the relationship between theology and philosophy, Bavinck argues that 'Theology is not in need of a specific philosophy. It is not per se hostile to any philosophical system and does not, a priori and without criticism, give priority to the philosophy of Plato or of Kant, or vice versa. But it brings along its own criteria, tests all philosophy by them, and takes over what it deems true and useful.'[56] Just as Bavinck and the Protestant theologians appropriated Thomas eclectically, as dealt with in chapter 4, their approach to philosophy was similarly eclectic and worked out within the parameters of biblical authority. Ultimately, what Ratzinger perceived as a dangerous threat to the Thomistic synthesis (i.e. *sola Scriptura*), the Reformation accepted as the vital principle for the Christian faith.

Case study 2: *Fides et Ratio* (1998) and the Thomistic synthesis between faith and reason

The 1998 encyclical *Fides et Ratio* (*FR*) by John Paul II is another instance in which the long wave of Thomas's influence is alive and

---

56 H. Bavinck, *Reformed Dogmatics*, vol. 1, ed. J. Bolt (Grand Rapids, MI: Baker Academic, 2003), p. 609.

well in the Roman Catholic theological method.[57] Unlike Benedict XVI's speech that implied Thomism throughout, *FR* celebrates the 'enduring originality' of Thomism and understands the relationship between faith and reason on the basis of the Thomist account of the interdependence between nature and grace. The latter is upstream from the former. In a programmatic sentence, *FR* affirms that 'as grace builds on nature and brings it to fulfilment, so faith builds upon and perfects reason' (n. 43; see also n. 75). The nature–grace interdependence is particularly evident in how *FR* conceives the relative autonomy of reason and the weak consequences of sin.

The encyclical reaffirms the Thomist thesis sanctioned by Vatican Councils I and II of the existence of two orders of knowledge, each of which has its own principles and objects of knowledge (nn. 9, 13, 53, 55, 67, 71, 73, 75, 76). Faith and reason, therefore, operate in distinct, though not separate, spheres. If, on the one hand, reason has its own area of autonomy concerning faith, on the other, faith cannot disregard the contribution of reason which, while pertaining to another order of knowledge, is nevertheless indispensable for a correct exercise of faith. Reason opens to faith and faith is grafted onto reason. In line with the Thomist vision, *FR* considers faith something beyond the 'natural' realm of reason and brings it to completion.

According to *FR*, if properly understood and practised, there is no conflict between faith and reason but only harmony and collaboration. It is no coincidence that the encyclical begins with the programmatic statement according to which 'faith and reason are like two wings on which the human spirit rises to the contemplation of truth' (n. 1). *FR* argues for the autonomy of reason. This autonomy reflects 'the autonomy of the creature' (n. 15) and manifests itself on methodological (nn. 13 and 67) and normative (nn. 67, 73, 77) levels. Within the Thomist framework in which '[f]aith

---

57 https://www.vatican.va/content/john-paul-ii/en/encyclicals/documents/hf_jp-ii_
enc_14091998_fides-et-ratio.html (accessed 21 August 2023). As an introduction see E. J.
Echeverria, 'Once Again, John Paul II's Fides et Ratio', *Philosophia Reformata* 69:1 (2004),
pp. 38–52. For a more critical reading, see L. Jaeger, 'La foi et la raison: à propos de la lettre
encyclique: Fides et ratio', *Fac-Réflexion* 46–47 (1999), pp. 35–46.

intervenes not to abolish reason's autonomy' (n. 16), autonomy is conceived as 'legitimate' (nn. 75 and 79) and 'valid' (nn. 75, 106).

From an evangelical perspective, the Thomist picture of *FR* is flawed because it envisions an unwarranted autonomy to reason. According to the Bible, all of existence, reason included, must be lived *coram Deo* (in the presence of God), and this excludes the idea that reason can be divorced from faith as if it were a self-subsisting faculty or detached from the reality of God. Life finds its frame of reference in the broken or re-established covenant with God. Any human activity is experienced in the context of the covenant between God and humankind. Reason, therefore, is essentially religious: either in a broken-covenantal framework due to sin or in a reconciled-covenantal framework brought about by Jesus Christ.

In continuity with the non-tragic vision of sin proper to Thomism, *FR* also presents a biblically deficient doctrine of sin concerning its impact on reason. The fragility, fragmentation and limitations of reason are recognised (nn. 13 and 43), as well as an inner weakness (n. 75) and a certain imperfection (n. 83). Sin intervenes in the structure of reason, bringing wounds, obstacles, obfuscation, debilitation and disorder (nn. 23, 82, 71). However, according to *FR*, the 'capacity' of reason to know the transcendent dimension 'in a true and certain way' (n. 83) remains, as well as its ability to grasp some truths (n. 67), to rise towards the infinite (n. 24) and to reach out to the Creator (n. 8). The very fact that *FR* often refers to reason in an absolute sense highlights the effective intangibility of reason with respect to sin. Ultimately, *FR* is an invitation to nurture 'trust in the power of human reason' (n. 56), demonstrating that sin has only had a marginal impact. According to *FR*, even if touched by sin, reason has retained its potential and its autonomous status. Again, this is present-day Thomism in a climactic expression.

From an evangelical point of view, the encyclical does not account for the biblical teaching regarding the radical and tragic effects that sin has determined in every area of life, including reason and the exercise of reason. For the Bible, sin has introduced a corruptive distortion to the point where there is no longer any reason that is only partially affected by sin, but all reason is entirely imbued with sin. The noetic effects of sin undermine any naive confidence in the intrinsic capacities of reason and require abandoning any claim of absolute or partial neutrality of reason concerning sin.

The encyclical is critical towards numerous thought trends present in today's world. Among these, the pope lists the danger of 'biblicism', which is defined as a 'fideistic tendency' which 'tends to make the reading of Sacred Scripture or its exegesis the only truthful point of reference' (n. 55). As was the case with Benedict XVI who criticised the 'Scripture alone' principle of the Reformation, so John Paul II took issue with it, even to the point of using derogatory language. Here is the full text:

> One currently widespread symptom of this fideistic tendency is a 'biblicism' which tends to make the reading and exegesis of Sacred Scripture the sole criterion of truth. In consequence, the word of God is identified with Sacred Scripture alone, thus eliminating the doctrine of the Church which the Second Vatican Council stressed quite specifically. Having recalled that the word of God is present in both Scripture and Tradition, the Constitution *Dei Verbum* continues emphatically: 'Sacred Tradition and Sacred Scripture comprise a single sacred deposit of the word of God entrusted to the Church. Embracing this deposit and united with their pastors, the People of God remain always faithful to the teaching of the Apostles'. Scripture, therefore, is not the Church's sole point of reference. The 'supreme rule of her faith' derives from the unity which the Spirit has created between Sacred Tradition, Sacred Scripture and the Magisterium of the Church in a reciprocity which means that none of the three can survive without the others (n. 55).

The recognition of the triad of Tradition–Scripture–Magisterium as the combined reference point for Roman Catholicism places the encyclical in the wake of the Council of Trent (1545–63), which rejected the 'Scripture alone' principle of the Reformation. The point is further reinforced when John Paul II writes that 'theology makes its own the content of Revelation as this has been gradually expounded in Sacred Tradition, Sacred Scripture and the Church's living Magisterium' (n. 65). There is a sense in which the 'Scripture alone' principle is misrepresented as if it entails disregard of tradition. This is not the mainstream Reformation position, neither yesterday nor today.[58] In Thompson's words, 'Sola Scriptura meant for him [Luther in this case] that all other authorities, as venerable as they may be, stand under the authority of Scripture and are to be tested by what is taught in Scripture. At the point of the final word, Scripture stands alone.'[59] For Reformation theology, Scripture is not the only, but the ultimate and supreme authority. However, even if FR had interpreted the 'Scripture alone' principle correctly, its criticism would stand because for Rome the relationship between Scripture, Tradition and Magisterium is thought of in terms of a 'single sacred deposit', making it impossible to uphold the supreme and ultimate authority of Scripture.

In FR we find the traditional doctrine of biblical authority to which the Reformers of the sixteenth century and the evangelicals of the following centuries objected, i.e. Scripture is intertwined with the Tradition of the Church past and present. The re-presentation of the Tridentine doctrine that directly contradicts the Reformation principle is central to FR and stems from its re-appropriation of the Thomist account of the 'peaceful' relationship between faith and reason. In short, FR grounds its rejection of sola Scriptura on its Thomistic foundations and reproduces the dynamics of the development of the Roman Catholic doctrine, i.e. updating without changing.

FR thinks of 'Scripture alone' as a danger to the Thomistic synthesis upon which the Roman Catholic theological system stands.

---

58 See Vanhoozer, Biblical Authority after Babel, pp. 109–46; K. A. Mathison, The Shape of Sola Scriptura (Moscow, ID: Canon Press, 2001); M. Barrett, God's Word Alone: The Authority of Scripture (Grand Rapids, MI: Zondervan, 2016).

59 M. D. Thompson, 'Sola Scriptura' in Barrett (ed.), Reformation Theology, p. 161.

Whereas *FR*, in continuity with Thomistic and Tridentine Roman Catholicism, incorporates the Bible into Tradition and allows the Bible to speak only through the voice of the Magisterium, the evangelical faith recognises the Bible as *norma normans non normata*, i.e. the rule that rules without being ruled, as the post-Reformation Protestant theologians would say:[60] something that Thomas got close to but never fully endorsed, thus opening the ground for the triadic view of revelation (Bible–Tradition–Magisterium) that has become the standard Roman Catholic position. The Roman Catholic traditions that appropriated Thomas interpreted him as building Christian theology in such a way as to exclude 'Scripture alone' as the foundation of the theological method.

To summarise what we have covered in this chapter: the ontological optimism based on the nature–grace interdependence, the expanded catholicity spurred by the doctrines of analogy and participation, and the *pax Thomistica* with its incompatibility with *sola Scriptura* are all primary trajectories of Thomas's legacy. They do not exhaust it, yet they belong to the centre of it, and an evangelical reading of Aquinas must come to terms with what lies at the core of his thought.

---

60 R. A. Muller, *Post-Reformation Reformed Dogmatics, vol. 2: Holy Scripture* (Grand Rapids, MI: Baker Academic, 2003).

6

Thomas Aquinas for evangelicals today

In a 2012 article for the Gospel Coalition, Oliphint writes:

> Thomas Aquinas is among the top philosophical theologians in the history of the church. His genius cannot be doubted. His significant influence extends, not simply to the Roman Catholic Church, but into many aspects of the Reformation as well. Like so many in church history, Thomas wears neither a black hat nor a white hat, but a grey hat. How dark or light the grey is depends on a complex multitude of factors.[1]

I agree. Neither a black nor a white hat, but a grey hat: this colourful comment encapsulates a realistic, middle-of-the-ground approach to Thomas that reflects both historic evangelical proximities to and distances from him. There is a sense in which the greyness that evangelical readers perceive in Thomas explains the prevalent eclecticism in Protestant appropriations and criticisms of Thomas since the Reformation: on the one hand, appreciating his being an interpreter of the Christian tradition and a significant contributor to it; on the other, showing various degrees of perplexity about his endorsement of Roman Catholic theological and devotional views that are alien to the Protestant faith, and also about the traditions of thought that bore his name and further solidified anti-Protestant stances.

---

1   K. S. Oliphint, 'Aquinas: A Shaky Foundation', *The Gospel Coalition* (7 November 2012): https://www.thegospelcoalition.org/article/aquinas-a-shaky-foundation (accessed 25 August 2023).

Thomas can hardly be given a simplistic label. This is perhaps less true for Roman Catholic interpreters but is certainly true for evangelical evaluations. It is important to end this book with a chapter that provides suggestions for evangelically engaging with Thomas by retrieving and updating the eclecticism practised over the centuries, with Scripture as the ultimate authority. The hope is to promote evangelical discernment and moderation at a time when even the reception of Thomas can become (indeed, has become) a polarising issue. It is one thing to assess the strengths and weaknesses of previous versions of evangelical eclecticism, as was done in chapter 4, all of them facing Thomas and Thomism in a pre-Vatican II age, in the context of the anti-Protestant use of Thomas by centuries of Roman Catholic apologetics shaped around the Council of Trent and neo-Thomism. It is another thing to build upon the collected wisdom of the past (with its lighter and darker tones) to face the challenge of framing an evangelical constructive approach to Thomas today, given that Thomas's appropriation by mainstream Roman Catholicism has been 'updated' since Vatican II in a 'catholic' direction, as was seen in chapter 5, and that significant sectors of evangelical thought today seem to be eager to retrieve Thomas in a very positive and generous way.

Are evangelicals Thomists?

One way of tackling the challenge of framing an evangelically responsible approach to Thomas is to ask what it means to be a 'Thomist' today. Of course, different answers could be given. Yet priority should be given to those for whom Thomas is a primary identity marker. According to Dominican scholar Romanus Cessario, a Thomist is someone for whom Thomas is not only a reference point or a respected voice among others but a 'sure guide' in matters of philosophical theology and Christian doctrine.[2] Cessario seems to indicate that being a Thomist is first and

---

2   R. Cessario, *A Short History of Thomism* (Washington, DC: Catholic University of America Press, 2005), p. 35.

foremost a matter of embracing Thomas wholesale, considering him a 'sure guide' for the whole of Christian theology and practice. Are evangelicals Thomists in this sense? Certainly not.

An interesting voice in this debate is distinguished evangelical theologian John Frame, who wrote a chapter in his latest book entitled 'Why I Am Not a Thomist'.[3] Frame concurs that Thomas is 'possibly the most influential among Christian thinkers' (81); he had a 'significant influence on Protestant theological formulations, including their creeds and confessions' (82) to the point where 'Protestant writers like John Owen have used a number of Aquinas's terms, concepts and arguments' (82). Frame also acknowledges that modern Protestant scholarship on post-Reformation theology (e.g. Richard Muller, Paul Helm, Carl Trueman) is asking that Thomistic themes be engaged with 'more respect' than Van Til and other critics have demonstrated (83). He even positions himself in a 'more favorable' way than Van Til. Frame gives voice to historic evangelical appraisals of Thomas when he says that Thomas is 'one of the most brilliant and penetrating thinkers I have ever encountered, and certainly an impressive Christian man'.[4] Given these remarks, why would Frame boldly state that he is not a Thomist? The issue revolves around an unwarranted 'appeal to authority'. When theologians say that the Aristotle–Aquinas approach amounts to Christian orthodoxy or that 'Protestants have an *obligation* to follow Aquinas' (84, italics in the text),[5] this is where the alleged evangelical appreciation of Thomas becomes problematic and needs to be questioned. For all the respect and even admiration for Thomas, his theology cannot become the ultimate standard for evangelical theology. Frame rightly remembers that the chief task of theology remains '[t]o ascertain what Scripture says, over and

3 J. M. Frame, 'Why I Am Not a Thomist' in *On Theology: Explorations and Controversies* (Bellingham, WA: Lexham Press, 2023), pp. 81–88. Page numbers of quotations from this chapter will appear in the main text.

4 J. M. Frame, 'Scholasticism for Evangelicals: Thoughts on *All That Is in God* by James Dolezal' in *On Theology*, p. 102.

5 Here Frame quotes J. Dolezal, *All There Is in God* (Grand Rapids, MI: Reformation Heritage Books, 2017), as an example of Protestants embracing Thomas as a test of orthodoxy. Frame deals with Dolezal's book in his 'Scholasticism for Evangelicals', pp. 101–18.

above all the competing historical figures' (88). While paying attention to historical theology and receiving its voices as part of the
ministerial choir of authorities that need to be heard (e.g. creeds,
Councils, Church Fathers and Mothers), Scripture remains the
supreme definer and arbiter of Christian truth.

If, in order to be a Thomist, a person needs to consider
Thomas a 'sure guide', then no evangelical of yesterday or today fits
this description. This assessment is also shared by scholars who
are more inclined than Frame to give a rather positive account
of Thomas. For example, after stressing that Protestants across
the centuries have found in Thomas an important resource for
Christian doctrine due to his inclusion in the broad catholic tradition, Carl Trueman rightly argues that '[t]heir use of Thomas
did not turn Protestants into "Thomists" in any party sense'.[6] No
overlap between Thomism and Protestantism is to be found in
history nor is it feasible to envisage it today. There seems to be
consensus on this across the evangelical spectrum.[7]

Where is the difference between the positions represented by
Frame and Trueman? As already mentioned, Frame takes issue with
the 'obligation' to follow Thomas not only on matters that separate
Protestants from his theology that is traditionally associated with
Roman Catholicism, e.g. sacramentology and ecclesiology – all
evangelicals disagree with Thomas on those – but also with the formulations of his doctrine of God regarding the use of 'pure being'

---

6   Trueman, 'Thomas Aquinas: Not Just for Catholics Any More'. Even J. V. Fesko, himself
    favourably inclined to Thomas and Thomism, argues that Reformed theologians who used the
    scholastic (and Thomistic) categories of 'infused habits' in their doctrine of sanctification were
    'not unreconstructed Thomists': J. V. Fesko, 'Aquinas's Doctrine of Justification and Infused
    Habits in Reformed Soteriology' in Svensson and VanDrunen (eds), *Aquinas Among the
    Protestants*, p. 257. As a matter of fact, as Fesko rightly points out, Thomas had used 'infused
    habits' in the context of his doctrine of justification whereas the Reformed theologians referred
    to them in the context of sanctification. Thomas viewed habits as stepping stones towards
    justification; the Reformed considered them as outcomes of it. Theirs was therefore an eclectic
    use of Thomas, not an endorsement of his theology.

7   When present-day supporters accuse critics of totally rejecting Thomas, I think they have a
    straw man in view. I have never read a serious evangelical scholar argue that Thomas is to
    be rejected *totally*. On the other hand, when critics accuse supporters of being compromised
    'Thomists' they have a straw man in view. I have never encountered evangelicals wanting to be
    identified with Thomas as buyers of a package deal. As demonstrated, evangelicals have been
    and continue to be eclectic in their appropriation of Thomas.

metaphysical language. To be clear, in line with Protestant appropriations of the creeds in the formulation of their Confessions of faith after the Reformation, Frame is open and willing to endorse the 'pure being' language of the doctrine of God (with its corollary attachments regarding aseity, divine simplicity and impassibility) to the extent that it reflects biblical personalism and does not become a self-referential philosophical grid detached from and untouched by biblical revelation. If so, these metaphysical descriptors of God return to the Aristotelian Prime Mover of pagan theology instead of being shaped by the attributes of divine lordship according to Scripture. According to Frame, 'God is both metaphysically absolute and fully personal' (85), the latter being somewhat obscured in Thomas. In Aquinas's theology proper, Frame sees a tension between biblical and Aristotelian categories that makes it a not always biblically consistent account of the doctrine of God: the outcome in Thomas is still a picture of God too heavily dependent on a Greek conceptual framework. This is why Thomas cannot be taken blindly as a 'sure guide' even in the doctrine of God, let alone become a test of orthodoxy. Frame is not saying that Thomas is, therefore, totally unreliable and should be rejected; he is saying that he cannot be taken as the most biblically faithful expositor of the doctrine of God in Church history. Biblically speaking, Thomas's theology has no entirely safe area, even his doctrine of God.

Of a different opinion is Trueman whereby Protestant theology at its best was consistent with Thomas on this point and just reiterated 'the creedal, classical doctrine of God', which rested on 'a tradition of metaphysics that both shared'. This school of thought represented by Trueman sees Thomas's language and conceptuality not only formally committed to Scripture (which all readers of Thomas are aware of, given his high view of Scripture) but also accomplishing an unsurpassed and perhaps unsurpassable level of biblical fidelity on theology proper. For Trueman, all that Thomas wrote on the doctrine of God was received by the Protestant Reformation as it stood (practically photocopied, as it were) and is to be received likewise today. This is why, according to this view, evangelicals have the obligation to follow him on theology proper.

This is the crux of the matter. While no evangelicals would subscribe to the total rejection of Thomas or the total embracement
of Thomas, the critical point is about the biblical reliability of his
doctrine of God and the general outlook of his metaphysics and
epistemology that undergird it. This is the issue at stake. One com-
plicating factor of the debate is that Thomas's theology has not yet
received an in-depth and comprehensive Protestant interpretation.
The eclecticism practised over the centuries has fostered a selective reading of Thomas, but not a systemic one. Most Protestant
theologians have used Thomas because he was the standard work
of medieval Christianity to reckon with and they have criticised
him on several doctrinal points, but no one has produced a critical
appraisal of his theology from a Protestant viewpoint. This past-
due homework created a vacuum and this vacuum is perhaps why
Thomas's legacy is creating some controversy in evangelical circles.

Perhaps it would be helpful at this point to provide a quick
comparison with Augustine, another giant of Church history.
Protestant theology has unanimously considered itself as stemming from the Augustinian tradition, especially regarding the
orientation of his doctrine of grace. Yet Augustine is also strongly
reclaimed by Roman Catholicism, especially regarding his high
view of the institutional Church. To deal with the crux, in his
studies on Augustine, B. B. Warfield (1851–1921) suggested the
'two children in the womb' theory whereby the Father would
have had both the doctrine of grace and the Church struggling in
his theology in an unresolved tension. The tension could only be
resolved later. According to Warfield's interpretation, 'the ultimate
triumph of Augustine's doctrine of grace over Augustine's doctrine
of the Church' took place at the time of the Reformation.[8] This
Protestant account of Augustine helps us to navigate the complexity

---

8   B. B. Warfield, 'Augustine' [1908] in *Studies in Tertullian and Augustine* [1930] (Westport, CT:
     Greenwood Press, 1970), p. 130. See also 'Augustine and His Confessions' [1905], especially
     pp. 283–85. Warfield inaugurated a flow in Protestant Augustinian studies that in recent
     decades has seen the valuable contribution of scholars like David Wright, Gerald Bray and
     Nick Needham. For a present-day Protestant reading of Augustine in many ways consonant
     with Warfield's, see B. B. Green, *Augustine of Hippo: His Life and Impact* (Fearn, Tain, Scotland:
     Christian Focus Publications, 2020).

of his theology and to have a compass in dealing with it. Certainly, Augustine is not Thomas, and the flowing thoughts of the former are not to be found in the stability of the 'cathedral' of the latter. The point is that the kind of analysis that Warfield did on the legacy of Augustine, whatever its merit, is lacking in evangelical scholarship on Thomas. Evangelical eclecticism has not yet produced a comparable and reliable compass.

Contours of an evangelical engagement with Thomas

Recent decades have seen evangelical theology express a renewed interest in the thought of Thomas Aquinas. This is all well and good. Rooted in the Bible, evangelicalism at its best has always thought of itself in continuity with the apostolic gospel as it was proclaimed and taught in the early church, the medieval period, the Protestant Reformation, and evangelical revivals up to the present day. In this positive retrieval, there is also the danger of an idealisation of Thomas (as if he was always right and always working with purely evangelical motives) and a wholesale and unwarranted appreciation of 'tradition' (as if it was a monolithic body that is organically related to Scripture). To both affirm the evangelical interest in Thomas and suggest some caveats in practising it, here are five principles that can be useful to bear in mind. They surely call for further study and improvement.

1. Scripture alone is ultimate and tradition (Thomas included) is always second

In reading Thomas, evangelical theology must always practise the *sola Scriptura* principle (the Bible alone is the inspired written Word of God and the ultimate authority in all matters of life), the *tota Scriptura* principle (the whole Bible is inspired by God and needs to be received as a whole), and the *Scriptura sui ipsius interpres* principle (the Bible is its own interpreter). As Protestant theologians, always remember that Scripture is the *norma normans non normata* (i.e. the norm of norms which cannot be normed, the standard according to which all other standards are measured). Thomas is important, but not decisive; Thomas can be useful (although often distorting and deviant), but never definitive; Thomas can be enriching, but only to the extent that he is faithful to Scripture. At the end of his letter to Sadoleto, John Calvin wrote, 'We hold that the Word of God alone lies beyond the sphere of our judgment and that Fathers and Councils are of authority only in so far as they accord with the rule of the Word, [but] we still give to Councils and Fathers such rank and honour as it is meet for them to hold, under Christ.'[9]

This leads to a theologically sober and realistic view of tradition, of which Thomas is a cornerstone. As the Protestant Reformation taught us, one can and must hold the Word of God over every theological and spiritual achievement of the past while, at the same time, treasuring the inheritance that generations of believers have consigned to subsequent ones. In J. I. Packer's words, which can be applied to Thomas's legacy, 'Tradition, after all, is the fruit of the Spirit's teaching activity from the ages as God's people have sought understanding of Scripture. It is not infallible, but neither is it negligible, and we impoverish ourselves if we disregard it.'[10]

2. Thomas is a giant of Church history who needs to be appropriated eclectically

The best Protestant theologians have read and studied Thomas, since he was the main exponent of medieval theology, having neither reverential fears nor inferiority complexes, but facing him head-on, with an attitude inspired by evangelical boldness and the biblical principle *omnia probate, quod bonum est tenete,*

---

9 John Calvin's *Letter to Sadoleto* (1539): https://www.monergism.com/john-calvins-letter-cardinal-sadoleto-1539 (accessed 31 August 2023). Notice the reversed Roman Catholic argument presented by John H. Newman (1801–90): talking about the Fathers (but the reference could be applied to Thomas too) he argues that 'They do not say, "This is true, *because* we see it in Scripture" – about which there might be differences of judgment – but, "this is true, because in matter of fact it is held, and has ever been held, by all the Churches, down to our times, without interruption, ever since the Apostles"': *Discussions and Arguments*, II.1 (London: Longmans, 1891), p. 46.

10 J. I. Packer, 'Upholding the Unity of Scripture Today', *Journal of the Evangelical Theological Society* 25:4 (1992), p. 414.

'Prove all things; hold fast that which is good' (1 Thessalonians 5:21). Protestant theologians at their best (from Peter Martyr Vermigli to Herman Bavinck, through Francis Turretin) have generally exercised theological discernment, which has allowed them to appreciate aspects of Thomas's theology that were in line with biblical faith and to reject his teaching where it conflicted with Scripture. In other words, they did not embrace the Thomist system as such – even his metaphysics and epistemology as integrated components of it – but broke it down into its parts as far as possible with integrity and used it eclectically. This is true even as far as issues like his 'natural theology' which, despite the resemblances with Protestant accounts, departs from them on key points because of the structures of Thomas's thought that are embedded in the nature–grace interdependence.[11] Eclecticism has its own risks if it loses sight of the fact that Thomas is a 'world view' thinker rather than only a brilliant medieval expert on some topics. His system is a whole and needs to be approached as such. There is room for eclectic appropriations if they show awareness of the deeper structures of the architecture of his thought. Ideas have consequences, and Thomas's have ripple-effects in all directions.

Evangelical scholarship can neither reject him as a hopelessly compromised theologian (the anti-Thomas temptation), nor elevate him as the chief parameter of Christian orthodoxy (the Roman Catholic temptation). Rather, it should treat Thomas as an unavoidable conversation partner in the history of Christian thought, to be read critically and generously in the light of the 'Scripture alone' principle that the Protestant Reformation recovered for the whole church. This approach is not original but seems to be the historic and best evangelical approach to Thomas Aquinas.

---

11 See D. McIlroy, 'A Trinitarian Reading of Aquinas's Treatise on Law', *Angelicum* 84 (2007), pp. 277–92. Apart from the examples already given in chapter 4, another instance of eclecticism can be seen in G. Vos, *Natural Theology* (Grand Rapids, MI: Reformation Heritage Books, 2022). Vos's lectures date back to 1888–93 and have been seen as proof of his 'Thomism' by J. V. Fesko in the Introduction. On closer examination, Vos departs from Thomas on some crucial points and cannot be listed as a Thomist theologian without unduly forcing his thought. See J. Baird, 'What Indeed Hath Thomas to Do with Vos? A Review Article', *Westminster Theological Journal* 84 (2022), pp. 149–60.

3. Thomas has many ambivalences and serious problems in his system

Whatever the multiple brilliant insights in his thought, Thomas's system, including his metaphysics and epistemology, contains tendencies and trajectories that lead to structural flaws. Chapters 2 and 5 have already suggested that Thomas's world view does present several critical issues for evangelicals. Only a few hints can be suggested here.

As argued by Schwöbel, 'Thomas's account of grace remains constantly ambivalent. On the one hand it looks back to Augustine, on the other hand, it points forward to the dissolution which Augustinianism would undergo in the fourteenth century . . . Thomas intends to insist on the sole efficacy of divine grace; but the way in which he develops this theme already points in the opposite direction.'[12] In his doctrine of grace, despite its Augustinian superficial outlook, significant elements make it significantly milder if not different: 'Man's free will cooperates as it is moved by God – a theme in Augustine – but Aquinas's stress is not on God working but on the infused grace. In this, Aquinas gives greater scope for human freedom and shows a subtle shift towards semi-Pelagianism.'[13] According to Thomas humanity had not completely lost its *capacitas* (capacity) for grace as if sin had not produced the breaking of the covenant with God, consequently leading to total corruption. Thomas's thought is pervaded with ontological optimism that translates into epistemological optimism (stressing the positive role of reason), moral optimism (underlining the role of virtues as human habits), and, in the post-Vatican II interpretation, soteriological optimism (all humanity participates in one way or another in the mystery of salvation).

Thomas's ambivalence lies at the core of his thought, and, because of its central place, erupts everywhere in his theology, though in different ways and levels of intensity. Unlike Augustine whose thought was an unfinished work-in-progress, Thomas's is

---

12 Schwöbel, 'Reformed Traditions', p. 333.

13 Letham, *Gamechangers*, pp. 93–94.

characterised by a high degree of internal coherence and consistency. Apart from the metaphor of the cathedral, Spezzano likens it to a brain, 'a myriad of interrelated networks connecting each point to many others'.[14] From his point of view, it is not easy to separate Thomas's classical theism (Trinity, Christology), and consider it sound, from his soteriology, ecclesiology, sacramentology, Mariology and devotional life, and consider them flawed. The latter part of his thought is argued in terms of the former. They are not detachable modules, nor disconnected atoms. All his theology is formed and shaped around the same parameters that include Scripture but are not ultimately submitted to it.[15] Likewise, it is not easy to distinguish his metaphysics and epistemology, and consider them entirely acceptable, from his Roman Catholic theology which is so different from the evangelical account of the gospel,[16] and consider it awkward. Thomas's thought is an integrated system that needs to be appreciated as such and appropriated eclectically, but not gullibly.

4. Roman Catholicism is the full outcome of Thomas's theology and legacy

Thomas laid the foundations for the theological framework typical of Roman Catholicism as a system, i.e. the nature–grace interdependence,[17] which is highly problematic from the biblical point of view. Evangelical theology must be aware (and biblically proud) of operating, not with a purely ontological scheme mainly deduced from philosophical categories and leading to ontological optimism as Thomas does, but with the historical-redemptive

14 D. Spezzano, 'Aquinas on Nature, Grace, and the Moral Life' in Levering and Plested (eds), *The Oxford Handbook on the Reception of Aquinas*, p. 658.

15 Referring to scholasticism Bavinck argues that '[w]hile in theory Scholasticism included Scripture among the sources of theology, calling it the supreme source, in fact it did not draw its material from Scripture but from the councils (and Aristotle?) and the church fathers . . . Scripture was no more than a point of departure': Bavinck, *Reformed Ethics*, vol. 1, p. 425. *Mutatis mutandis*, the same remarks could be made regarding Thomas's theological method.

16 E.g. see the chart 'Twenty Watershed Doctrines on Which Evangelicals Do Not Agree with Thomas Aquinas', *Pro Pastor* 1:1 (2022), pp. 41–47.

17 Apart from ch. 5, for a brief presentation and pointed critique, see G. R. Allison, *Roman Catholic Theology and Practice* (Wheaton, IL: Crossway, 2014), pp. 46–55.

motif of the Bible: Creation–Sin–Redemption, however formulated. Here again, the difference is critical.

Thomas is the acknowledged authority behind many non-biblical developments in medieval and modern Roman Catholicism, from Trent to Vatican I and II. One cannot fail to see the distorting elements present at the heart of his system, which has generated several departures from the biblical faith, e.g. in the areas of Catholic soteriology, ecclesiology, sacramentology, and devotions. While he has a high view of Scripture, it resembles more that of the Council of Trent than the Reformation. In his Bible exegesis and interpretation, among brilliant insights, there are flaws and problematic applications. Moreover, he has a view of justification that somewhat overlaps with a forensic understanding of justification, yet significantly departs from it at crucial points. In both the formal and the material principles of the Reformation, Thomas is much closer to Roman Catholicism than mainstream Protestantism.

Thomas has been fully and convincingly appropriated by Roman Catholic theology for centuries, especially in its anti-Protestant polemical stance. One cannot naively assume that he is a proto-Protestant unless one acknowledges the persistent unfoundedness of all Roman Catholic interpretations of Thomas, with all their variations, over the last 750 years and the many magisterial affirmations of Aquinas. While Thomas is a 'sure guide' for Roman Catholics, the same does not apply to the heirs of the Reformation.

5. Neither infatuation nor disparagement: a call for evangelical maturity

In our current cultural climate, the reference to the metaphysics of Thomas, capable of keeping Plato, Aristotle and the Bible together – in short, the entire pre-modern Western tradition – produces an anxiety-relieving effect in some sectors of evangelical theology. Thomas primarily symbolises the 'great tradition' that unites Christian antiquity and modernity.[18] In a world sceptical and

---

18 See C. Carter, *Contemplating God with the Great Tradition: Recovering Classical Trinitarian Theism* (Grand Rapids, MI: Baker, 2021).

suspicious of any meta-narrative, Thomas's metaphysics and epistemology exert some apologetic appeal in claiming to harmoniously
combine faith and reason and to challenge scepticism in the name
of the reasonableness of faith.[19] In the ruined landscape of present-
day culture, Thomas Aquinas looks like an impressive cathedral
that reassures, comforts and inspires. However, the remedy may be
worse than the problem, especially if it leads to an infatuation with
Thomas and the idealisation of his thought.

There is a recent phenomenon of former evangelicals converting
to Roman Catholicism because of the attraction exerted by the
intellectual density and spiritual depth of Thomas. It generally
began with people thinking they could affirm his metaphysics
and ethics without embracing his theology. Upon further study,
they became convinced that Thomas's thought could not be split
into disconnected pieces, and conversions to Roman Catholicism
followed.[20] Maybe, as Barrett points out, it is untrue to say that
'Thomas is the gateway to Roman Catholicism',[21] but, at the same
time, one does not need to be naive about the attraction of the
Roman Catholic 'full package' that many find in Thomas when they
begin to be absorbed into his theological vision.[22]

A disparaging attitude towards Thomas is equally problematic.
Thomas belongs to a pre-Reformation age when the Western
Church had not yet committed itself to what Rome would officially
endorse at the Council of Trent. Although he is behind much of
what Roman Catholicism would transform into an anti-Protestant
stance, he is still part of a 'fluid' time in Church history. This is
to say that Thomas needs to be read with spiritual empathy and

---

19 As is the case with the 'classical' approach to apologetics championed by R. C. Sproul, J.
Gerstner and A. Lindsey, *Classical Apologetics: A Rational Defense of the Christian Faith and a
Critique of Presuppositionalist Apologetics* (Grand Rapids, MI: Zondervan, 1984).

20 D. M. Beaumont (ed.), *Evangelical Exodus: Evangelical Seminarians and Their Paths to Rome*
(San Francisco, CA: Ignatius Press, 2016) and R. J. Snell and R. P. George (eds), *Mind, Heart
and Soul: Intellectuals and the Path to Rome* (Charlotte, SC: TAN Books, 2018).

21 M. Barrett, '25 Myths about Thomas Aquinas', *Credo Magazine* (23 June 2022): https://
credomag.com/article/25-myths-about-thomas-aquinas (accessed 28 August 2023).

22 K. J. Stewart, 'Why Are Younger Evangelicals Turning to Catholicism and Orthodoxy?' in *In
Search of Ancient Roots: The Christian Past and the Evangelical Identity Crisis* (Downers Grove,
IL: IVP, 2017), pp. 253–73.

critical discernment like Peter Lombard, Bonaventure, Duns Scotus and other medieval theologians: benefiting from their insights and lessons, raising issues when they depart from Scripture in their systems.

Finally, we must be neither 'Thoma-phobic' (i.e. fearing the study of Thomas) nor 'Thoma-laters' (i.e. elevating him as an absolute standard for Christian orthodoxy). Evangelical theology needs to pursue a realistic reading of Thomas under the supreme authority of Scripture and in the service of the cause of the gospel. More than naively embracing Thomas or dismissingly rejecting him, let evangelical eclecticism be retrieved under the authority of Scripture. There is no better way than this to come to terms with Thomas Aquinas.

Bibliography

Works by Thomas Aquinas

To consult the complete works of Thomas in Latin, see https://www.
corpusthomisticum.org/iopera.html

The complete English translation of Thomas Aquinas's works was origi-
nally compiled by Father Joseph Kenny OP (1936–2013) and can be found
here: https://isidore.co/aquinas/

Unless otherwise indicated, quotations from the works of Thomas Aquinas
are taken from this translation. References to Thomas's commentary on
Romans are taken from J. Mortensen and E. Alancórn (eds), *Commentary
on the Letter of Saint Paul to the Romans* (Lander, WY: Aquinas Institute,
2012).

For another online version of the *Summa Theologiae*, translated by the
Fathers of the English Dominican Province (Cincinnati, OH: Benziger
Bros. edition, 1947): https://aquinas101.thomisticinstitute.org/st-index

I abbreviated the *Summa Theologiae* as *ST* and the *Summa contra Gentiles*
as *SG*. I cite *ST* from the three parts in four sections as I, I–II, II–II and
III, indicating questions with q. and articles with a.

For a continually updated bibliography of Thomas Aquinas in English,
see Thérèse Bonin, *Thomas Aquinas in English: A Bibliography*: https://
aquinas-in-english.neocities.org/

Roman Catholic magisterial documents

Fourth Lateran Council, 1215
Constitution 2 on the Error of Abbot Joachim

John XXII, bull *Redemptionem misit*, 1323

Council of Trent, 1545–63
Sixth, Seventh, Thirteenth, Fourteenth, Twenty-Second and Twenty-Third Sessions

Sixtus V, bull *Triumphantis Hierusalem*, 1558
Leo XII, encyclical letter *Aeterni Patris*, 1879
Leo XIII, letter to the minister of the Ordo Fratrum Minorum, 1885
Pius X, encyclical *Pascendi Dominici gregis*, 1907
Pius XI, encyclical *Studiorum ducem*, 1923

First Vatican Council, 1869–70
Dogmatic constitution *Dei Filius*, 1870

Second Vatican Council, 1962–65
Decree on Priestly Training *Optatam Totius*, 1965
Declaration on Christian Education *Gravissimum educationis*, 1965

Pope Paul VI, apostolic letter *Lumen Ecclesiae*, 1974
John Paul II, encyclical *Fides et Ratio*, 1998
Benedict XVI, *General Audience*, 2 June 2010
Benedict XVI, speech at the University of Regensburg (Germany) 'Faith, Reason and the Universities: Memories and Reflections', 12 September 2006

Francis, Bull of Indiction of the Extraordinary Jubilee of Mercy *Misericordiae Vultus*, 2015
Francis, encyclical *Fratelli tutti*, 2020
Francis, Address to the Participants in the International Thomistic Congress, 2022

Codex of Canon Law, 1983

Secondary literature

'What Can Protestants Learn from Thomas Aquinas?', *Credo Magazine* 12:2 (2022): https://credomag.com/magazine_issue/what-can-protestants-learn-from-thomas-aquinas (accessed 2 January 2023).

'"Praeambula fidei" e nuova apologetica' – 'The "Praeambula fidei" and the New Apologetics', *Doctor Communis* 1–2 (2008), available here: https://

Bibliography

www.vatican.va/roman_curia/pontifical_academies/san-tommaso/publications/dc10.pdf (accessed 17 May 2023).

'San Tommaso e la salvezza', ed. S.-T. Bonino and G. Mazzotta, *Doctor Communis* 4 (2020).

'San Tommaso e l'analogia', ed. S.-T. Bonino, G. Mazzotta, L. F. Tuninetti, *Doctor Communis* 5 (2023).

'Twenty Watershed Doctrines on Which Evangelicals Do Not Agree with Thomas Aquinas', *Pro Pastor* 1:1 (2022), pp. 41–47.

Allen, M., 'Disputation for Scholastic Theology: Engaging Luther's 97 Theses', *Themelios* 44:1 (2019), pp. 105–19.

Allison, G. R., *Roman Catholic Theology and Practice* (Wheaton, IL: Crossway, 2014).

Armstrong, C. R., *Medieval Wisdom for Modern Christians: Finding Authentic Faith in a Forgotten Age with C. S. Lewis* (Grand Rapids, MI: Brazos Press, 2016).

Bagchi, D. V. N., 'Sic et Non: Luther and Scholasticism' in C. R. Trueman and R. S. Clark (eds), *Protestant Scholasticism: Essays in Reassessment* (Carlisle: Paternoster Press, 1999), pp. 3–15.

Baird, J., 'What Indeed Hath Thomas to Do with Vos? A Review Article', *Westminster Theological Journal* 84 (2022), pp. 149–60.

Ballor, J. J., 'Deformation and Reformation: Thomas Aquinas and the Rise of Protestant Scholasticism' in M. Svensson and D. VanDrunen (eds), *Aquinas Among the Protestants* (Oxford: Wiley Blackwell, 2018), pp. 27–48.

Ballor, J. J., Gaetano, M. T., and Sytsma, D. S. (eds), *Beyond Dordt and De Auxiliis: The Dynamics of Protestant and Catholic Soteriology in the Sixteenth and Seventeenth Centuries* (Leiden, the Netherlands: Brill, 2019).

Barrett, M., '25 Myths about Thomas Aquinas', *Credo Magazine* (23 June 2022): https://credomag.com/article/25-myths-about-thomas-aquinas

Barrett, M., *God's Word Alone: The Authority of Scripture* (Grand Rapids, MI: Zondervan, 2016).

Baschera, L., 'Aristotle and Scholasticism' in T. Kirby, E. Campi and F. A. James III (eds), *A Companion to Peter Martyr Vermigli* (Leiden, the Netherlands: Brill, 2009), pp. 133–59.

Bauerschmidt, F. C., 'Thomas Aquinas' in K. L. Johnson and D. Lauber (eds), *T&T Clark Companion to the Doctrine of Sin* (London: Bloomsbury T&T Clark, 2016), pp. 199–216.

H. Bavinck, *Reformed Dogmatics*, 4 vols [1895–1901], ed. J. Bolt (Grand Rapids, MI: Baker Academic, 2003–08).

Bavinck, H., *Reformed Dogmatics* vol. 1, ed. J. Bolt (Grand Rapids, MI: Baker Academic, 2003).

Bavinck, H., *Reformed Ethics*, vol. 1, ed. J. Bolt (Grand Rapids, MI: Baker Academic, 2019).

Bavinck, J. H., *An Introduction to the Science of Mission* (Phillipsburg, NJ: P & R Publishing, 1960).

Beaumont, D. M. (ed.), *Evangelical Exodus: Evangelical Seminarians and Their Paths to Rome* (San Francisco, CA: Ignatius Press, 2016).

Beckwith, F. J., *Never Doubt Thomas: The Catholic Aquinas as Evangelical and Protestant* (Waco, TX: Baylor University Press, 2019).

Bellarmine, R., *Controversies of the Christian Faith* [1583–1596] (Saddle River, NJ: Keep the Faith, 2016).

Bellarmine, R., *On the Most Holy Sacrifice of the Mass* [1583–1596] (Columbia, SC: Mediatrix Press, 2020).

Berti, E., *Le prove dell'esistenza di Dio nella filosofia* (Brescia: Morcelliana, 2022).

Beumer, J., 'Gratia supponit naturam: zur Geschichte eines theologischen Prinzips', *Gregorianum* 20 (1939), pp. 381–406, 535–52. Italian edition: *Gratia supponit naturam: storia di un principio teologico*, ed. S. Billeci (Venice: Marcianum Press, 2020).

Bianchi, L., *Il vescovo e i filosofi: la condanna parigina del 1277 e l'evoluzione dell'aristotelismo* (Bergamo: Ed. Pierluigi Lubrina, 1990).

Biffi, I., 'Il commento alle Sentenze' in *Alla scuola di Tommaso* (Milan: Jaca Book, 2007), pp. 1–80.

Biffi, I., 'Una teologia sapienziale' in *Alla scuola di Tommaso* (Milan: Jaca Book, 2007), pp. 81–97.

Biffi, I., 'Una introduzione alla *Summa contra Gentiles* di San Tommaso' in *Sulle vie dell'Angelico: teologia, storia, contemplazione* (Milan: Jaca Book, 2009), pp. 385–404.

Billeci, S., *Gratia Supponit Naturam nella teologia di Joseph Ratzinger* (Trapani: Il Pozzo di Giacobbe, 2020).

Boersma, H., *Nouvelle Théologie and Sacramental Ontology: A Return to Mystery* (Oxford: Oxford University Press, 2009).

Bolognesi, P., 'La teologia come disciplina elenctica', *Studi di Teologia* NS 46I (2011), pp. 131–45.

Bolognesi, P., *Tra credere e sapere: dalla Riforma protestante all'Ortodossia riformata* (Caltanissetta: Alfa & Omega, 2011).

Bolognesi, P., 'Un cristiano riformato: Girolamo Zanchi (1516–1590)', *Studi di Teologia* 55 (2016), pp. 3–24.

Bolt, J., 'Doubting Reformational Anti-Thomism' in M. Svensson and D. VanDrunen (eds), *Aquinas Among the Protestants* (Oxford: Wiley Blackwell, 2018), pp. 129–48.

Bonaventure, St., *The Life of St. Francis of Assisi* [1260] (Charlotte, NC: TAN Books, 2010).

Bonino, S.-T. (ed.), *Grandi opere del Tomismo nel Novecento* (Rome: Urbaniana University Press, 2020).

Bouillard, H., *Conversion et grâce chez saint Thomas d'Aquin* (Paris: Aubier, 1944).

Bowlin, J., 'Contemporary Protestant Thomism' in P. Van Geest, H. Goris and C. Leget (eds), *Aquinas as Authority* (Leuven, Belgium: Peeters, 2002), pp. 235–51.

Boyle, J. F., *Aquinas on Scripture: A Primer* (Steubenville, OH: Emmaus Academic, 2023).

Bray, G., *Biblical Interpretation: Past & Present* (Downers Grove, IL: IVP, 1996).

Bray, G., *God Has Spoken: A History of Christian Theology* (Wheaton, IL: Crossway, 2014).

Brock, C., *Orthodox Yet Modern: Herman Bavinck's Use of Friedrich Schleiermacher* (Bellingham, WA: Lexham Press, 2020).

Brock, C., 'Herman Bavinck the Neo-Thomist? A Reevaluation of Influence' in J. Eglinton and G. Harinck (eds), *Neo-Calvinism and Roman Catholicism* (Leiden, the Netherlands: Brill, 2023), pp. 114–33.

Brock, C. and Gray Sutanto, N., 'Herman Bavinck's Reformed Eclecticism: On Catholicity, Consciousness and Theological Epistemology', *Scottish Journal of Theology* 70:3 (2017), pp. 310–32.

Brock, C. and Gray Sutanto, N., *Neo-Calvinism: A Theological Introduction* (Bellingham, WA: Lexham Press, 2022).

Broeyer, F. G. M., 'Traces of the Rise of Reformed Scholasticism in the Polemical Theologian William Whitaker (1548–1595)' in W. J. van Asselt and E. Dekker (eds), *Reformation and Scholasticism: An Ecumenical Enterprise* (Grand Rapids, MI: Baker Academic, 2001), pp. 155–80.

Bromiley, G. W., *Historical Theology: An Introduction* (Grand Rapids, MI: Eerdmans, 1978).

Calvin, J., *Letter to Sadoleto* (1539): https://www.monergism.com/john-calvins-letter-cardinal-sadoleto-1539

E. Campi and J. C. McLelland (eds), *Commentary on Aristotle's Nicomachean Ethics*, The Peter Martyr Library, vol. 9 (Kirksville, MO: Truman State University Press, 2006).

Carter, C., *Contemplating God with the Great Tradition: Recovering Classical Trinitarian Theism* (Grand Rapids, MI: Baker, 2021).

Centi, T. S., *Tommaso d'Aquino: nel segno del sole* (Milan: Ares, 2023).

Cessario, R., *Le thomisme et les thomistes* (Paris: Cerf, 1999).

Cessario, R., *A Short History of Thomism* (Washington, DC: Catholic University of America Press, 2005).

Cessario, R., 'Sixteenth-Century Reception of Aquinas by the Council of Trent and Its Main Authors' in M. Levering and M. Plested (eds), *The Oxford Handbook of the Reception of Aquinas* (Oxford: Oxford University Press, 2021), pp. 159–72.

Cessario, R., *The Seven Sacraments of the Catholic Church* (Grand Rapids, MI: Baker Academic, 2023).

Cessario, R. and Cuddy, C., *Thomas and the Thomists: The Achievement of Thomas Aquinas and His Interpreters* (Minneapolis, MN: Fortress Press, 2017).

Chenu, M.-D., *Introduzione allo studio di S. Tommaso d'Aquino* (Florence: Libreria Editrice Fiorentina, 1953).

Chenu, M.-D., *Aquinas and His Role in Theology* [1959] (Collegeville, MN: Liturgical Press, 2002).

Chesterton, G. K., *San Thomas Aquinas: The Dumb Ox* (1933): https://archive.org/details/thedumbox/mode/2up (accessed 17 May 2023).

Colli, A. (ed.), 'Albert the Great and Holy Scripture', *Divus Thomas* 122 (2019).

Congar, Y., 'La théologie au Concile: le "théologiser" du Concile' in *Situation et tâches présentes de la théologie* (Paris: Cerf, 1967).

Cooper, A. G., 'The Reception of Aquinas in *Nouvelle Théologie*' in M. Levering and M. Plested (eds), *The Oxford Handbook of the Reception of Aquinas* (Oxford: Oxford University Press, 2021), pp. 424–41.

Crisp, O., 'On Being a Reformed Theologian', *Theology* 115:1 (2012), pp. 14–25.

Cuddy, C., 'Sixteenth-Century Reception of Aquinas by Cajetan' in M.

Bibliography

Levering and M. Plested (eds), *The Oxford Handbook of the Reception of Aquinas* (Oxford: Oxford University Press, 2021), pp. 144–58.

Daly, G., *Transcendence and Immanence: A Study in Catholic Modernism and Integralism* (Oxford: Oxford University Press, 1980).

Dauphinais, M., David, B. and Levering, M. (eds), *Aquinas the Augustinian* (Washington, DC: Catholic University of America Press, 2007).

Davies, B., 'The Limits of Language and the Notion of Analogy' in B. Davies and E. Stump (eds), *The Oxford Handbook of Aquinas* (Oxford: Oxford University Press, 2012), pp. 390–400.

Davies, B., *Thomas Aquinas's Summa Theologiae: A Guide and Commentary* (Oxford: Oxford University Press, 2014).

Davies, B., *Thomas Aquinas's Summa Contra Gentiles: A Guide and Commentary* (Oxford: Oxford University Press, 2016).

Davies, B. and Stump, E. (eds), *The Oxford Handbook of Aquinas* (Oxford: Oxford University Press, 2012).

De Chirico, L., *Evangelical Theological Perspectives on Post-Vatican II Roman Catholicism* (Oxford: Peter Lang, 2003).

De Chirico, L., 'The Joy of the Gospel: A Window into Francis's Vision', *Vatican Files* N. 69 (2 December 2013): https://vaticanfiles.org/en/2013/12/69-the-joy-of-the-gospel-a-window-into-francis-vision

De Chirico, L., 'Would You Ever Ask a Muslim to Pray for You? Pope Francis Did', *Vatican Files* N. 139 (1 July 2017): https://vaticanfiles.org/en/2017/07/139-would-you-ever-ask-muslims-to-pray-for-you-pope-francis-did

De Chirico, L., 'Do Atheists Go to Heaven? Pope Francis Says Yes', *Vatican Files* N. 149 (1 May 2018): https://vaticanfiles.org/en/2018/05/149-atheists-go-heaven-pope-francis-says-yes

De Chirico, L., *Same Words, Different Worlds: Do Roman Catholics and Evangelicals Believe the Same Gospel?* (London: Apollos, 2021).

De Chirico, L., 'Robert Bellarmine and His Controversies with the Reformers: A Window on Post-Tridentine Roman Catholic Apologetics', *European Journal of Theology* 31:1 (2022), pp. 21–42.

De Chirico, L., '"The Clay of Paganism with the Iron of Christianity": Cornelius Van Til's Critique of Roman Catholicism' in J. Eglinton and G. Harinck (eds), *Neo-Calvinism and Roman Catholicism* (Leiden, the Netherlands: Brill, 2023), pp. 249–62.

De Chirico, L., 'Retrieving Elenctics: Kuyper, Machen, and Van Til on Roman Catholicism' in B. G. Green (ed.), *Thinking God's Thoughts After*

Him: Essays in the Van Til Tradition (Eugene, OR: Wipf and Stock, forthcoming).

De Franceschi, S. H., *Thomisme et théologie moderne: l'école de saint Thomas à l'épreuve de la querelle de la grâce (XVIIe–XVIIIe siècles)* (Paris: Artège Lethielleux, 2018).

De Franceschi, S. H., 'Uniformité de doctrine et orthodoxie au temps de la synthèse bellarminienne: le statut doctrinal de Thomas d'Aquin dans la Compagnie de Jésus à la veille des Congrégations de auxiliis' in *Ripensare Bellarmino tra teologia, filosofia e storia* (Rome: Gregorian & Biblical Press, 2023), pp. 131–58.

De Lubac, H., *The Mystery of the Supernatural* [1965] (Chestnut Ridge, NY: Herder & Herder, 1998).

Di Maio, A., *Piccolo glossario bonaventuriano: prima introduzione al pensiero e al lessico di Bonaventura da Bagnoregio* (Rome: Aracne, 2008).

Dieter, T., 'Martin Luther and Scholasticism' in D. Marmion, S. Ryan and G. E. Thiessen (eds), *Remembering the Reformation: Martin Luther and Catholic Theology* (Minneapolis, MN: Fortress Press, 2017), pp. 55–74.

Domenici, G., 'La genesi, le vicende ed i giudizi delle controversie bellarminiane', *Gregoranium* 2:2 (1921), pp. 513–42.

Donnelly, J. P., *Calvinism and Scholasticism in Vermigli's Doctrine of Man and Grace* (Leiden, the Netherlands: Brill, 1976).

Donnelly, J. P., 'Calvinist Thomism', *Viator* 7 (1976), pp. 441–55.

Dorsche, J. G., *Thomas Aquinas, dictus doctor angelicus, exhibitus confessor veritatis evangelicae Augustana confessione repetitae* (1656): https://www.digitale-sammlungen.de/en/view/bsb11230518?page=2,3.

Duby, S. J., *God in Himself: Scripture, Metaphysics, and the Task of Christian Theology* (Downers Grove, IL: IVP, 2019).

Duby, S. J., 'Reformed Catholicity and the Analogy of Being' in J. Minich (ed.), *Reforming the Catholic Tradition: The Whole Word for the Whole Church* (Leesburg, VA: The Davenant Institute, 2019), pp. 47–76.

Duffy, S. J., *The Graced Horizon: Nature and Grace in Modern Catholic Thought* (Collegeville, MN: Liturgical Press, 1992).

Duffy, S. J., *The Dynamics of Grace: Perspectives in Theological Anthropology*, vol. 3 (Collegeville, MN: Liturgical Press, 1993).

Dulles, A., *A History of Apologetics* (San Francisco, CA: Ignatius Press, 2005).

Echeverria, E. J., 'Once Again, John Paul II's Fides et Ratio', *Philosophia Reformata* 69:1 (2004), pp. 38–52.

Bibliography

Eglinton, J., 'The Reception of Aquinas in Kuyper's *Encyclopaedie der heilige Godgeleerdheid*' in M. Levering and M. Plested (eds), *The Oxford Handbook of the Reception of Aquinas* (Oxford: Oxford University Press, 2021), pp. 452–67.

Elliott, M. W., 'Thomas Aquinas' in B. G. Green (ed.), *Shapers of Christian Orthodoxy* (Downers Grove, IL: IVP Academic, 2010), pp. 341–88.

Emery, G., 'Central Aristotelian Themes in Aquinas's Trinitarian Theology' in G. Emery and M. Levering (eds), *Aristotle in Aquinas's Theology* (Oxford: Oxford University Press, 2015), pp. 1–28.

Farrow, D., 'Theology and Philosophy: Recovering the Pax Thomistica' in *Theological Negotiations: Proposals in Soteriology and Anthropology* (Grand Rapids, MI: Baker, 2018), pp. 1–32.

Farrow, D., 'Thinking with Aquinas about Nature and Grace' in *Theological Negotiations: Proposals in Soteriology and Anthropology* (Grand Rapids, MI: Baker, 2018), pp. 33–64.

Farthing, J. L., *Thomas Aquinas and Gabriel Biel: Interpretations of St. Thomas in German Nominalism on the Eve of the Reformation* (Durham, NC: Duke University Press, 1988).

Feser, E., *Aquinas: A Beginner's Guide* (London: Oneworld Publications, 2009).

Fesko, J. V., 'Aquinas's Doctrine of Justification and Infused Habits in Reformed Soteriology' in M. Svensson and D. VanDrunen (eds), *Aquinas Among the Protestants* (Oxford: Wiley Blackwell, 2018), pp. 249–66.

Finnis, J., *Aquinas: Moral, Political, and Legal Theory* (Oxford: Oxford University Press, 1998).

Frame, J. M., 'Theology' in G. North (ed.), *Foundations of Christian Scholarship: Essays in the Van Til Perspective* (Vallecito, CA: Ross House Books, 1976), pp. 295–330.

Frame, J. M., *Cornelius Van Til: An Analysis of His Thought* (Phillipsburg, NJ: P & R Publishing, 1995).

Frame, J. M., *On Theology: Explorations and Controversies* (Bellingham, WA: Lexham Press, 2023).

Frugoni, C., *Francis of Assisi: A Life* (London: Continuum, 1997).

Gaboriau, F., *L'Écriture seule?* (Paris: FAC-éditions, 1997).

Garrigou-Lagrange, R., *La sintesi tomistica* [1950] (Verona: Fede & Cultura, 2015).

Geisler, N. L., 'A New Look at the Relevance of Thomism for Evangelical Apologetics', *Christian Scholar's Review* 4:3 (1975), pp. 189–200.

Geisler, N. L., *Thomas Aquinas: An Evangelical Appraisal* (Grand Rapids, MI: Baker, 1991).

Gemelli, A., 'Medievalismo', *Vita e Pensiero* 1 (1914), pp. 1–24.

Gerstner, J., 'Aquinas Was a Protestant', *Tabletalk* 18:5 (May 1994), pp. 13–15, 52.

Ghisalberti, A., 'Dio come essere e Dio come uno: la sintesi di Tommaso d'Aquino' in *Medioevo teologico: categorie della teologia razionale nel Medioevo* (Rome-Bari: Laterza, 1990), pp. 85–112.

Gilson, É., *Thomism: The Philosophy of Thomas Aquinas* [1922] (Toronto: Pontifical Institute of Medieval Studies, 2002).

Goergen, D. J., *St. Dominic: The Story of a Preaching Friar* (New York, NY: The Paulist Press, 2016).

Grabmann, M., *Die Geschichte der scholastischen Methode* [1909–1911]. Italian edition: *Storia del metodo scolastico, vol. 2: Il metodo scolastico nel XII e all'inizio del XIII secolo*, tr. M. Candela and P. Buscaglione Candela (Florence: La Nuova Italia Editrice, 1999).

Gray Sutanto, N., *God and Knowledge: Herman Bavinck's Theological Epistemology* (London: T&T Clark, 2020).

Green, B. G., *Augustine of Hippo: His Life and Impact* (Fearn, Tain, Scotland: Christian Focus Publications, 2020).

Grumett, D., 'Movements of *Ressourcement* in Theology: Foundations for a Council of Renewal' in C. E. Clifford and M. Faggioli (eds), *The Oxford Handbook of Vatican II* (Oxford: Oxford University Press, 2023), pp. 44–60.

Guarino, T. G., *The Disputed Teachings of Vatican II: Continuity and Reversal in Catholic Doctrine* (Grand Rapids, MI: Eerdmans, 2018).

Haak, C. J., 'The Missional Approach: Reconsidering Elenctics (part 1)', *Calvin Theological Journal* 44:1 (2009), pp. 37–48.

Haines, D., 'Thomas Aquinas on Total Depravity and the Noetic Effects of Sin', *Themelios* 48:2 (2023), pp. 366–80.

Helm, P., 'Nature and Grace' in M. Svensson and D. VanDrunen (eds), *Aquinas Among the Protestants* (Oxford: Wiley Blackwell, 2018), pp. 229–48.

Horton, M., *Justification*, vol. 1 (Grand Rapids, MI: Zondervan, 2018).

Hoye, W. J., *Divine Being and Its Relevance According to Thomas Aquinas* (Leiden, the Netherlands: Brill, 2020).

Huizinga, J., *The Autumn of the Middle Ages*, tr. R. J. Payton and U. Mammitzsch (Chicago, IL: University of Chicago Press, 1996).

Husinger, G., *Evangelical, Catholic, and Reformed: Doctrinal Essays on Barth and Related Themes* (Grand Rapids, MI: Eerdmans, 2015).

Hütter, R., *Aquinas on Transubstantiation: The Real Presence of Christ in the Eucharist* (Washington, DC: Catholic University of America Press, 2019).

Jaeger, L., 'La foi et la raison: à propos de la lettre encyclique: Fides et ratio', *Fac-Réflexion* 46–47 (1999), pp. 35–46.

Johnson, A. M., *Beyond Indulgences: Luther's Reform of Late Medieval Piety, 1518-1520* (University Park, PA: Penn State University Press, 2017).

Johnstone, B., 'The Debate on the Structure of the *Summa Theologiae*: From Chenu (1939) to Metz (1998)' in P. van Geest, H. Goris and C. Leget (eds), *Aquinas as Authority* (Leuven, Belgium: Peters, 2002), pp. 187–200.

Jordan, M., *Rewritten Theology: Aquinas After His Readers* (Oxford: Blackwell, 2006).

Keating, D. A., 'Justification, Sanctification, and Divinization in Thomas Aquinas' in T. G. Weinandy, D. A. Keating and J. P. Yocum (eds), *Aquinas on Doctrine: A Critical Introduction* (New York, NY: T&T Clark, 2004), pp. 117–58.

Kerr, F., *After Aquinas: Versions of Thomism* (Oxford: Blackwell, 2002).

Kerr, F., *Twentieth-Century Catholic Theologians* (Oxford: Blackwell, 2007).

Kerr, F., *Thomas Aquinas: A Very Short Introduction* (Oxford: Oxford University Press, 2009).

Kilcrease, J., 'Johann Gerhard's Reception of Thomas Aquinas's *Analogia Entis*' in M. Svensson and D. VanDrunen (eds), *Aquinas Among the Protestants* (Oxford: Wiley Blackwell, 2018), pp. 109–28.

Kilcrease, J. D., *Justification by the Word: Restoring Sola Fide* (Bellingham, WA: Lexham Press, 2022).

Koterski, J. W., 'The Doctrine of Participation in Thomistic Metaphysics' in D. W. Hudson and D. W. Moran (eds), *The Future of Thomism* (Mishawaka, IN: American Maritain Association and University of Notre Dame Press, 1992), pp. 185–96.

Kretzmann, N., *The Metaphysics of Theism: Aquinas's Natural Theology in Summa contra Gentiles 1* (Oxford: Clarendon Press, 1997).

Kretzmann, N. and Stump, E. (eds), *The Cambridge Companion to Aquinas* (Cambridge: Cambridge University Press, 1993).

Kristeller, P. O., *La tradizione aristotelica nel Rinascimento* (Padua: Antenore, 1962).

Bibliography

Kühn, U., *Via Caritatis: Theologie des Gesetzes bei Thomas von Aquin* (Berlin: Ev. Verlagsanstalt, 1964).

Kuyper, A. *Lectures on Calvinism* (Grand Rapids, MI: Eerdmans, 1931; 10th reprint 1978).

Lane, A. N. S., *John Calvin: Student of the Church Fathers* (Grand Rapids, MI: Baker, 1999).

Lantigua, D. M., 'Aquinas and the Emergence of Moral Theology during the Spanish Renaissance' in M. Levering and M. Plested (eds), *The Oxford Handbook of the Reception of Aquinas* (Oxford: Oxford University Press, 2021), pp. 173–90.

Lanza, L. and Toste, M. (eds), *Summistae: The Commentary Tradition on Thomas Aquinas's Summa Theologiae from the 15th to the 17th Centuries* (Leuven, Belgium: Leuven University Press, 2021).

Le Goff, J., *The Birth of Purgatory* (Chicago, IL: University of Chicago Press, 1986).

Leithart, P. J., 'Aquinas on Justification' (28 April 2005): https://theopolisinstitute.com/leithart_post/aquinas-on-justification (accessed 7 April 2023).

Leithart, P. J., 'Medieval Theology and the Roots of Modernity' in W. A. Hoffecker (ed.), *Revolutions in Worldview: Understanding the Flow of Western Thought* (Phillipsburg, NJ: P & R Publishing, 2007), pp. 140–77.

Letham, R., *Gamechangers: Key Figures of the Christian Church* (Fearn, Tain, Scotland: Christian Focus Publications, 2015).

Levering, M. and Dauphinais, M. (eds), *Reading Romans with St. Thomas Aquinas* (Washington, DC: Catholic University of America Press, 2012).

Levering, M. and Plested, M. (eds), *The Oxford Handbook of the Reception of Aquinas* (Oxford: Oxford University Press, 2021).

Lindholm, S., 'Jerome Zanchi's Use of Thomas Aquinas' in M. Svensson and D. VanDrunen (eds), *Aquinas Among the Protestants* (Oxford: Wiley Blackwell, 2018), pp. 75–90.

Long, S. A., *Natura Pura: On the Recovery of Nature in the Doctrine of Grace* (New York, NY: Fordham University Press, 2010).

Luna, C., 'L'édition léonine de saint Thomas d'Aquin', *Revue des sciences philosophiques et théologiques* 89:1 (2005), pp. 31–110.

Luy, D., 'Sixteenth-Century Reception of Aquinas by Luther and Lutheran Reformers' in M. Levering and M. Plested (eds), *The Oxford Handbook of the Reception of Aquinas* (Oxford: Oxford University Press, 2021), pp. 105–20.

Maas, K. D., 'Justification by Faith Alone' in M. Barrett (ed.), *Reformation Theology: A Systematic Summary* (Wheaton, IL: Crossway, 2017), pp. 511–48.

Maas, K. D., 'The First and Chief Article: Luther's Discovery of Sola Fide and Its Controversial Reception in Lutheranism' in M. Barrett (ed.), *The Doctrine on Which the Church Stands or Falls: Justification in Biblical, Theological, Historical, and Pastoral Perspective* (Wheaton, IL: Crossway, 2019), pp. 657–700.

Maritain, J., *The Angelic Doctor: The Life and Thought of St. Thomas Aquinas* [1930] (New York, NY: Lincoln MacVeagh; Toronto: Longmans, 1931).

Maritain, J., *Integral Humanism* [1936] (New York, NY: Scribner's, 1968).

Marshall, B., 'Beatus Vir: Aquinas, Romans 4, and the Role of "Reckoning" in Justification' in M. Levering and M. Dauphinais (eds), *Reading Romans with St. Thomas Aquinas* (Washington, DC: Catholic University of America Press, 2012), pp. 219–31.

Mathison, K. A., *The Shape of Sola Scriptura* (Moscow, ID: Canon Press, 2001).

Mayes, B. T. G., 'Seventeenth-Century Lutheran Reception of Aquinas' in M. Levering and M. Plested (eds), *The Oxford Handbook of the Reception of Aquinas* (Oxford: Oxford University Press, 2021), pp. 222–54.

McCool, G. A., *From Unity to Pluralism: The Internal Evolution of Thomism* (New York, NY: Fordham University Press, 1989).

McCormack, B. L. and White, T. J. (eds), *Thomas Aquinas and Karl Barth: An Unofficial Catholic-Protestant Dialogue* (Grand Rapids, MI: Eerdmans, 2013).

McCosker, P. and Turner, D. (eds), *The Cambridge Companion to the Summa Theologiae* (Cambridge: Cambridge University Press, 2016).

McGinn, B., *Thomas Aquinas's Summa Theologiae: A Biography* (Princeton, NJ: Princeton University Press, 2014).

McGrath, A. E., *Iustitia Dei: A History of the Christian Doctrine of Justification* (Cambridge: Cambridge University Press, 1986; 3rd edn 2005).

McIlroy, D., 'A Trinitarian Reading of Aquinas's Treatise on Law', *Angelicum* 84 (2007), pp. 277–92.

McInerny, R., *The Logic of Analogy: An Interpretation of St. Thomas* (The Hague: Martinus Nijhoff, 1961).

McInerny, R., *Praeambula Fidei: Thomism and the God of the Philosophers* (Washington, DC: Catholic University of America Press, 2006).

McLelland, J. C., 'Vermigli's "Stromatic" Theology' in T. Kirby, E. Campi and F. A. James III (eds), *A Companion to Peter Martyr Vermigli* (Leiden, the Netherlands: Brill, 2009), pp. 495–98.

Melville, G., *The World of Medieval Monasticism: Its History and Forms of Life* (Collegeville, MN: Liturgical Press, 2016).

Milbank, J., *The Suspended Middle: Henri de Lubac and the Debate Concerning the Supernatural* (Grand Rapids, MI: Eerdmans, 2005).

Milbank, J. and Pickstock, C., *Truth in Aquinas* (London: Routledge, 2001).

Mondin, B., *Dizionario enciclopedico del pensiero di San Tommaso d'Aquino* (Bologna: Edizioni Studio Domenicano, 2000).

Morra, G., 'La "Aeterni Patris" cent'anni dopo', *Sacra Doctrina* 92 (1980), pp. 5–19.

Muller, R. A., *Post-Reformation Reformed Dogmatics: The Rise and Development of Reformed Orthodoxy, ca. 1520 to ca. 1725*, 4 vols (Grand Rapids, MI: Baker, 1987–2003).

Muller, R. A., 'The Problem of Protestant Scholasticism: A Review and Definition' in W. J. van Asselt and E. Dekker (eds), *Reformation and Scholasticism: An Ecumenical Enterprise* (Grand Rapids, MI: Baker Academic, 2001), pp. 45–64.

Muller, R. A., 'Aquinas Reconsidered', *Reformation21* (19 February 2018): https://byk2739.tistory.com/712

Muller, R. A., 'Reading Aquinas from a Reformed Perspective: A Review Essay', *Calvin Theological Journal* 53:2 (2018), pp. 255–88.

Naro, M., *Protagonista è l'abbraccio: temi teologici nel magistero di Francesco* (Venice: Marcianum Press, 2021).

Needham, N., 'The Evolution of Justification: Justification in the Medieval Traditions' in M. Barrett (ed.), *The Doctrine on Which the Church Stands or Falls: Justification in Biblical, Theological, Historical, and Pastoral Perspective* (Wheaton, IL: Crossway, 2019), pp. 587–622.

Newman, J. H., *Discussions and Arguments*, II.1 (London: Longmans, 1891).

Nutt, R. W., 'The Reception of Aquinas in Early Twentieth-Century Catholic Neo-Scholastic and Historical Theologians' in M. Levering and M. Plested (eds), *The Oxford Handbook of the Reception of Aquinas* (Oxford: Oxford University Press, 2021), pp. 392–407.

Oakes, K., 'Karl Barth's Reception of Thomas Aquinas' in M. Levering and M. Plested (eds), *The Oxford Handbook of the Reception of Aquinas* (Oxford: Oxford University Press, 2021), pp. 468–82.

Oberman, H. A., *The Harvest of Medieval Theology: Gabriel Biel and Late Medieval Nominalism* (Cambridge, MA: Harvard University Press, 1963; repr. 2001).

Oliphint, K. S., 'Aquinas: A Shaky Foundation', *The Gospel Coalition* (7 November 2012): https://www.thegospelcoalition.org/article/aquinas-a-shaky-foundation (accessed 25 August 2023).

Oliphint, K. S., *Thomas Aquinas* (Phillipsburg, NJ: P & R Publishing, 2017).

Owen, J., 'Aristotle and Aquinas' in N. Kretzmann and E. Stump (eds), *The Cambridge Companion to Aquinas* (Cambridge: Cambridge University Press, 1993), pp. 38–59.

Ozment, S., *The Age of Reform, 1250–1550: An Intellectual and Religious History of Late Medieval and Reformation Europe* (New Haven, CT: Yale University Press, 1980).

Packer, J. I., 'Upholding the Unity of Scripture Today', *Journal of the Evangelical Theological Society* 25:4 (1992), pp. 409–14.

Parker, E. M., 'Fides Mater Virtutum Est: Peter Martyr Vermigli's Disagreement with Thomas Aquinas on the "Form" of the Virtues', *Reformation & Renaissance Review* 15:1 (2014), pp. 49–62.

Parker Jr, G. W., 'Reformation or Revolution? Herman Bavinck and Henri de Lubac on Nature and Grace', *Perichoresis* 15:3 (2017), pp. 81–95.

Pawl, T., 'The Five Ways' in B. Davies and E. Stump (eds), *The Oxford Handbook of Aquinas* (Oxford: Oxford University Press, 2012), pp. 115–34.

Pellegrini, L., *L'incontro di due 'invenzioni' medievali: università e ordini mendicanti* (Naples: Liguori, 2005).

Penone, D., *I domenicani nei secoli: panorama storico dell'Ordine dei frati predicatori* (Bologna: Edizioni Studio Domenicano, 1998).

Pera, C., *Le fonti del pensiero di S. Tommaso d'Aquino nella Somma teologica* (Turin: Marietti Editore, 1979).

Pesch, O. H., *Theologie der Rechtfertigung bei Martin Luther und Thomas von Aquin* (Mainz: Matthias-Grünewald-Verlag, 1967).

Pesch, O. H., *Tommaso d'Aquino: limiti e grandezza della teologia medievale. Una introduzione* (Brescia: Queriniana, 1994).

Pesch, O. H., *Hinführung zu Luther* (Mainz: Matthias-Grünewald-Verlag, 2004).

Pinckaers, S., 'The Place of Philosophy in Moral Theology', *L'Osservatore Romano* (15 June 1999), p. 15.

Porro, P., *Tommaso d'Aquino: un profilo storico-filosofico* (Rome: Carocci Editore, 2019; repr. 2021).

Poythress, V. S., *The Mystery of the Trinity: A Trinitarian Approach to the Attributes of God* (Phillipsburg, NJ: P & R Publishing, 2020).

Prouvost, G., *Thomas d'Aquin et les thomismes: essai sur l'histoire des thomismes* (Paris: Cerf, 1996).

Purdy, R. A., 'Norman Geisler's Neo-Thomistic Apologetics', *Journal of the Evangelical Theological Society* 25 (1982), pp. 351–58.

Ratzinger, J., *Introduction to Christianity*, 2nd edn (San Francisco, CA: Ignatius Press, 2004).

Ratzinger, J., *Opera Omnia*, vols 1–3 (Freiburg, Basel, Vienna: Herder Verlag, 2011).

Reeves, M., *Introducing Major Theologians* (Nottingham: IVP, 2015).

Reeves, M., 'The Holy Trinity' in M. Barrett (ed.), *Reformation Theology: A Systematic Summary* (Wheaton, IL: Crossway, 2017), pp. 189–216.

Renick, T. M., *Aquinas for Armchair Theologians* (Louisville, KY: Westminster John Knox Press, 2002).

Reymond, R. L., 'Dr. John H. Gerstner on Thomas Aquinas as Protestant', *Westminster Theological Journal* 59 (1997), pp. 113–21.

Robertson, C., 'Seventeenth-Century Catholic Reception Outside the *De auxiliis* Controversy' in M. Levering and M. Plested (eds), *The Oxford Handbook of the Reception of Aquinas* (Oxford: Oxford University Press, 2021), pp. 280–92.

Rowland, T., *Catholic Theology* (London: Bloomsbury T&T Clark, 2017).

Russell, J. B., *Dissent and Reform in the Early Middle Ages* (Eugene, OR: Wipf and Stock, 2005).

Santi, F., 'L'esegesi biblica di Tommaso d'Aquino nel contesto dell'esegesi biblica medievale', *Angelicum* 71:4 (1994), pp. 509–35.

Sarmenghi, A., *Rimuovere l'oscurità: conoscenza e amore nella Somma di Teologia di Tommaso d'Aquino* (Rome: Città Nuova, 2021).

Schaeffer, F., *Escape from Reason* (Downers Grove, IL: IVP, 1970).

Schaff, P., *History of the Christian Church, vol. 5: The Middle Ages. A.D. 1049-1294* [1907] (repr. Grand Rapids, MI: Eerdmans, 1960).

Schmitt, C. B., *Aristotle and the Renaissance* (Cambridge, MA: Harvard University Press, 1983).

Schwöbel, C., 'Reformed Traditions' in P. McCosker and D. Turner (eds), *The Cambridge Companion to the Summa Theologiae* (Cambridge: Cambridge University Press, 2016), pp. 319–42.

Bibliography

Smith, R. B., *Reading the Sermons of Thomas Aquinas: A Beginner's Guide* (Steubenville, OH: Emmaus Academic, 2016).

Smith, R. B., *Aquinas, Bonaventure, and the Scholastic Culture of Medieval Paris: Preaching, Prologues, and Biblical Commentaries* (Cambridge: Cambridge University Press, 2021).

Snell, R. J. and George, R. P. (eds), *Mind, Heart and Soul: Intellectuals and the Path to Rome* (Charlotte, SC: TAN Books, 2018).

Spezzano, D., 'Aquinas on Nature, Grace, and the Moral Life' in M. Levering and M. Plested (eds), *The Oxford Handbook on the Reception of Aquinas* (Oxford: Oxford University Press, 2021), pp. 658–72.

Sproul, R. C., Gerstner, J. and Lindsey, A., *Classical Apologetics: A Rational Defense of the Christian Faith and a Critique of Presuppositionalist Apologetics* (Grand Rapids, MI: Zondervan, 1984).

Stark, R., *God's Battalions: The Case for the Crusades* (San Francisco, CA: HarperOne, 2010).

Steffensmeier, L., 'Revisiting the Reformation: Aquinas and Luther on Justification' (2017), *Celebrating Scholarship & Creativity Day*, 136: https://digitalcommons.csbsju.edu/elce_cscday/136 (accessed 7 April 2023).

Steinmetz, D. C., 'The Scholastic Calvin' in C. R. Trueman and R. S. Clark (eds), *Protestant Scholasticism: Essays in Reassessment* (Carlisle: Paternoster Press, 1999), pp. 16–30.

Stephens, W. P., *The Holy Spirit of the Theology of Martin Bucer* (Cambridge: Cambridge University Press, 1970).

Stewart, K. J., 'Why Are Younger Evangelicals Turning to Catholicism and Orthodoxy?' in *In Search of Ancient Roots: The Christian Past and the Evangelical Identity Crisis* (Downers Grove, IL: IVP, 2017), pp. 253–73.

Strachan, O., 'Did Thomas Teach the Biblical God of Monergistic Salvation?', *Pro Pastor* 1:1 (2022), pp. 33–40.

Strange, D., *Make Faith Magnetic* (Epsom: The Good Book Company, 2021).

Subilia, V., *La giustificazione per fede* (Brescia: Paideia, 1976).

Svensson, M. and VanDrunen, D. (eds), *Aquinas Among the Protestants* (Oxford: Wiley Blackwell, 2018).

Swiezawski, S., *Redécouvrir Thomas d'Aquin* (Paris: Nouvelle Cité, 1989), pp. 135–39.

Sytsma, D. S., 'Thomas Aquinas and Reformed Biblical Interpretation: The Contribution of William Whitaker' in M. Svensson and D. VanDrunen (eds), *Aquinas Among the Protestants* (Oxford: Wiley Blackwell, 2018), pp. 49–74.

Sytsma, D. S., 'Vermigli Replicating Aquinas: An Overlooked Continuity in the Doctrine of Predestination', *Reformation & Renaissance Review* 20:2 (2018), pp. 155–67.

Sytsma, D. S., 'Sixteenth-Century Reformed Reception of Aquinas' in M. Levering and M. Plested (eds), *The Oxford Handbook of the Reception of Aquinas* (Oxford: Oxford University Press, 2021), pp. 121–43.

Thompson, M. D., 'Sola Scriptura' in M. Barrett (ed.), *Reformation Theology: A Systematic Summary* (Wheaton, IL: Crossway, 2017), pp. 145–87.

Torrell, J.-P., 'Thomas Aquinas', *Dictionnaire de Spiritualité*, vol. 15 (Paris: Beauchesne, 1991), cols 718–73.

Torrell, J.-P., *Saint Thomas Aquinas, vol. 1: The Person and His Work*, tr. Robert Royal (Washington, DC: Catholic University of America Press, 1996; rev. edn 2005); *vol. 2: Spiritual Master*, tr. Robert Royal (Washington, DC: Catholic University of America Press, 2003).

Torrell, J.-P., *La 'Somme' de Saint Thomas* (Paris: Cerf, 2011).

Torrell, J.-P., 'Saint Thomas and His Sources' in M. Levering and M. Plested (eds), *The Oxford Handbook of the Reception of Aquinas* (Oxford: Oxford University Press, 2021), pp. 1–20.

Trueman, C., 'Thomas Aquinas: Not Just for Catholics Any More', *Public Discourse* (19 August 2018): https://www.thepublicdiscourse.com/2018/08/39373 (accessed 2 January 2023).

Trueman, C. R., 'The Reception of Thomas Aquinas in Seventeenth-Century Reformed Orthodoxy and Anglicanism' in M. Levering and M. Plested (eds), *The Oxford Handbook of the Reception of Aquinas* (Oxford: Oxford University Press, 2021), pp. 207–21.

Turretin, F., *Institutes of Elenctic Theology*, 3 vols., ed. J. T. Dennison Jr (Phillipsburg, NJ: P & R Publishing, 1992–96).

Tutino, S., *Shadows of Doubt: Language and Truth in Post-Reformation Catholic Culture* (Oxford: Oxford University Press, 2014).

Tyerman, C., *God's War: A New History of the Crusades* (London: Penguin, 2007).

Tyn, T., *Metafisica della sostanza: partecipazione e analogia entis* (Bologna: Edizioni Studio Domenicano, 1991).

Van Nieuwenhove, R., *An Introduction to Medieval Theology* (Cambridge: Cambridge University Press, 2012).

Bibliography

Van Til, C., *A Christian Theory of Knowledge* (Phillipsburg, NJ: P & R Publishing, 1969).

Van Til, C., *The Reformed Pastor and Modern Thought* (Phillipsburg, NJ: P & R Publishing, 1971).

VanDrunen, D., 'The Contemporary Reception of Aquinas on the Natural Knowledge of God' in M. Levering and M. Plested (eds), *The Oxford Handbook of the Reception of Aquinas* (Oxford: Oxford University Press, 2021), pp. 596–611.

Vanhoozer, K. J., *Biblical Authority after Babel: Retrieving the Solas in the Spirit of Mere Protestant Christianity* (Grand Rapids, MI: Brazos, 2016).

Vanneste, A., *Nature et grâce dans la théologie occidentale* (Leuven, Belgium: Leuven University Press, 1996).

Vanni Rovighi, S., *Introduzione a Tommaso d'Aquino* (Rome-Bari: Laterza, 1973, 1999).

Vauchez, A., *Francis of Assisi: The Life and Afterlife of a Medieval Saint* (New Haven, CT: Yale University Press, 2012).

Veenhof, J., *Nature and Grace in Herman Bavinck* (Sioux Center, IA: Dordt College Press, 2006).

Vos, A., *Aquinas, Calvin, and Contemporary Protestant Thought: A Critique of Protestant Views on the Thought of Thomas Aquinas* (Washington, DC: Christian University Press, 1985).

Vos, G., *Natural Theology* [1888–1893] (Grand Rapids, MI: Reformation Heritage Books, 2022).

Walz, A., *I Domenicani al Concilio di Trento* (Rome: Herder, 1961).

Walz, A., 'San Tommaso d'Aquino dichiarato dottore della Chiesa', *Angelicum* 44 (1967), pp. 145–73.

Warfield, B. B., 'The Idea of Systematic Theology Considered as a Science' [1888], reprinted in *The Works of Benjamin B. Warfield*, vol. 9 (New York, NY: Oxford University Press, 1932), pp. 49–87.

Warfield, B. B., 'Augustine and His Confessions' [1905] in *Studies in Tertullian and Augustine* [1930] (Westport, CT: Greenwood Press, 1970), pp. 229–85.

Warfield, B. B., 'Augustine' [1908] in *Studies in Tertullian and Augustine* [1930] (Westport, CT: Greenwood Press, 1970), pp. 113–32.

Wawrykow, J. P., *A–Z of Thomas Aquinas* (London: SCM Press, 2005).

Webster, J., 'Perfection and Participation' in T. J. White (ed.), *The Analogy of Being: Invention of the Antichrist or the Wisdom of God?* (Grand Rapids, MI: Eerdmans, 2011), pp. 379–93.

Weisheipl, J. A., *Friar Thomas d'Aquino: His Life, Thought and Work* (New York, NY: Doubleday, 1983).

White, T. J. (ed.), *The Analogy of Being: Invention of the Antichrist or the Wisdom of God?* (Grand Rapids, MI: Eerdmans, 2011).

White, T. J., 'Imperfect Happiness and the Final End of Man: Thomas Aquinas and the Paradigm of Nature-Grace Orthodoxy', *The Thomist* 78 (2014), pp. 247–89.

White, T. J., 'Thomas Aquinas and Karl Barth on the Analogy of Being', *Doctor Communis* 5 (2023), pp. 213–42.

Wicks, J., 'Thomism Between Renaissance and Reformation: The Case of Cajetan', *Archiv für Reformationsgeschichte* 68 (1977), pp. 9–32.

William of Tocco, *The Life of St. Thomas Aquinas* [1323] (Saint Marys, KS: Angelus Press, 2023).

Zeller, W., 'Lutherische Orthodoxie und mittelalterliche Scholastik: das Thomas-Verständnis des Johann Georg Dorsch', *Theologie und Philosophie* 50 (1975), pp. 527–46.

Zuppi, M., 'Foreword' to M. Naro, *Protagonista è l'abbraccio: temi teologici nel magistero di Francesco* (Venice: Marcianum Press, 2021), p. 16.

Index of names

Index of names

Dekker, E. 100n., 106n.
Di Maio, A. 20n.
Dieter, T. 98n., 99n.
Dionysius the Areopagite 8, 23, 30, 51, 53,
  61, 128
Dolezal, J. 161n.
Domingo de Soto 73–5, 80, 103
Dominic of Guzmán 10, 17
Donnelly, P. 107
Dooyeweerd, H. 121n.
Dorsche, J. G. 102–4
Duby, S. J. 143n., 150n.
Duffy, S. J. 45, 131, 132n.
Dulles, A. 37, 52
Duns Scotus 152, 172

Echeverria, E. J. 154n.
Eglinton, J. 36n., 116n., 118n.
Elliott, M. W. 44, 52n., 56n.
Emery, G. 63n.

Faggioli, M. 145n.
Farrow, D. 60n., 129n., 133n., 136, 150
Farthing, J. L. 97n.
Feser, E. 7.n.
Fesko, J. V. 162n., 167n.
Finnis, J. 4n.
Frame, J. M. 36n., 119n., 143n., 161–3
Francis (Pope) 3, 9, 134, 148–9
Francis of Assisi 17–8
Frederick II 14, 22
Frugoni, C. 17n.

Gaboriau, F. 43
Garrigou-Lagrange, R. 4, 35n., 85
Geisler, N. 5, 59n., 122
Gemelli, A. 12n.
George, R. P. 171n.
Gerhard, J. 110
Gerstner, J. 122n., 171n.
Ghisalberti, A. 53n.
Gilson, E. 4, 42, 59n., 88
Goergen, D. J. 17n.
Goris, H. 55n., 123n.
Grabmann, M. 15n.
Gray Sutanto, N. 114n., 117n., 118n.
Green, B. G. 44n., 114n., 164n.
Gregory X 25
Gregory of Nazianzus 127

Gregory the Great 51
Grumett, D. 145n.
Guarino, T. G. 2, 88n., 145, 147–8
Guinness, O. 122

Haak, C. J. 112n.
Haines, D. 129n.
Hall, C. 3n.
Harinck, G. 36n., 118n.
Helm, P. 135n., 161
Henry, C. 121n., 122
Hilary of Poitiers 51
Hoeffecker, W. A. 13n.
Holmes, A. 122
Horton, M. 46n., 47, 48n., 50, 51n.
Hoye, W. J. 142n.
Hudson, D. W. 144n.
Huizinga, J. 12
Husinger, G. 150n.

Innocent III 13
Irenaeus 127

Jaeger, L. 154n.
James III, F. A. 106n., 107n.
Jerome 51
John XXII 1, 8, 9, 70–2
John Chrysostom 51
John of Damascus 53, 128
John Paul II (see Woytyła, K.) 2, 8–9, 37,
  60, 90, 153, 154n., 156–7
Johnson, A. M. 96n.
Johnson, K. L. 56n.
Johnstone, B. 55n.
Jordan, M. 132n.

Kannard, C. 10
Kant, I. 153
Karlstadt, A. 98n.
Keating, D. A. 51n.
Kerr, F. 3n., 7n., 26n., 87n., 137n.
Kilcrease, J. D. 45n., 110
Kirby, T. 106n., 107n.
Kleutgen, J. 118
Koterski, J. W. 144n.
Kretzmann, N. 33n., 40
Kristeller, P. O. 100
Kühn, U. 121
Kuyper, A. 91, 114–16, 118n., 119

Index of names

Index of names

Russell, J. B. 17n.
Ryan, S. 98n.

Sadoleto, J. 166
Santi, F. 41n.
Sarmenghi, A. 61, 136n.
Schaeffer, F. 5, 120, 121n., 122, 129n.
Schaff, D. 94
Schaff, P. 94n.
Schmitt, C. B. 101
Schwöbel, C. 99, 109, 168
Smith, R. B. 20n., 41n.
Snell, R. J. 171n.
Spezzano, D. 169
Sproul, R. C. 171n.
Stark, R. 14n.
Steffensmeier, L. 51n.
Steinmetz, D. C. 101n.
Stephens, W. P. 105
Stewart, K. J. 171n.
Strachan, O. 50n.
Strange, D. 113n.
Stump, E. 33n., 62n., 142n.
Subilia, V. 45n.
Svensson, M. 101n., 103n., 106n., 110n.,
   113n., 135n., 162n.
Swiezawski, S. 135
Sytsma, D. 79n., 102, 103n., 106n., 107n.

Tetzel, J. 96
Theodora D'Aquino 22
Thiessen, G. E. 98n.
Thompson, M. D. 157n.
Tolkien, J. R. R. 12
Torrell, J.-P. 7n., 22n., 25, 27n., 32n., 34, 41,
   42n., 44, 55n., 57n., 68n., 71
Trueman, C. R. 98n., 101n., 111, 123n.,
   161–3
Trutfetter, J. 98
Tuninetti, L. F. 142n.
Turner, D. 99n.
Turretin, F. 111–13, 167
Tyerman, C. 14n.

Tyn, T. 2n.

Urban II 14
Urban IV 31
Urban V 69

Van Asselt, W. J. 100n., 106n.
Van Geest, P. 55n., 123n.
Van Til, C. 5, 35–6, 114n., 119–20, 121–2,
   143n., 161
VanDrunen, D. 60n., 101n., 103n., 106n.,
   110n., 113n., 135n., 162n.
Vanhoozer, K. J. 137, 157n.
Vanneste, A. 127n.
Vanni Rovighi, S. 3n., 54n.
Vauchez, A. 17n.
Veenhof, J. 117n.
Vermigli, P. M. 101, 105–7, 167
Victorines 106
Von Balthasar, H. U. 87, 131
Von Harnack, A. 152
Vos, A. 5, 121
Vos, G. 167n.

Waldo, P. 17
Warfield, B. B. 113, 164–5
Wawrykow, J. P. 46n.
Webster, J. 144n.
Weinandy, T. G. 51n.
Weisheipl J. A. 22n., 25–6, 27n., 52n., 54n.
Whitaker, W. 27n., 108n.
White, T. J. 123n., 132–3, 143n., 144n.
William de la Mare 70
William of Tocco 21, 71
Wojtyła, K. (see also John Paul II) 9
Wolterstorff, N. 121n.
Wright, D. F. 164n.

Yocum, J. P. 51n.

Zanchi, J. 102–4, 106n.
Zeller, W. 102n.
Zuppi, M. 149

Index of topics

Index of topics

Printed in the USA
CPSIA information can be obtained
at www.ICGtesting.com
CBHW071418270424
7438CB00005B/20